THE GERMANIC HERO

Politics and Pragmatism
in Early Medieval Poetry

THE GERMANIC HERO

Politics and Pragmatism
in Early Medieval Poetry

BRIAN MURDOCH

THE HAMBLEDON PRESS

LONDON AND RIO GRANDE

Published by The Hambledon Press 1996
102 Gloucester Avenue, London NW1 8HX (UK)
P.O. Box 162, Rio Grande, Ohio 45674 (USA)

A description of this book is available from the British Library and from
the Library of Congress

ISBN 1 85285 143 0

Typeset by Carnegie Publishing Ltd, 18 Maynard St, Preston
Printed on acid-free paper and bound in Great Britain by
Cambridge University Press

060997-5000X5

Contents

Preface   vii

1   About Heroes: Otto, Sigurðr, Hamðir and Byrhtnoð   1

2   Coping with Necessity: Hildebrand, Gunnarr
    and Völundr   33

3   Youth, Education and Age: Beowulf, Ernst of
    Bavaria and Heinrich of Kempten   61

4   In the Hands of the Church: Waltharius the
    Visigoth and Louis of the West Franks   89

5   Shifting Perspectives: Roland   118

6   Damage and Damage Limitation:
    The Nibelungs, Hilde and Kudrun   147

Bibliography of Primary Texts   176

Index to Secondary Literature   182

Index   186

Preface

These chapters were originally given as the Waynflete Lectures at Magdalen College, Oxford in the Michaelmas Term, 1994; I have tried to preserve the immediacy of the lecture form whilst expanding and providing the text with notes and references—although such is the bulk of secondary literature in this area that no claims to complete familiarity with it could possibly be made. The aim was to try to examine for a non-specialist audience (hence I have translated all quotations) the literary presentation of the early Germanic hero—a restriction which was itself partly pragmatic—as a warrior characterised by the political constraints in which he operated. He was not a *miles gloriosus*, still less a sword-wielding barbarian concerned solely with how to establish a reputation for himself. We do sometimes meet apparent heroes that seem to come into that category, but these are not really heroes as such: the hero is defined by the way in which his *res gestae* arise from, and are determined within a political construct, not by his acts of inviduality. Prowess is not enough.

The Waynflete Lectures were in their turn based on material offered over a period of many years at Stirling, in which period I also translated *Kudrun* and *Waltharius*, as well as some of the shorter poems, realising in the process that this remains one of the best ways of getting to know a medieval text. I have to acknowledge with gratitude the Sabbatical Committee of Stirling University and more particularly the German Department and its head, Dr Bruce Thompson, for allowing me a sabbatical. I am especially grateful, too, of course, to the President and Fellows of Magdalen College for a Visiting Fellowship and for the invitation to give the lectures.

I benefitted enormously from the period in Oxford, and from discussion with colleagues in German studies and at Magdalen. I hope that those I do *not* name will forgive me if I mention my particular gratitude to Professor Nigel Palmer, Dr Almut Suerbaum, Dr Annette Volfing and Mr Seb Coxon, as well as Mrs Olive Sayce—an enthusiastic and hospitable group of specialists in medieval German studies. At the equally hospitable Magdalen College, thanks are due to Dr Ralph Walker and Dr Richard Sheppard in particular. I remain grateful, finally, for the contact over the years not only with students, but with other scholars in the field. Most notable amongst these (and on various continents) are Professors Ute Schwab, George Gillespie and Winder McConnell, and Dr Rod Fisher, to all of whom I offer thanks for many kindnesses, and apologies (to these and to those named already) if my views are too divergent from their own. The fine modern poem with which I opened the lectures, 'Thermopylae 1941' by J. E. Brookes, is quoted by kind permission of the Salamander Oasis Trust and the poet.

Stirling, July 1995

'Weland gave the Sword! The Sword gave the Treasure, and the Treasure gave the Law. It's as natural as an oak growing.'

Kipling, Puck of Pook's Hill

About Heroes

Otto, Sigurðr, Hamðir and Byrhtnoð

It seems appropriate to open a consideration of the early medieval Germanic hero in literature with a poem in a Germanic language—in this case modern English—which alludes to a *classical* hero. John Brookes's 'Thermopylae 1941'—one of the finest poems of the Second World War—has a British soldier deposited in Greece just before the Germans invaded, and he is well aware of the historical implications of his present situation, one of which is that he and his colleagues are at best a rearguard.[1] He recalls Leonidas at the first battle of Thermopylae, and he tells an Australian colleague about him:

> I said to Blue,
> my Aussie mate, 'There was this famous chap
> Leonidas, he was the Spartan who
> defended it with just 300 men
> against an army'.

---

1   The poem, written on 25 August 1941, is in the Oasis anthology *Poems of the Second World War*, ed. Victor Selwyn (London: Dent, 1985), pp. 178–81, and also in the most recent anthology from the Salamander Oasis Trust, *The Voice of War*, ed. Victor Selwyn (London: Michael Joseph, 1995), pp. 120–23. I am indebted to Victor Selwyn for information and comments on the poem. The image of Thermopylae was used in a more predictable manner in earlier war poems, of course: see Joachim Freiherr von der Golß, *Deutsche Sonette* (Berlin: Cassierer, 1916), p. 11 ('Leonidas'). There the German soldier is ordered to face death nobly, washed and garlanded in the dark hour of death.

The pragmatic Australian is unimpressed, however:

> Bluey took a draw
> upon his cigarette. 'Well stuff 'im then!'
> A pungent comment on the art of war.

Later, but still with the image of dead Leonidas in his mind, the narrator tells Bluey how Leonidas and his men wore flowers in their long hair to show that they were free men. Bluey, however, is not only pragmatic, but bald, and dismisses them as:

> 'a load of bloody poufdahs!' Thus he laid the ghost
> of brave Leonidas.

All through the poem the heroism and implicitly the apparent foolhardiness of Leonidas run side by side until, at the last moment, when the narrator is already preparing to meet death as bravely as possible, like Leonidas, the British troops are withdrawn. The narrator experiences relief, while Bluey is annoyed that the orders didn't come sooner so that they need not have dug a trench; the final lines are revealing:

> But as we drove away I must confess
> It felt like a desertion. Those few men
> With flowers in their hair were heroes! Yes!

There are various points here: our narrator has *one* view of Leonidas, and Bluey is allowed to voice another. Were they heroes or were they fools? For the narrator there is no certainty, even after the relief of the withdrawal, that it might not have been better to be a hero. John Brookes's poem has, however, a number of other implications. Leonidas was indeed killed, so that in effect his grand gesture *was* worthy of Bluey's dismissal, even if the comments on his presumed sexual preferences were less relevant. The strategic withdrawal of the Allied troops from Greece in 1941 was in military terms the better idea, and in a way it, too, is celebrated in the poem. However, for all that the Persians were in a military sense the victors at Thermopylae, Leonidas did conquer something: death. One of the points of John Brookes's poem is that the narrator (and then, of course, his Aussie mate) had heard of Leonidas, so that the

Spartan leader's act did live on in this poem as well as countless earlier ones. Thus it could (and here does) function as an inspiration. In historical-political terms, finally, the sacrifice of Leonidas managed to allow for the escape and regrouping of the rest of his army. Various perceptions are possible.

The aim of these studies is to look at the presentation and reception of the hero, looking not at classical figures like Leonidas, but at heroes who have a Germanic origin in common, to try and see how the hero was presented, what his role was, and how that role depended upon a broader scheme of things. The emphasis will be on the political implications of heroic literature to a large extent, because Germanic heroic literature *is* largely political (though not all critics have accepted the point); but although I am much concerned, too, with the hero as a literary phenomenon, I shall not be looking at heroic poetry as using (or indeed defined by the use of) an oral-formulaic style or the ring-composition which has been the focus of attention for scholars such as Milman Parry, Albert Lord and more recently Alain Renoir.[2] I am concerned here not with heroic poetry, in fact, but with the hero in poetry. The aim is to try to present the Germanic hero—a restriction which is itself pragmatic and by no means teutonicising, by the way—in the hope that common traits will emerge which can then be reused to confirm what I would see as a preliminary rough definition: that the early medieval Germanic hero is a warrior in a realistic context, who is characterised in literature by the part he plays within a set of predetermined political and social constraints. Although concerned with the preservation of his reputation (something which interacts with the literary presentation of the hero), he is not a sword-wielding barbarian concerned solely with how to establish his own fame.

---

2   The most succinct work on formulaic composition remains Albert B. Lord's *The Singer of Tales* (Cambridge, Mass.: Harvard UP, 1960). This refers in detail to his work with Milman Parry. There is a Germanic focus in Alain Renoir, *A Key to Old Poems: The Oral-Formulaic Approach to the Interpretation of West-Germanic Verse* (University Park and London: Pennsylvania State UP, 1987), for which Albert Lord provided a foreword. On ring-composition, see for example Bernard Fenik, *Homer and the Nibelungenlied* (Cambridge, Mass.: Harvard UP, 1986).

We do sometimes—rarely—meet heroes who seem to come into that category, but even though these may indeed include one or two of the most famous medieval warrior-figures of all, it can be argued that such fame-seekers fall outside the definition of the Germanic hero, the value of whose *res gestae*, whose acts of fame, are given meaning only within a political construct. Individual prowess is not enough. The hero must conquer the blows that fate aims against his own person because he is committed, too, to the conquest of chaos. Over all else in Germanic writings about the hero is the acknowledgement of a need for stability, for the imposition (and in a warrior society, or indeed any society except in Plato's ideal republic, it *is* an imposition) of law and order, of control. Often this implies what looks like an aggressive *Realpolitik*. Going outside the Germanic world for a moment, a useful distinction has been drawn between the Greek hero represented by Achilles as a seeker after personal glory, and the Roman Aeneas, who needs to be part of a society.[3] Although Germanic writings present us with a whole range of very different heroes, so that one would hardly be able to establish a norm, they do seem to fit—with a very few exceptions—into the latter pattern.

Although I have tried to include as wide a range of works as possible I have still had to neglect the (mostly later) Middle High German Dietrich epics on the one hand and the Icelandic prose sagas on the other. I have concentrated upon early poetic texts, in most of which the heroes themselves are not necessarily aware that they *are* heroes in any modern sense. Indeed, most of the languages concerned have no absolutely clear word for that state. I do not intend to enter upon an etymological investigation of, or even to speculate upon the word *hero*, which might be, indeed, a somewhat Germanic approach, and which has in any case been done more thoroughly, most recently by Klaus von See in a paper with the intriguing title 'Held und Kollektiv' [Hero and Collective].[4]

3   R. Deryck Williams, *Aeneas and the Roman Hero* (London: Macmillan, 1973), pp. 28–30.
4   Klaus von See, 'Held und Kollektiv'. *Zeitschrift für deutsches Altertum* 122 (1993), 1–35.

It is probably more useful to keep in mind the fact that the modern German word *Held*, for example, has a medieval equivalent—*helt* in Middle High German—which is invariably contextualised, and means simply 'warrior'. If it needs to be made clear that the warrior is a particularly brave one, then he will be described in Middle High German, for example, as *ein helt guot*, 'a noble warrior', whilst a hero-king may well be praised in Old English for his special achievements with some equally thin-looking formula, such as *Þat wæs god cynyng*.[5] For the Germanic *helt*, to be a *good* warrior is simply to do his appointed task properly, and he cannot (or at least he ought not to) set out to be a hero in more recent senses of the word. The hero is placed in the literary foreground because of some notable action, and if he is to be dealt with at all in literature he will have certain powers and be of a certain stature in any case; but for the Germanic hero, any special *fame* (rather than just the maintaining of his good reputation) is an end-effect rather than an aim.[6] Glory is something which happens *to* a warrior, and this is the real and still not always recognised difference from the central figure in the romance, in which the knight may deliberately set out on a quest for fair fame. The central figure in the romance (we now use the word 'hero' very loosely in that literary sense, too) may seek glory. The Germanic hero is concerned with the *preservation* of his reputation; naturally he is pleased if he knows that after his death songs will be sung about him. But his concern is usually expressed negatively: that the wrong songs are *not* sung about him.

In the present age, the word 'hero' has broadened semantically, sometimes, though not necessarily, being weakened or amended in

---

5   There are intensifications, and of course there are other similar words. This is documented in Eva-Maria Woelker, *Menschengestaltung in vorhöfischen Epen des 12. Jahrhunderts* (Berlin, 1940; repr. Nendeln/Liechtenstein: Kraus, 1969).

6   The point is summed up very clearly by Markus Diebold, *Das Sagelied* (Berne and Frankfurt/M.: Lang, 1974), p. 80. 'Heldentum um seiner selbst Willen ist der heroischen Dichtung fremd . . . Die Helden setzen sich mit ihren ausserordentlichen Fähigkeiten für eine ganz bestimmte Aufgabe ein'. [Heroism for its own sake is foreign to heroic poetry . . . a hero sets out upon a quite specific task, using his own special capabilities].

the process.[7] The word has descended more recently, too, to the subculture of popular entertainment—Superman is a name of some interest, and so is Captain Marvel—and indeed, the very word 'hero' has been subjected to such visible devaluation that the term 'super-hero' has entered this albeit limited vocabulary. The use of the word for film and later pop stars has helped its degeneration. Modern political hero-cults have also made us wary, but we are certainly more familiar with Wilfred Owen's statement that his poetry of the First World War was 'not about heroes'. The literature of the First World War did indeed demythologise the facile notion of the hero found in German, for example, in overused and sanitising compounds such as *Heldentod,* 'a hero's death'. That notion of the warrior hero, already obsolescent at Bull Run, was surely blown out of existence at the Somme. In a sense this is true, but it was really only one particular view of the hero that was destroyed, and it was a view that was less medieval than Victorian, elevated to a kind of social norm by Carlyle. In its popular form it conflated the medieval warrior-hero with the fame-seeker of the romance and added a dash of *miles gloriosus,* taken at face value rather than as the satirical figure that he always was. What Wilfred Owen and others rightly set out to demythologise was a specific, distorted and dishonest idea of heroism imposed uncomprehendingly and unrealistically from outside, not the inner desire by an individual to keep his own reputation, to do his duty as he saw it when *in extremis,* to keep faith with his origins (family or country) and his political allegiance, and make no disgrace for his posterity. That Hollywood

7   There is a concise survey of the development of the word and its ramifications by Morton W. Bloomfield in his essay 'The Problem of the Hero in the Later Medieval Period'. in *Concepts of the Hero in the Middle Ages and the Renaissance,* ed. Norman T. Burns and Christopher Reagan (London: Hodder and Stoughton, 1976), pp. 27–48. See also von See, 'Held und Kollektiv'. We might now include under the heading of heroism, for example, the passive virtues of the saint (which causes some problems of overlap in medieval genres, too): fortitude in the sense of bearing suffering with patience, rather than in the sense of simple strength, *fortitudo* in a classical sense. Germanic heroes have to suffer the blows of fate, but they also react, and their *suffering* is not usually passive.

has *re*-mythologised that particular distortion of the warrior-hero in the figure of Rambo is unfortunate. Far more in accord with the medieval Germanic hero are the words of a private soldier in the First World War, who promised in a letter home just before his death in 1915 that he would take care of himself to an extent 'consistent, as I have said before with my duty'.[8] This externally generated imperative, coupled with a clear denial of overt glory-seeking, is a central and defining feature of the medieval Germanic hero.[9]

The history and geography of the early medieval heroic world are at least realistic, even if things are sometimes adapted so that Theoderic the Goth can serve at the court of a king who died the year before he was born, or so that you can see Mount Etna from Devon. We may range historically into an almost mythical past in the story of Wayland, into Germanic tribal history in *Beowulf*, into more recent (but still very clearly past) history in some texts, and be faced with contemporary or near-contemporary events in others.

8   The letter from a soldier named Harvey Steven is cited by Hilda D. Spear, 'A City at War: Dundee and the Battle of Loos'. in *Intimate Enemies*, ed. Franz Karl Stanzel and Martin Löschnigg (Heidelberg: Winter, 1993), pp. 149–63 (citation on p. 162). In terms of film, probably the only modern echo of the medieval hero is to be found in the Western; there is case to be made for viewing *High Noon* as an heroic narrative. The point has been touched on occasionally: see D. G. Mowatt and Hugh Sacker, *The Nibelungenlied: An Interpretative Commentary* (Toronto: Toronto University Press, 1967), p. 26 and Winder McConnell, 'Death in *Kudrun*,' *Fifteenth-Century Studies* 17 (1990), 229–43. On Hollywood films and the hero, see von See, 'Held und Kollektiv'.

9   See for example on the hero in general H. M. Chadwick, *The Heroic Age* (Cambridge: CUP, 1912); C. M. Bowra, *Heroic Poetry* (London: Macmillan, 1952); Jan de Vries, *Heroic Song and Heroic Legend*, trans. B. J. Timmer (London: OUP, 1963); Gwyn Jones, *Kings, Beasts and Heroes* (London: OUP, 1972); W. H. T. Jackson, *The Hero and the King* (New York: Columbia UP, 1982). See more recently the chapter by Roberta Frank on 'Heroic Ideals and Christian Ethics'. in the *Cambridge Companion to Old English Literature*, ed. Malcolm Gooden and Michael Lapidge (Cambridge: CUP, 1991). It is hardly necessary to note that these are just a few examples from a very large secondary literature. Other indispensable works in the study of the heroic epic in general are aimed in the first instance at specific texts—such as Tolkien on *Beowulf*—and will be noted as appropriate, as will be older studies like those of W. P. Ker.

7

All this imposes upon us differences in the way in which we can or should approach (or utilise) the historical backgrounds of such divergent texts. All of them show us, however, the acts of important figures within Germanic social units—the *res gestae populi Germanici*. The defining quality in the different varieties of classical historiography—I quote Charles Fornara—was the 'direct concern with the description of *res gestae*, man's actions in politics, diplomacy and war, in the far and near past'.[10] This could even serve as a definition for the literature of the Germanic hero.

It is especially difficult with works that are in essence historical to determine how and whether they can or should be interpreted in accordance with the history they contain, with the history of the period in and perhaps for which they were written, or from a contemporary viewpoint. It has been argued that modern moral values should not even be applied to the heroic warrior, and that although war is a political device in the works concerned, our twentieth-century experience of war has distorted the perception of medieval fighting to the point of unrecognisability. The manifold pitfalls of the intentionalist fallacy, of an excessively Whig historiography or of anachronistic expectations have to be avoided with care, but the works in question sometimes appear surprisingly modern, both on the personal level—as in Hildebrand's existential dilemma of finding himself unable to prove who he is—and on the broader political front. In fact, most of the works present situations (rather than models) with political and ethical implications which can be related to our own times just as much as to the time in which the work was written or even (in so far as it is identifiable) the age in which the work is set.

10 For further material in this direction, see the useful historiographic summary by Charles William Fornara, *The Nature of History in Ancient Greece and Rome* (Berkeley etc.: University of California Press, 1983). The quotation is from p. 3. On history and literature, see George M. Trevelyan, *Clio, A Muse* (London: Longmans, 1914) and C. V. Wedgewood, *Truth and Opinion* (London: Collins, 1960). A final and thought-provoking text in this area is Helen Cam's essay on *Historical Novels* (London: Historical Association, 1961).

The wide range of different situations set up in Germanic heroic literature remains essentially realistic, and because of that its messages are applicable on a wider scale. But Clio is, and always was a muse, and the literary aspects remain important, too. Oh yes, heroic literature tells a story. Except with those heroic poems which present very recent actions (and sometimes even then) it is usually unhelpful to dwell too much on the history that lies behind the literary hero. Equally, the texts we have must stand as we have them; the vigorous literary search for an ur-text is rarely very productive. Studies of *Kudrun*, a fine work as it stands, sometimes postulate an original in which Kudrun did not herself appear, and this has always seemed to be somewhat unhelpful in critical terms.

Concentrating on the *hero* as such means that we are not limited to what is usually seen as 'the heroic epic',[11] and in any case, to insist on too rigid a canon always means that a great deal is lost. My corpus will be broader, though I am not sure that anyone would get away with insisting on a general term like 'medieval Germanic political novel in verse', even though *Staatsroman* is sometimes encountered. In the introductory paper in a volume devoted to the concept of the hero, Bernard Huppé declared in 1970 that Germanic heroes, especially in the early period, were very few and far between. Thus he dismissed out of hand *Waltharius*, as 'an academic exercise which cannot seriously be considered as a work of art', the *Ludwigslied* as 'far from being either heroic or a work of art' and the *Hildebrandslied* as a 'mere scrap'. Since Huppé did allow the *Battle of Maldon*, which is also a fragment, perhaps he meant 'scrap' in a different sense.[12] I have to confess, however, that I propose to examine all of those works in some detail. Germanic

11 As a matter of fact even the validity of concepts like 'germanisches Heldenlied', [Germanic heroic poem] has been called into question: see Werner Schröder, 'Ist das germanische Heldenlied ein Phantom?'. *Zeitschrift für deutsches Altertum* 120 (1991), 249–56.
12 Bernard F. Huppé, 'The Concept of the Hero in the Early Middle Ages'. in Burns and Reagan, *The Concept of the Hero*, pp. 1–26 (see esp. p. 1). Huppé seems not to be interested in Old Norse. It is comforting, of course, if not surprising, that other critics *do* accept precisely this range of works as 'hero-stories': T. A. Shippey, *Old English Verse* (London: Hutchinson, 1972), p. 26.

does not mean only German, so that we may include not only Anglo-Saxon and Old Norse, but writings about Germanic heroes in Latin and even Old French. The saga of Roland at Roncesvalles really involves a Germanic hero, even if the best text, the *Chanson de Roland* happens to have come down to us in a Romance language. Professor Huppé would not approve, however, of the inclusion here of the hero in the so-called 'minstrel epic' in German. We still lack a better term for poems of this kind; 'pre-courtly romance' is unsatisfactory and I am again unsure that something like 'medieval science-fiction' would ever find general favour. What is worse, I shall even approach the Germanic hero via a work by a writer who is normally classified as a late medieval *chivalric* poet, Konrad von Würzburg. His tale of Heinrich von Kempten and the anonymous 'minstrel epic' of Duke Ernst both compare interestingly with that of *Beowulf*, and thus allow us to span half a millennium. Given the equation in medieval thought of hero with warrior, all the heroes so far mentioned are male, and this is inevitable. It does not mean, however, that women are devoid of heroic virtues: Kudrun, in the epic which bears her name, suffers exile and privation heroically whilst maintaining her reputation and that of her family. Although the role of women is not to fight—not one of action in that sense—they have other and equally important political roles within a warrior society, especially in the earlier period. While it is true that Aude, Roland's lady, seems to have entered the *Chanson de Roland* only so that she can die of shock when she hears of his death, women of power and influence can also be foregrounded. This is the case most notably in the—still neglected—epic of *Kudrun* once more.[13]

The standard studies of heroic poetry, most notably those by Bowra and Chadwick, and going back further, that of W. P. Ker, have made very clear that the individual hero takes a variety of

13 It is a pity that some recent studies of women in this context (which are occasionally perhaps a little over-selective) take so little account of *Kudrun*: see for example Roberta Frank, 'Quid Hinieldus cum Feminis: The Hero and Women at the End of the First Millennium'. in *La funzione dell'eroe germanico: storicità, metaforo, paradigma*, ed. Teresa Pàroli (Rome: Il Calamo, 1993), pp. 7–25.

roles—the father of his people, the breaker of cities, the champion, the king. They have made clear, too, that the hero, although endowed with great powers, is nevertheless at base human. Achilles, Siegfried and, for that matter, Superman, all have their weak spots, and where a hero *does* appear to be invincible, this is not necessarily a positive thing—Hildebrand complains that no one has ever conquered him, old as he is, and it is because of that that he has to fight his own son. So, too, the inner imperative—which has to have a source—that motivates the hero to act in the way he thinks he must, *may* lead to disaster. It may often look like arrogance, although this will be a recurrent problem in the interpretation of writings about the Germanic hero. In medieval Germanic literature, the notions of hero and warrior are virtually interchangeable, and the political context is usually (though not always) the politics of the sword. We are also limited, by and large, to the deeds of a single class. Gregory of Tours opened his history of the Franks with a declaration that he will describe 'wars waged by kings'.[14] and the politics with which we are concerned are linked in broad terms with the notion of feudality. However, the presentation of feudal loyalty can be appreciated on a more universal level because it is loyalty not only to a hierarchical overlord, but also, and because of that, to the self, and indeed to the idea of stability within the constraints of the society.[15] Nor indeed does the emphasis on the power of the sword imply a philosophy *of* violence. The essence is stability, the use of force frequently the *ultima ratio*

14 Gregory of Tours' *Historia Francorum* is edited by W. Arndt, Bruno Kusch and W. Levison in the *Monumenta Germaniae Historica,* Scriptores rerum Merovingicarum i, pt i (Berlin: MGH, rev. edn 1937–51).
15 See for example F. L. Ganshof, *Feudalism,* 3rd. English ed. tr. Philip Grierson (New York: Harper and Row, 1964), which remains one of the (many) standard works on the complex notion of feudalism, though it concentrates on the legal sense of the word rather than on broad political structures. An earlier work with interesting comments is that by Lucie Sandrock, *Das Herrscherideal in der erzählenden Dichtung des deutschen Mittelalters* (Emsdetten: Lechte, 1931). See also another standard work, Walter Ullmann, *Medieval Political Thought* (Harmondsworth: Penguin, 1965). On the military aspects, see H. W. Koch, *Medieval Warfare* (London: Bison, 1978), pp. 37–44 and 57–64.

regum.[16] For the individual hero, warrior or king, however, subordination to the good of the state even within the feudal pattern is in most cases the underlying principle.

The Germanic hero, then, will be a warrior of stature and importance within a feudal society, and he is normally shown in foregrounded action, carrying out a task of importance which it is his duty to complete, driven by an inner imperative which is dependent also upon the social constraints which he has accepted. To waver from this—however unacceptable the task—would damage his reputation. The Germanic hero's task is to conquer. This might well be, and indeed often is, meant in a simple military sense: to extend his or his country's power; but it can equally well combine with ethical impulses—a conquest of the self; and it can imply in broader political-philosophical terms the conquest of chaos. All literature, finally, is of itself a conquest of death, and for the hero in literature this is a recurrent motif. In poems about the hero, the hero himself often refers to poems will be made about that hero later, a kind of circularity best illustrated by the fact that in the poem of *Beowulf* itself we hear that a song is sung about Beowulf. But the songs must be the right ones, and it is Roland, for example, who makes the point very clearly that heroes should behave so that 'male chançun n'en deit estre cantee' (line 1466) [malicious songs shall not be sung about their deeds].[17]

Military conquest will often be the climax of the whole narrative of the hero's exploits. 'Gilobot si thiu godes kraft, Hluduuig uuarth

16 However, the considerations leading to such a decision might accord more with the precepts of Machiavelli in *The Prince* or with gun-boat diplomacy than with modern views. Much of what Machiavelli has to say applies well, incidentally, to the politics of early medieval Germanic heroic writings, most notably the stress on the need for a prince to demonstrate his power, or to rely on what he can control: Niccolò Machiavelli, *The Prince*, trans. George Bull (Harmondsworth: Penguin, 1961).

17 *Das altfranzösische Rolandslied nach der Oxforder Handschrift*, ed. Alfons Hilka, 4th edn by Gerhard Rohlfs (Tübingen: Niemeyer, 1953). There are translations by Dorothy Sayers (Harmondsworth: Penguin, 1957), D. D. R. Owen (London: Unwin, 1972); and Glyn Burgess (Harmondsworth: Penguin, 1990).

sigihaft' [praise be to God, Louis was victorious] ends the Old High German *Ludwigslied*, a poem about an historical battle.[18] Indeed, a Germanic warrior leader without a victory to his name was rather to be pitied, which brings us to an historical figure who enjoyed an a priori political prominence for the simple reason that he was emperor, Otto II. His poetic heritage as a Germanic hero, however, is a little limited, and I fear he is something of a negative example, his deeds being represented by a single strophe in a Latin pem in praise of the three Saxon emperors named Otto, who ruled between 936 and 1002. The poem was written during the reign of Otto III, and was probably performed in front of him, so that he gets a predictably favourable set of comments. Otto I—Otto the Great—is also lauded for his exploits, but Otto II gets fairly short shrift. Of the ninth and tenth strophes of the *Modus Ottinc*, one of the so-called *Carmina Cantabrigensia*, the first is about Otto the Great, the second about his son:[19]

Parva manu
cesis Parthis
ante et post

18   The *Ludwigslied* is in Elias v. Steinmeyer, *Die kleineren althochdeutschen Denkmäler* (Berlin and Zurich: Weidmann, repr. 1963), no. 16 (cited), and in Wilhelm Braune, *Althochdeutsches Lesebuch*, 16. edn Ernst Ebbinghaus (Tübingen: Niemeyer, 1965), no. 36, with modern German translation in Horst Dieter Schlosser, *Althochdeutsche Literatur* (Frankfurt/M.: Fischer, 2nd edn, 1989), pp. 274–7, and an English translation in J. Knight Bostock, *A Handbook on Old High German*, 2nd edn by K. C. King and D. L. McLintock (Oxford: Clarendon, 1976), pp. 239–41. The *Hildebrandslied* is in Steinmeyer, *Denkmäler*, no. 16 and Braune, *Lesebuch*, no. 28, with modern German translation in Schlosser, *Literatur*, pp. 264–7, and English translation by Brian Murdoch, *Lines Review*, 109 (1989), 20–22.

19   Karl Strecker, *Die Cambridger Lieder (Carmina Cantabrigensia)* (Berlin: Monumenta Germaniae Historica, 1926, 2nd edn, 1955), poem 11; text and facsimile in Karl Breul, *The Cambridge Songs* (Cambridge: CUP, 1915). Text and modern German translation in Horst Kusch, *Einführung in das lateinische Mittelalter* (Berlin: VEB Verlag der Wissenschaften, 1957), I, 210–17. On the work see Franz Bittner, *Studien zum Herrscherlob in der mittellateinischen Dichtung* (Volkach: n. pub. [diss. Würzburg, 1961], 1962), p. 157f, and Annette Georgi, *Das lateinische und deutsche Preisgedicht des Mittelalters* (Berlin: Schmidt, 1969), p. 131f.

sepe victor
communem cunctis
movens luctum
nomen, regnum, optimos
hereditans
mores filio
obdormivit.

Adolescens
post hunc Otto
imperavit
multis annis
cesar iustus
clemens, fortis
unum modo defuit:
nam inclitis
raro preliis
triumphabat.

Otto the Great, we are told, defeated the Magyars (they are called Parthians here) *parva manu*, with a mere handful of warriors, the classic heroic situation: 'with a few warriors only he defeated the Magyars, and was often victorious before this and afterwards, and everyone sorrowed when he died and passed on his name, empire and great inheritance to his son'. He was victorious, then, both before and after that one particularly noteworthy battle (the defeat of the Magyars on the Lech in 955), and we may note that he left all this to his son. Inheritance and indeed heredity will play a part in other heroic works, and when we are specifically concerned with an hereditary ruling dynasty (as we normally shall be, since the hereditary principle of rule is rarely questioned), such things are clearly even more important. But now comes the son's strophe: 'After this young Otto was emperor, a just ruler, mild and strong, but one thing was missing—he was seldom able to rejoice in a victory'. The whole poem is a panegyric, so that Otto II is, like his father, a just, mild and firm ruler. But then comes the sting in the tail of the only one of the dozen strophes of the poem that is concerned with him at all; *unum modo defuit*, one thing was missing for him—he was rarely able to glory in a famous battle.

Straightforward conquest in battle is not (though a work like the *Modus Ottinc* might seem to imply this) an end in itself. Victory in battle will usually have larger political implications, and the reference to Otto the Great bequeathing his *regnum*, a stable and protected state, to his son, is an indication of this. With the enhancement of the hero's reputation comes very frequently something more solid, such as the possibility of political expansion; the development of reputation must invariably enhance the position of a warrior or a king, which is also why Otto II needed a victory. It can also lead to the acquisition of wealth, which itself implies power. The ownership or payment of gold plays a role of central importance in very many of the works, and that role cannot be underestimated.

Beside conquests of this kind, however, the hero is faced frequently with the need for another conquest, the conquest of the self, the coming-to-terms with a situation. Hildebrand must accept that he will either kill or be killed by his own son, just as Hagano in *Waltharius* has to come to terms with the necessity of fighting his closest friend. But we need to remember that the presentation of the hero is selective and set upon a broad historical base, even when a short poem shows only one incident. We are shown, in effect, the interesting times, and we may recall the famous imprecation along the lines of 'may you live in interesting times'. In the many and detailed studies of *Beowulf*, too, with all the concentration on the defeat of the monsters, less attention has been paid to a few lines which seem to be of very considerable importance.[20] To be

---

20 But see John Gardner, 'Fulgentius' *Expositio Vergiliana Continentia* and the Plan of *Beowulf*: Another Approach to the Poem's Style and Structure'. *Papers on Language and Literature* 6 (1970), 227–62. See also W. F. Bolton, *Alcuin and Beowulf* (New Brunswick: Rutgers UP, 1978). *Beowulf* is cited from F. Klaeber, *Beowulf and the Fight at Finnsburg* (Boston: Heath, 3rd edn, 1950); see also A. J. Wyatt, *Beowulf*, rev. edn by R. W. Chambers (Cambridge: CUP, 1952); C. L. Wrenn, *Beowulf*, rev. edn by W. F. Bolton (London: Harrap, 1973); Michael Swanton, *Beowulf*, ed. and transl. (Manchester: MUP, 1978) There is also a translation by Michael Alexander, *Beowulf* (Harmondsworth: Penguin, 1973); Alexander has also produced an edition of the text in the same series (Harmondsworth: Penguin, 1995).

fair to the critics, the poet hardly draws attention to the lines in question himself, but still they constitute the fulcrum upon which the whole work balances:

> syððan Bēowulfe   brāde rīce
> on hand gehwearf;   hē gehēold tela
> fiftig wintra . . . (lines 2207–9)

[And then the broad kingdom came into the hands of Beowulf; he ruled it well for fifty years.]

Other heroes are far less successful in holding back chaos than is Beowulf. Man is in time, and Beowulf is eminently successful in doing his job while he—literally—has time.

Only in the literary mode can the hero actually conquer time and even death. Whether the victory is over an army or over one's own inclinations, that victory must be recorded for posterity, and this is immanent in the heroic poem itself, an end to be desired. The clearest explicit statement of this point comes in a well-known strophe of the Old Norse *Hávamál*, the Song of Oðin:

> Deyr fé
> deyja frændr,
> deyr sjalfr hit sama;
> ek veit einn
> at aldri deyr:
> dómr of dauðan hvern (77)

'Cattle die, friends die, you yourself will die', the verse runs, but the seer knows one thing that will not die: 'the reputation of the dead hero'. Indeed, reputation is sometimes all that the hero *can* leave behind. To examine more closely the interaction of heroic reputation and its necessary literary reflection we may follow Otto II, an emperor whose reputation is deficient, with a very different case indeed, an individual warrior whose reputation is almost excessive. That warrior is the Norse hero Sigurðr, whom we perhaps know better in a later literary incarnation as the Siegfried of the Nibelung story. Here the historical background is so remote as to be entirely unhelpful, and the relationship between Sigurðr the hero and the unspectacular Frankish king who married the historical Brünhild and was murdered by the hired assassins of Fredegonda the Concubine need not concern us. It must be stressed that even as a literary figure, however, he is not typical. Sigurðr (like Siegfried in the German *Nibelungenlied*) is an anomaly in many ways, a warrior who operates *outside* a political context. However, one—in literary terms very odd—poem about him is worth considering not for what it says about the hero's deeds as such, but about his thoughts and attitudes, and more especially for the way everything (and I chose the word carefully) is presented. The poem is the *Grípisspá*, the 'Prophecy of Gripir' from the Old Norse *Elder Edda*.[21] After a fairly straightforward genealogy of the hero Sigurðr, the prose introduction tells us how he arrived at the hall of Grípir, who in this text is Sigurðr's uncle, and who is also 'var allra manna vitastr ok framvíss', [the most forward-seeing of all men]. This is the key to the work, a poem which tells the entire story of Sigurðr (in the Norse version) in a kind of future perfective. Grípir is no enigmatic oracle, but is entirely specific about the course of the hero's life. In the Greek tale, the identity of Oedipus's father and mother was at least in doubt. Here there is none whatsoever. Nor, indeed, is there any question of Sigurðr trying to avoid any part of the fate mapped out for him. In spite of critics like Ker, who wanted to separate the Norse works from those of a more clearly Christian southern Germania, Christian warriors also express a kind of fatalism in the notion that men's lives are determined by God,

21 Although it is clearly a late work, it is the first of the Sigurðr poems in the Codex Regius. On the date and position of the work, see Theodore M. Andersson, *The Legend of Brynhild* (Ithaca and London: Cornell UP, 1980), p. 102–7, where the text is given a date in the first part of the thirteenth century. Its overview character clearly makes it a later work, but it is in this feature that its fascination also lies. On the position in the Edda-codex, see W. P. Ker, *The Dark Ages* (Edinburgh and London: Blackwood, 1904), p. 290. Text of the *Hávamál* and the *Grípisspá* in *Sæmundar-Edda*, ed. Finnur Jónsson (Reykjavik: Kristjánsson, 2nd edn, 1926), pp. 268–84 (cited) and also Gustav Neckel, *Edda. Die Lieder des Codex Regius*, 4th edn rev. Hans Kuhn (Heidelberg: Winter, 1962) English translations in: Henry Adams Bellows, *The Poetic Edda* [1923] (repr. New York: Biblo, 1969) and Patricia Terry, *Poems of the Vikings* (New York: Bobbs-Merrill, 1969).

and indeed God sometimes indicates to the warriors what will happen. How those warriors behave is also left up to them. In response to his initial request for a glimpse into the future, Sigurðr is first of all assured that he will be a great man. Then he asks for more details, which are promptly given, causing him to request more, so that we, the audience, are given a complete synopsis of the Sigurðr saga. But for the hero himself, all of it is cast in the future mode, so that the entire poem underlines the inescapability of fate. Having been told that he will defeat Fafnir and Regin, and will release a valkyrie, Sigurðr agrees that he will set off on his path. It is when he asks for *further* information, though, that Grípir hesitates:

> farit es Sigurðr
> Þats fyrir vissak
> skala fremr an svá
> fregna Grípi. (strophe 19)

[I have told Sigurðr all I can foresee; do not ask Grípir to tell you any more.]

But this simply adds to the audience's suspense, and Sigurðr is assured not only that his actions will be blameless, but that

> Þvit uppi mun
> meðan öld lifir,
> naddéls boði,
> nafn Þitt vesa. (strophe 23)

[As long as the world lives, your name will be a cry to battle.]

That is, Sigurðr's name will be one of those of the famous Germanic warriors used to inspire others to fight, a custom mentioned in Tacitus and still noted as being in use at the battle of Hastings.

Pressed by Sigurðr, Grípir now tells, or rather foretells, the actual fate of the warrior, his betrothal to Brynhildr and his subsequent betrayal of her (through no fault of his own, he is assured) in favour of Guðrun, right down to his death at the hands of Guðrun's brothers. Again, however, the reaction of Sigurðr is of interest: he asks constantly for reassurance of blamelessness, and expresses no horror (and certainly no disbelief) at what will happen to him. Indeed, it *will* now happen, although the *poem* has told us the story already. This is a very un-Greek work, oracular though it might be; such a state of mind would hardly be possible after the pronouncements of a Greek oracle, say, where the tragedy might lie in the attempt to avoid fate. Sigurðr is perfectly well aware that it is quite impossible to conquer fate—he actually says so, his last words before he takes his leave of Grípir: 'munat sköpum vinna', [no-one shall escape fate]. But he has, significantly, just been been told once again that in all this, his *reputation* will be intact, and that this must be his consolation; in fact, he will be the most famous of men. This, then, is his conquest of death, given to him, as it were, in advance of the deeds which will inevitably happen. This is not a literal work in any sense, else we should have to suppose that Sigurðr now embarks on his adventures in a kind of sequel, knowing precisely what will happen to him. The poem as we have it, however, is also the kind of poem that Sigurðr wishes to be made about him after the events, and that Grípir tells him actually will be made.

A brief excursus is necessary at this point, although it links very much with the Sigurðr poem. It is often assumed that the hero is associated with tragedy, indeed, that the heroic epic is a tragic mode. Heiko Uecker states quite categorically that 'der Held endet meistens tragisch' [the hero usually comes to a tragic end], as if this were part of a definition.[22] Other critics have made the same point, but it is at best questionable. Indeed, the nature of the hero seems precisely *not* to end tragically, but with the hero reassured by the knowledge that he will be remembered well. Taking this a little further, it is part of the point that knowledge of the hero's deeds does not end at all. That the *Grípisspá* ends with a beginning, so to speak, takes away the implicit notion that the *ending*—even if it can be identified at all—is somehow the most important point. The time-spread in the heroic work is always significant. To end tragically is not the

---

22 Heiko Uecker, *Germanische Heldensage* (Stuttgart: Metzler, 1972), p. 3.

The Germanic Hero

same as to die bravely anyway and, indeed, by no means every hero is killed; the term 'tragic' also begs other questions. The notion of a tragic saint has been discussed and dismissed, since the overt promise of heaven cannot but detract from tragedy, and this will apply in the case of some Christian Germanic heroes. Even in those not overtly Christian, the afterlife is in the song itself, and for this reason the Sigurðr of the *Grípisspá* is not tragic. Indeed, it is rare to find in Germanic literature a clear example of a tragic hero in the classical sense, where tragedy is brought about by some flaw in the character leading to a genuine act of *hubris*.[23] One example is the story of Hamðir, whose tale (unaffected, incidentally, by Christianity) is told in the Eddic *Hamðismál*. Briefly, Hamðir and his brother are sent to avenge their sister Svanhildr, killed by her husband, Jörmunrekkr (Ermanaric), king of the Goths. When an illegitimate half-brother, Erpr, offers to help, he is mocked as a bastard, challenges the brothers and is killed. But by doing this, the brothers 'lose a third of their strength', and although they attack and maim Jörmunrekkr he is still able to shout out for help. At the end, Hamðir realises very clearly that his treatment of Erpr was fatal: 'Af væri nú höfuð / ef Erpr lifði' (strophe 28) [Jörmunrekkr's head would have been off as well if Erpr were still alive] he says, meaning that it would then have been impossible for the Goth to call out. Such clear causality is rare, however, and it is here treated with resignation.[24]

The *Grípisspá* is a very curious work in literary terms, but a final and contrasting short work, the Anglo-Saxon *Battle of Maldon*,

---

23 The Marxist perception of the tragic hero as a victim of historical necessity (in which the tragic fall need not itself be perceived as pessimistically, because it might usher in a new age) is sometimes tried as an interpretative model, but rarely with success. See for example K. H. Ihlenburg, *Das Nibelungenlied: Problem und Gehalt* (Berlin/O.: Akademie, 1969).

24 Text and commentary in Ursula Dronke, *The Elder Edda* i (Oxford: Clarendon, 1969), pp. 161–242. Strophe numbers vary in other editions, as in Jónsson, *Sæmundar-Edda*, pp. 432–9; English translation in Terry, *Poems of the Vikings*, pp. 237–41. On the background, see R. C. Boer, *Die Sagen von Ermanarich und Dietrich von Bern* (Halle/S.: Waisenhaus, 1910). The work is commented upon in Alois Wolf, *Gestaltungskerne und Gestaltungsweisen in der altgermanischen Heldendichtung* (Munich: Fink, 1965), pp. 16–36.

shows us a contemporary hero who can illustrate the problem of reputation within a political context and in more straightforward narrative terms, even though it raises the question of *hubris* without providing a satisfactory answer.[25] It is set not in the distorted and distant past of the *Edda* poems, but in more recent and better documented times. The battle in question took place in 991, when a Viking force sailed up the River Blackwater, where they were met by the Anglo-Saxons led by the ealdorman of Essex, Byrhtnoð, who was by this time an old man. His heroic stature seems to have been undiminished, however, and this may be taken quite literally if we believe a report from the eighteenth century (an age when antiquaries were much given to exhuming the famous and long dead) that when Byrhtnoð's bones were disinterred at Ely Cathedral in May 1769, he was found to have been very tall and robust, just as he is described in later medieval documents. This assumes, of course, that the bones were indeed those of Byrhtnoð, and one of the means of identification was—*pace* the modern detective story—precisely the fact that the head was missing.[26]

25 Texts are *The Battle of Maldon*, ed. E. V. Gordon (London: Methuen, 2. corr. ed., 1954), with supplement by D. G. Scragg (Manchester: MUP, 1976), and ed. D. G. Scragg (Manchester: MUP, 1981). There is a text (cited) and translation (by Donald Scragg) in the splendid millennium volume, *The Battle of Maldon AD 991*, ed. Donald Scragg (Oxford: Blackwell, 1991), cited here. Another useful edition is that by Bill Griffiths, *The Battle of Maldon* (Pinner: Anglo-Saxon Books, 1991). Further translations are in Michael Alexander, *The Earliest English Poems* (Harmondsworth: Penguin, 1966), pp. 111–23; Kevin Crossley-Holland, *The Battle of Maldon and Other Old English Poems*, ed. Bruce Mitchell (London: Macmillan, 1966). Griffiths' book has a useful annotated bibliography. Secondary works on the text are very numerous; for recewnt examples, see D. G. Scragg's millenary volume noted above (which also has a bibliography), and also *The Battle of Maldon: Fiction and Fact*, ed. Janet Cooper (London: Hambledon, 1993), with a good range of interesting essays.

26 See Marilyn Deegan and Stanley Rubin, 'Byrhtnoth's Remains: a Reassessment of his Stature'. in Scragg, *Battle*, pp. 289–93. The article reproduces the eighteenth-century material, but finds, rather sadly, that Byrhtnoð was not—as claimed—six feet nine, but only about six feet in height; he was taller, admittedly than most of the early bishops who were similarly exhumed and measured. Nevertheless, the medieval sources other than the poem are fairly unanimous in stressing his relative height.

No matter: we have the poem to attest to his stature as a Germanic hero. There are various medieval accounts of Byrhtnoð and his fate, most notably in the roughly contemporary *Life of St Oswald*, and in the twelfth-century *Liber Eliensis*, but we may begin—as Margaret Ashdown did some sixty years ago—with the reports in the *Anglo-Saxon Chronicle* (it is there in all five surviving texts) as interestingly brief and in one case slightly confused. I cite the Laud version:

> Her was Gypeswic ge hergod. 7 æfter Þam swiðe
> raðe wæs Brihtnoð ealdorman ofslagen æt Mældune.
> 7 on Þam geare man ge rædde þt man geald ærest
> gafol Deniscan mannum. for Þam mycclan brogan
> Þe he worhtan be Þam sæ riman. þt wæs ærest
> .x. Þusend punda, ðæne ræd ge rædde Siric
> arceb.[27]

[In 991 Ipswich was laid waste, and not long after this Earl Byrhtnoð was killed at Maldon. And in that year it was agreed that payment should be made for the first time to the Vikings, because of the great terror that they caused along that shore. The first payment was of ten thousand pounds, as advised by Archbishop Si(ge)ric.]

Just that: Byrhtnoð was killed, and after that the Vikings had to be paid off, something which has sometimes been seen as rather less than heroic, although medieval sources usually make no comment. In a Victorian history of the Anglo-Saxons, however— that by the children's writer Thomas Miller, which was much reprinted, and even included in *Bohn's Illustrated Library*—the decision of King Æthelred to pay the Danegeld makes him into

---

27 Cited from Charles Plummer and John Earle, *Two of the Saxon Chronicles (787–1001 AD)* (Oxford: Clarendon, 1889). All the texts, including this, are there with translation in Scragg, *Battle of Maldon AD 991*, discussed by Janet M. Bately. The earlier work by Margaret Ashdown remains useful: *English and Norse Documents relating to the Reign of Ethelred the Unready* (Cambridge: CUP, 1930), pp. 1 and 22–108.

a 'dastardly sovereign' paying a 'disgraceful grant' as a 'cowardly measure'. Sigeric is contrasted with St Dunstan, who 'would have seen England drenched with Saxon blood . . . ere he would have seen his country degraded by such an unmanly concession'.[28] Kipling made similar noises, rather more famously, in 1911 in a poem called 'Dane-geld', though without reference to Maldon. The absolutely clear-cut up-and-at-'em demands of Thomas Miller and others were easy to make, it has to be said, from the safe vantage point of 900 years distance.[29] Byrhtnoð's boldness appealed to the Thomas Millers, and if Sigeric sanctioned an unmanly concession, Byrhtnoð is most famous for granting a concession of a different kind. In the Anglo-Saxon poem, Byrhtnoð is asked by the Viking leader to allow him to lead his men across the causeway separating Northey Island from the mainland, to be able to fight; Byrhtnoð allows this, and is killed as a result. John Brookes's Australian soldier would probably have thought him a fool for doing so, but the poem does seem to be in line with those unreflective Victorian views as far as the payment of tribute is concerned.

The engagement proper opens with a demand by the Vikings for tribute which will—and the Viking argument is an interesting one—avoid bloodshed: 'ne Þurfe we us spillan' [we need not kill each other.] Byrhtnoð replies angrily to the Viking, telling him first that their tribute will be spear-points, and secondly that treasure cannot be gained that easily. Gold rings are referred to, incidentally, rather than the coinage, some of it minted at Maldon itself, that

28 Thomas Miller, *History of the Anglo-Saxons* (London: Bogue, 2nd edn, 1850), p. 241. The work first appeared in 1848, and the *Dictionary of National Biography* does at least comment that in spite of reaching five editions, it was 'adversely criticised in the *Westminster Review* for July, 1856'. Miller, a prolific writer, lived from 1807 to 1874.

29 Although Kipling was making a more general point, and his views *were* reapplied fairly extensively. See Roberta Frank's article 'The Battle of Maldon: Its Reception, 1726–1906,' in Cooper, *Maldon*, pp. 237–47. Frank cites Kipling (but not Miller). Included in Kipling's *School History of England* in 1911, Marghanita Laski also included it in her BBC series in 1973, *Kipling's English History* (London: BBC, 1974).

was actually paid (as present-day Danish museum collections testify) in such vast quantities[30] Byrhtnoð says that his country—*Æþelredes eard*, Æthelred's land (he is also a feudal vassal)—will not pay, but he does agree to the request from the Vikings to let them cross the causeway.

One issue in the poem is that of cowardice in general, and the payment of tribute *might* perhaps have been thought of by Byrhtnoð as a cowardly way out—even a dastardly one—although tribute is paid and offered elsewhere—notably in *Waltharius*—by other Germanic heroes when there is no alternative or as a way of avoiding war. There are, however, not moral, but perfectly sound economic grounds for *not* paying tribute *if it can be avoided*, and this is surely the point. It is hardly likely that Byrhtnoð was motivated exclusively by an insistence on personal fame and glory at the expense of his own life and the lives of his men, by an overwhelming desire not to have future generations— the Thomas Millers yet unborn—call him dastardly or cowardly. Even Sigurðr's insistence on reputation was framed as a response to the fate mapped out for him, and there are several differences here at Maldon. The brief but much-cited passage in which the point is made does seem to be pejorative in its reference to Byrhtnoð's pride:

> Ða se eorl ongan   for his ofermode
> alyfan landes to fela   laþere ðeode . . . (line 89f)

---

30 A graphic illustration of the payments under the reign of Æthelred II is provided by Georg Galster, *Sylloge of Coins of the British Isles . . . Anglo-Saxon Coins of Æthelræd II* (London: British Academy/OUP, 1966), which documents nearly 1700 Anglo-Saxon coins in the Royal Collection in the National Museum in Copenhagen, and points out that there are far more such coins in Danish museums than in British ones. For those minted at Maldon (Mældune), see plate 42. Several were minted by a moneyer named Ælfwine, but the name is not uncommon. See the paper by D. M. Metcalfe and W. Lean, 'The Battle of Maldon and the Minting of Crux Pennies in Essex'. in Cooper, *Maldon*, pp. 205–34. We shall see an interesting reversal of the situation in the *Hildebrandslied*, incidentally, when tribute is offered rather than demanded, and rejected in very similar terms, albeit on an individual basis.

[The earl allowed too much land to the wicked people out of pride.]

Unlike Sigurðr, however, Byrhtnoð does *not* know how everything will work out, and he says very clearly indeed that 'God ana wat / hwa Þære wælstowe wealdan mote' (line 94f) [only God knows the outcome of the battle.] Men, including Byrhtnoð, do not.[31]

So too, that word *ofermod* (usually rendered as 'pride') has provoked more scholarly argument than any other word in the poem, ranging from interpretations that see it as derogatory to others which see it as meaning something like 'exuberance'. It is likely that the problem of *ofermod* will never really be resolved, but if it is a criticism levelled by the narrator it is by no means a prominent one, and it is taken up by no one in the work.[32] Frederick Whitehead's argument is a telling one, however, that if Byrhtnoð is clearly culpable, then what is the point of loyalty to him? Byrhtnoð falls and is hacked to pieces by the Vikings, and it is at this point (as most critics have indicated) that the whole tenor of the poem changes. Not Byrhtnoð's pride, but his death is the turning-point of the piece, and if his decision as a military commander may have

31 I am not even sure that W. P. Ker's link between Byrhtnoð and the awareness of death expressed by Achilles is a fair one: *Epic and Romance* (London: Macmillan, 1908), p. 12, referring to *Iliad*, xix, line 420. In one of the Icelandic sagas a seer appears who thinks that she ought not to be able to foresee the future because she is a Christian; however, her prophecies are concerned with specific events that will happen to a community, rather than of a hero's life: see Francis Berry, *Thoughts on Poetic Time* (Abingdon: Abbey, 1972), p. 7. The significance of the passage cited is pointed out by Hans Erik Andersen, *'The Battle of Maldon: The Meaning, Dating and Historicity of an Old English Poem* (Copenhagen: U. Copenhagen Press, 1991); see also the review by David J. Williams in the *Modern Language Review* 89 (1994), 959f.

32 *Ofermod* does seem to be a pejorative term, though it is not terribly common, and appears in verse elsewhere only in *Genesis B*, where it is indeed applied to Lucifer. Amongst the many studies of the passage, see importantly Frederick Whitehead, '*Ofermod* and *Demesure*'. *Cahiers de civilisation médiévale* 3 (1960), 115–17, and also N. F. Blake, 'The Battle of Maldon'. *Neophilologus* 49 (1965), 332–45, and Helmut Gneuss, 'The Battle of Maldon 89; Byrhtnoð's *ofermod* Once Again'. *Studies in Philology* 73 (1976), 117–37.

been in the last analysis wrong, events after his death place it in a different context.

Precisely *why* Byrhtnoð gave the Vikings that advantage has been much discussed in military terms, and here the advantage we have of being able to relate the work closely to historical events comes into play. In spite of critical references to Byrhtnoð's 'gullibility' his 'lack of military experience', his 'mistakes' and even an excess of 'piety'—all of which are very hard to support from the poem or, indeed, from anywhere else—it has quite properly been questioned whether the decision attributed to Byrhtnoð in the poem actually *would* have been so foolhardy. 'Quixotic and generous' are somewhat more positive, but equally suspect terms, and it goes too far to invoke, as some critics have, notions of fair play and sportsmanship. One might wonder whether it is even necessary in historical terms to refer somewhat apologetically, as Tolkien did, for example, to Byrhtnoð having 'died for his folly. But it was a noble error'.[33]

The situation as it stood and in which Byrhtnoð found himself—it was not one of his own making, by the way, like Roland's final stand at Roncesvalles—was a stalemate. To assume, as Bowra did, that Byrhtnoð should have held the Vikings at bay until they gave up and went somewhere else, is a little naïve.[34] The Viking force would simply have attacked elsewhere on the same coast, but allowing them to come forward and fight with a Saxon army that

33 J. R. R. Tolkien, 'The Homecoming of Beorhtnoth, Beorhthelm's Son'. in *The Tolkien Reader* (New York: Ballantine, 1966), p. 23 (originally in *Essays and Studies of the English Association*, NS 6, 1953, 1–18). M. W. Grose and D. McKenna use the term 'quixotic' in their *Old English Literature* (London: Evans, 1973), p. 76f, but treat the whole thing rather like a sporting event, something which strikes as a misleading interpretation at best, and potentially absurd. On Byrhtnoð's generalship, see both W. A. Samouce, 'General Byrhtnoth'. *Journal of English and Germanic Philology* 52 (1963), 129–35 and (countering this, but in many places equally unsupportable), A. D. Mills, 'Byrhtnoð's Mistake in Generalship'. *Neuphilologische Mitteilungen* 67 (1966), 14–27. The negative reasons cited for Byrhtnoð's concession are all from Mills.

34 Bowra, *Heroic Poetry*, p. 122.

was actually prepared might have led to a great propaganda victory. Anglo-Saxons typically fought in line formation at close quarters with long spears, a technique which led them to victory under Ælfred at Ethandune in 878.[35] Demands for tribute would have been easier to reject, too. Apart from the *Anglo-Saxon Chronicle*, most of the medieval sources refer to the battle, moreover, as having been close. The *Life of St Oswald*, a Latin work written between 997 and 1005, says that the Vikings were severely damaged, 'Dani quoque mirabiliter sunt uulnerati,' and the twelfth-century *Liber Eliensis* is even more specific; the Anglo-Saxon force nearly put them to flight: 'pene in fugam eos converterat'.[36] In the event, the battle *was* lost, and the poem, it is true, does not mention how close the fight was; yet it still makes a long-term propaganda point in the role that the dead Byrhtnoð plays, if such a term is permissible, within the poem and afterwards. The first consequence of Byrht-noð's death is negative, in that a number of his followers—more than expected—abandon the fight, a detail mentioned in the *Life of St Oswald* as well. They do not remember their obligations to the dead man, the poet tells us, or else they would not have fled. This leaves, however, the *comitatus*, the close group of *heorðgeneatas*, 'hearth-comrades', for whom the dead earl remains an inspiration to the last. Placed in a new situation in which they have had no determining say, these close associates are set up in contrast to those who fled, and they accept the clear choice either of avenging their lord or dying with him, just as the disciples swear to do for Christ in the Old Saxon *Heliand*. Indeed, there it is St Thomas who puts the idea into words, the one disciple less sure than the others of the reality of Christ's sacrifice. He notes, furthermore, that they must do so to safeguard their reputation later on amongst

35 C. R. Dodwell, *Anglo-Saxon Art: A New Perspective* (Manchester: MUP, 1982), p. 286 stresses this point. On the details of fighting, see Charles W. Whister, *Ethandune 878: King Alfred's Campaign from Athelney* (London: Nutt, [1900]).

36 See Michael Lapidge, 'The Life of St Oswald'. and Alan Kennedy, 'Byrhtnoth's Obits and Twelfth-Century Accounts of the Battle of Maldon'. in Scragg, *Battle*, pp. 51–8 and 59–80. Citations are from the texts given in these papers.

men.[37] In the *Battle of Maldon,* one of the inner group, Ælfwine, is given an important speech in which he asserts first of all his own lineage, and then indicates that death or glory are not direct alternatives, since death may be unavoidable, but then would attract fame. Ælfwine himself does not seek even posthumous glory, however; it is once again that people should not sing the wrong songs about him. In literary terms the wish in the poem is again self-fulfilling, since the poem itself represents the right sort of song. Those, too, who flee the field after Byrhtnoð falls—Godric, Godrinc and Godwig—have in the literary mode already suffered the fate that Ælfwine wants to avoid. Ælfwine's speech is first of all general, and then personal:

> nu mæg cunnian   hwa cene sy.
> Ic wylle mine æÞelo   eallum gecyÞan,
> Þæt ic wæs of Myrcon   miccles cynnes;
> wæs min ealda fæder   Ealhelm haten,
> wis ealdorman   woruldsælig.
> Nu sceolon me on Þære Þeode   Þegenas ætwitan
> Þæt ic of ðisse fyrde   feran wille,

37 A point made in relation to the *Battle of Maldon,* though without drawing further parallels between Christ and Byrhtnoð, in the fascinating Belfast inaugural lecture in 1971 by the late Ronald G. Finch, *Heroes in Germany—Ancient and Modern* (Belfast: The Queen's University, 17 November 1971), p. 18, with reference to *Heliand,* lines 3996–4002. The lecture is of some importance overall. Ute Schwab's paper '*The Battle of Maldon:* A Memorial Poem'. in Cooper, *Maldon,* pp. 63–85, develops the point (p. 80), which had been made before (though not, as Schwab thought, exclusively), in another important study, that by Rosemary Woolf, 'The Ideal of Men Dying with their Lord'. *Anglo-Saxon England* 5 (1976), 63–81, which compares the poem with the *Germania* of Tacitus. Woolf's paper is reprinted in her collected essays, *Art and Doctrine,* ed. Heather O'Donoghue (London: Hambledon, 1986), pp. 175–96, and she discusses the question of *ofermode* in her essay 'The Devil in Old English Poetry' in the same volume, p. 8f. (pp. 1–14). See for the Old Saxon text *Heliand und Genesis,* ed. Otto Behaghel, 8th edn by Walther Mitzka, 9th edn by Burkhard Taeger (Tübingen: Niemeyer, 1984), with English translations by Marianne Scott, *Heliand* (Chapel Hill: U. North Carolina Press, 1966) and G. Ronald Murphy, *The Heliand* (London and New York: OUP, 1992), plus a German version by Felix Genzmer, *Heliand* (Stuttgart: Reclam, 1966).

eard gesecan   nu min ealdor ligeð
forheawen æt hilde.   Me is Þæt hearma mæst . . .
(lines 215–23)

[Now we shall see who is bold. I want to make my lineage
known to all men—that I come from a great Mercian family,
grandson of the wise and rich ealdorman Ealhelm. Mercian
warriors will not be able to mock me for wanting to leave
this force, now that my lord has been hacked down. That
is the worst thing of all to me . . .]

Precisely what the last comment refers back to is unclear—the
loss of Byrhtnoð or the possibility of mockery. Either would be
appropriate. The same point about avoiding mockery is voiced by
the next speaker, Leofsunu, as well. The speech of Ælfwine is far
more central than the celebrated and of course immensely moving
words of exhortation spoken towards the end by Byrhtwold:

Hige sceal Þe heardra,   heorte Þe cenre,
mod sceal Þe mare,   Þe ure mægen lytlað (lines 312f)

[Our minds shall be stronger, our hearts bolder,
our courage greater, as our power decreases.]

Those sentiments, however memorable and, indeed, inspiring for
later generations in comparable contexts, are here the expression of
their immediate situation. The motivation to continue fighting depends, though, upon the dead Byrhtnoð. The words of Ælfwine—that
his lord 'ligað forheawen'—recur in a variety of forms: 'nu ure Þeoden
lið . . .' (line 231), 'He læg Þegenlice ðeodne gehende . . .' (line
294), 'Her lið ure ealdor eall forheawen . . .' (line 314) ['now that
our lord lies here', 'he lay beside his lord as a warrior should', 'here
lies our earl, cut down']. The last follows those much-quoted words
of Byrhtwold, and the exhortation as such depends upon the love
of and feudal obligation to Byrhtnoð, whose death can inspire men
to battle, just as the poem itself might inspire men to battle later.
Whatever the reason for the military leader Byrhtnoð's decision in
giving the Vikings passage across the causeway the individual warrior—the other kind of hero in the work—has two choices only: to
keep his word to his accepted overlord, Byrhtnoð (who is categorised

as the paymaster too, as *beahgifan*, 'giver of gold rings') or to be a coward like Godric, who is pilloried by the poet both directly and through Ælfwine. This is clearly of such importance that the poet felt constrained to make quite clear that another Godric, referred to just before the text breaks off, is *not* the one who fled. Ælfwine and the rest take over the central place in the poem after Byrhtnoð falls, and they are warriors of stature in their own rights. Of course we cannot speak here of a heroism of the common man—that would not come, perhaps, until more modern wars—but they compare for all that with the soldier of 1915 whose words were cited earlier.[38]

The battle of Maldon was lost to the Vikings, and within twenty years Cnut was on the throne; but the Anglo-Saxon poem presents the military defeat as a triumph of the heroic ethos in which the moral integrity of Byrhtnoð's *comitatus*, at least, remained intact, and which, as a poem, is his and their memorial, allowing Byrhtnoð to inspire others because he fell in an honourable attempt to preserve the position of *Æþelredes eard*, even if at the last his attempt to do so failed. It is clear that the Anglo-Saxon poem does not present the whole picture of the Viking invasions.[39]

---

38 See Andrew Rutherford, *The Literature of War: Studies in Heroic Virtue* (Basingstoke: 1989). Rutherford has a chapter on 'The Common Man as Hero' in the First World War, noting how the ordinary soldier remained committed to the activity which he nevertheless condemned (see p. 80). That the other warriors are as important as Byrhtnoð, something made clear in a recent paper by W. G. Busse and R. Holtei in *Neophilologus* 65 (1981), 614–21, with the provocative title '*The Battle of Maldon*: A Historical, Heroic and Political Poem'.

39 A very recent collection of essays on the poem has the subtitle 'Fiction and Fact,' and in an essay on '*The Battle of Maldon*: Fact or Fiction?' Donald Scragg points to its presentation perhaps of the truth, but not of the whole truth, such as the fact that the Vikings did eventually win rather more than this one battle, Cooper, *Maldon*, pp. 19–31. There has been some debate about who led the Vikings at Maldon, and in spite of a reference in the Parker *Chronicle* to 'Unlaf'. the *communis opinio* is that it was probably *not* the celebrated Olaf Tryggvason. But the poet would doubtless have been satisfied to know that it is Byrhtnoð's name that has survived as the song's hero, rather than any of the Vikings. The conquering *sælida* or *sæmann*, are presented so neutrally throughout as to be literally unmemorable except as the force against which the named and characterised Anglo-Saxons have to fight. Clearly negative references are few and far between.

Unlike the *Ludwigslied*, which celebrates a real victory, and the *Song of Roland*, which pretends to do so even though it is really about a calamity, the *Battle of Maldon* shows us a defeat, but places in the foreground the victory of inescapable duty, the duty of those involved at different levels within a political context. The warriors do their appointed tasks to the best of their abilities and are praised; they are condemned if they avoid those duties. The poem is in the last analysis a kind of *Bewältigung der Vergangenheit*, a justification of an event in which Byrhtnoð's heroic concession serves to explain why the battle was lost.[40]

Of the poems so far looked at, the *Modus Ottinc* reminds us that the Germanic hero must be seen to be tested (a motif we shall encounter with another king in the *Ludwigslied*). The *Grípispá* demonstrates (in a peculiar but memorable literary manner) the need for the hero always to have acted in accordance with his own concept of duty in the face of a completely unavoidable and potentially evil turn of events. Sigurðr must act in such a way as to prevent later reproach, even if the poem gives us no indication of the social or political reasons why the hero should feel that impulse. In the *Battle of Maldon* we return to a clearer historical and political sphere. Byrhtnoð attracts (perhaps) a modicum of reproach in the reference to pride, but once he is dead his act attracts no opprobrium. Godric, though, who is mentioned three times—more than most others in the work—is firmly branded as a coward. And yet Byrhtnoð and the warriors are not, as has often been assumed, actively seeking glory. What they are concerned to do is what they feel to be their duty; the heroes keep faith, with

---

40 This would apply whether the poem was composed fairly soon after the battle itself or whether, as some critics think, it is a deliberately historical piece written fifty or more years later. See on the point C. L. Wrenn, *A Study of Old English Literature* (London: Harrap, 1967), p. 186f, and in particular J. B. Bessinger, 'Maldon and the *Óláfsdrápa*: An Historical Caveat'. *Comparative Literature* 14 (1962 = *Festschrift for Arthur G. Brodeur*), 23–35, and N. F. Blake, 'The Genesis of the Battle of Maldon'. *Anglo-Saxon England* 7 (1978), 119–29. Bessinger speaks of 'an historical awkwardness' in interpretations of *Maldon*, but it is not impossible to link the events there described with the historical situation and the crossing of the causeway.

themselves (Offa's kinsman and Eadric), with their family (Ælfwine), with their overlord (the *comitatus*), or with Æthelred's kingdom (Byrhtnoð), and this may lead to fame after death, but the private acceptance of public duty is the key, and their reward is the everlasting song itself.[41]

41 I would not agree entirely with the emphases placed by Roberta Frank, 'The Battle of Maldon and Heroic Literature', in Scragg, *Battle*, pp. 196–207, but would place the speeches by Ælfwine and Leofsunu in the foreground, and question whether there is any glory-seeking in the work at all. Tolkien, 'Homecoming', stresses the heroic nature of the followers, but possibly places too much emphasis on the supposed folly of the leader. See Paul Kocher, *Master of Middle-Earth* (Harmondsworth: Penguin, 1974), pp. 165–75, who goes further even than his subject, Tolkien. To refer to 'criminal folly' by Brythnoð is hard to justify.

2

Coping with Necessity

Hildebrand, Gunnarr and Völundr

Tucked away in the introduction to E. V. Gordon's primer of Old Norse is a comment which bears repeating on a regular basis to combat a common misconception about the Germanic hero. It is worth quoting in full:

> The chief evil in life which men had to face in those violent days was death by the sword. That is why Norse authors usually have feuds or battles as the setting of heroic story. Their motives in doing so are often misunderstood, for many critics have attributed to them a delight in battle and killing for its own sake; but, on the contrary, they saw in it the greatest evil, the one that required the most heroic power to turn into good.[42]

Whether or not the hero is always able to turn things to the good is a matter of debate, but it *is* the mark of the Germanic hero that he copes with, rather than seeks out, the blows of fate, even though he may be described as actually fighting with a will; and given his status, the way in which he does so can affect not only his own life, but that of the society in which he lives. Fate, however, can be

---

42 E. V. Gordon, *An Introduction to Old Norse* (London: OUP, 1927), p. xxx. The establishing of a reputation is not the primary aim, as is implied for example in Michael D. Cherniss, *Ingeld and Christ: Heroic Concepts and Values in Old English Christian Poetry* (The Hague: Mouton, 1972), p. 83f.

malicious—*wewurt*, cruel fate, is the appropriate variation applied in one of the texts—so that sometimes all that the hero can do is choose to accept. Three very different early poems demonstrate various ways in which different heroes respond to and act in situations in which they are (sometimes literally) trapped. In the first, the Old High German *Hildebrandslied*, fate blocks every possible exit for the hero, so that he has no choice but to follow a particular course of action demanded by the political framework in which he operates. In the second, the Norse *Atlakviða*—the so-called lay of Atli or Attila—the hero, the Burgundian king Gunnarr, both accepts and uses his own inevitable destruction to a political end. The third piece is one of the most unusual of the hero poems, another Edda-poem, the *Völundarkviða*, the tale of Völundr (whom we know better perhaps as Wayland the Smith), which shows us a hero cast down by fate's blows, but taking revenge with a completeness that is as watertight as fate's own entrapment of Hildebrand in the German poem.

The Old High German *Hildebrandslied* is a literary and philological nightmare. Preserved on the two spare outside pages of a manuscript (and both now back in Germany after a series of adventures and an entirely unofficial sojourn in the USA after the Second World War), the work is incomplete, although only a very small amount appears to be missing from the end and there is no excuse for ignoring the work on the grounds that it is a fragment. The verse form, albeit clearly the Germanic alliterative line, is ragged and there are lines that cannot with the best will in the world be scanned. On a couple of occasions, passages have been copied badly, and in another place there is a well-founded suspicion that there is a portion missing and/or some lines misplaced. Furthermore, the work as we have it is written in a language which is genuinely impossible, a mixture of High and Low German caused by the unsuccessful attempt to convert a poem in High German—in the Bavarian dialect, in fact—into Low German, using a few Anglo-Saxon letters into the bargain. The alliteration only works in High German, and some of the Low German forms are actually incorrect, but still it is possible to find in the text a word of four letters,—*chud*, the modern German *kund* and English *couth*, 'known'— the first two letters of which are Bavarian, while the last two (with the missing nasal that we have in *kund*) point to Low German.

A Bavarian original takes us further southwards, and some of the names indicate that the stage before the one we have was Lombardic—Lombardic being the Germanic language of northern Italy in the sixth century. In fact, a reconstruction of the poem in Lombardic was published as recently as 1959, which is something of an achievement, given that it printed a poem which may or may not have existed in a language in which we possess very little material indeed. We might take the work back even further,—indeed philologists have tried to do so—from the Lombards to the Goths, because the context of the work is the world of the Goths and the Huns in the fifth century. That is, there are references in the text to a distorted view of history not uncommon in Germanic heroic literature in which Theoderic (or Dietrich) the Ostrogoth, king of Rome and murderer of the philosopher Boethius, is perceived as an exile, having been driven out of his 'rightful' kingdom by Odoaker, the man he killed to *get* that kingdom. In this literary version of history Theoderic is conflated with his father, Theodemer, and seen as an ally of Attila, king of the Huns, who in reality died just before the real Theoderic was born. But no matter: this is history rewritten for the successful, and it gives us a context. It is possible that there may indeed have been a Gothic version of the *Hildebrandslied*, and people tried in the nineteenth century to reconstruct that as well.

The plot of the poem—a fight between a father and his son—is well-established, and occurs elsewhere in literature: in Greek, in Old Irish, and indeed in modern English, in Matthew Arnold's 'Sohrab and Rustum'. Whilst acknowledging the antiquity of the ideas, we have nevertheless to accept the imperfect Old High German text that we have, and in fact, in spite of some adverse criticism of it, it will do very well indeed.[43] A. T. Hatto was perfectly justified when in 1973 he wrote a paper comparing the various versions, nailing his colours to the mast in his title: 'On

43 Willy Krogmann, *Das Hildebrandslied in der langobardischen Urfassung hergestellt* (Berlin: Schmidt, 1959). See also Siegfried Gutenbrunner, *Von Hildebrand und Hadubrand: Lied-Sage-Mythos* (Heidelberg: Winter, 1976), a complex and thought-provoking book of considerable importance to the study of the poem, but the chart on p. 139 genuinely takes us back to the neolithic period.

the Excellence of the *Hildebrandslied*.[44] The work has, to be fair, continued to attract a wide range of critical responses, and simply as representatives perhaps I can mention three works from the last decade or so: Rosemarie Lühr's two volumes of *Studien zur Sprache des Hildebrandsliedes*, which devotes over 800 pages to the language of a poem which has rather fewer than 450 words; Jacques Bril's *L'Affaire Hildebrand' ou le meutre du fils*, which is a psychological study; and, as a curiosity, Gustav Süßmann's privately published volume which proves conclusively (for its author, that is) that the *Hildesbrandslied* is a forgery by its first publisher, Johann Georg von Eckhart.[45] My own approach will be more literary than the

44 Text of the poem cited from Steinmeyer, *Die kleineren althochdeutschen Denkmäler*, no 1. It is also in Braune, *Althochdeutsches Lesebuch*, no. 28, with a modern German translation in Schlosser, *Althochdeutsche Literatur*, pp. 264–7. English translations by Francis A. Wood, *The Hildebrandslied* (Chicago: U. Chicago P., 1914), and in Charles W. Jones, *Medieval Literature in Translation* (New York: McKay, 1950), p. 499f, Bruce Dickens, *Runic and Heroic Poems of the Old Teutonic Peoples* (Cambridge: CUP, 1915), pp. 78–85, and Brian Murdoch, *Lines Review*, 109 (1989), 20–22. See A. T. Hatto, 'On the Excellence of the *Hildebrandslied*'. *Modern Language Review* 68 (1973), 820–38; see also Werner Hoffmann, 'Das *Hildebrandslied* und die indo-germanischen Vater-Sohn-Kampf-Dichtungen'. *Beiträge* (Tübingen) 92 (1970), 26–42. I am here less concerned with the battle between father and son as such than with the reaction of the hero to the extreme situation, variations on which recur in Germanic and other heroic writing. For further references see Brian Murdoch and J. Sidney Groseclose, *Die althochdeutschen poetischen Denkmäler* (Stuttgart: Metzler, 1976), pp. 31–41, and H. van der Kolk, *Das Hildebrandlied: Eine forschungsgeschichtliche Darstellung* (Amsterdam: Scheltema and Holkema, 1967). The bibliography is very large, as it is for most of the works included in these studies.

45 Rosemarie Lühr, *Studien zur Sprache des Hildebrandsliedes* (Frankfurt/M. and Berne: Lang, 1982); the book is of course a useful one, and there are similarly extensive studies of the language of equally brief works such as the *Ludwigslied*. Neither Lühr's nor Bril's work is to be compared with that by Süßmann; and lest the extent of Lühr's book be used as ammunition against philological publications as such, a 1964 paper on physics had twice as many authors as paragraphs (see R. L. Weber, *A Random Walk in Science*, London: Institute of Physics, 1973, p. 84). See also Jacques Bril, *L''Affaire Hildebrand' ou le meutre du fils* (Paris: PUF, 1989) and Gustav Süßmann, *Das Hildebrandlied—gefälscht?* (Staufenberg: Eigenverlag Gustav Süßmann, 1988).

first, more pragmatic than the second, and I hope less eccentric than the third.

The plot of the work is easily summarised: a father has to fight with a warrior whom he discovers to be his son, and must kill him or die at his hands. Hildebrand is Theoderic's faithful retainer and vassal, and in our poem has fled with Theoderic from the anger of Odoaker, presumably to the court of the Huns. He left behind a bride and a baby son, and on his return has to face that son, now grown up, in single combat. The most unusual feature about Hildebrand is his age, and it is a feature of some importance. In spite of advanced years, Hildebrand has never been defeated, and he tells us so:

> ih wallota sumaro enti wintro sehstic ur lante
> dar man mih eo scerita in folc sceotantero
> so man mir at burc enigeru banun nigifasta.
> (lines 50–3)

[For thirty years I've been a wanderer, and I was always placed in the first battle-line, and before no fortress was I felled.]

Hildebrand's apparent invincibility works against him, however, because—as he himself comments in the next lines—he has been spared only to kill or be killed by his own son:

> nu scal mih suasat chind suertu hauwan
> breton mit sinu billiu eddo ih imo ti banin werdan.

[Now my own child will cut me down with his weapon, or I shall be his doom.]

The language is a little garbled in this section, but the sense is clear. Hildebrand is indeed a great fighter, and thus far a victorious one, as indeed he will be again. But the irony of all this is not just that he now has to fight his own son; it is that his son, whilst proud of his unknown father's reputation as a warrior, cannot believe that a warrior as bold in battle can still be alive. The apparent invincibility of the hero, even if not actually magical, can be a disadvantage if it is literally unbelievable.

The story is presented by a narrator who sets the scene for us in fewer than ten lines; but every point he gives us in those few lines is of importance for the understanding of the work. The names of the two warriors who are to fight each other, Hildebrand and Hadubrand, already indicate relationship, and we are told (though the protagonists do not know this yet) that they are father and son—*sunufatarungo* is a single compound in Old High German, and this brings them closer together.[46] They come as the chosen champions from two different armies; the narrator has set those armies in place, and even though they do not play any active role in the story, they do not go away. If we, as modern readers, must be reminded not to think of these armies as modern battalions but as smaller groups, we must also take care not to forget them: they form a silent audience for, and the political underlay of, the entire work.

Next, we are shown the two warriors arming, but although some of the phrases used here are formulaic, the matter is not to be overlooked. It is true that formulaic phrases can sometimes indicate that the content is of secondary importance, but this is not the case here. We must remember that armour: it is all a warrior possesses and it will be of great significance later. Finally, as the battle is about to start, we are given the lead-in to the dialogue that comprises most of the rest of the work (with a notable exception later when the narrator makes another highly significant insertion).[47] Hildebrand addresses Hadubrand, we are

46 Important studies of this aspect of the work (discussed—and on occasion over-interpreted—by most critics of the work of course, and part of one of the oldest European literary motifs) are those by Wolfgang Harms, *Der Kampf mit dem Freund oder Verwandten in der deutschen Literatur bis um 1300* (Munich: Eidos, 1963), pp. 18–29, and also Herbert Kolb, 'Hildebrands Sohn'. in *Studien zur deutschen Literatur des Mittelalters*, ed. Rudolf Schützeichel and Ulrich Fellmann (Bonn: Bouvier, 1979), pp. 51–75. See also Birgit Meinecke, *Chind und barn im Hildebrandslied* (Göttingen: Vandenhoeck und Ruprecht, 1987), and Joseph Harris, 'Hadubrand's Lament'. in *Heldensage und Heldendichtung im Germanischen*, ed. Heinrich Beck (Berlin: de Gruyter, 1988), pp. 81–41.

47 See the interesting early work by Wilhelm Luft, *Die Entwickelung des Dialoges im alten Hildebrandsliede* (Berlin: PhD diss., Fr. -Wilhelms Univ., 1895).

told, because he is the older man, and although he wishes to establish the credentials of this young warrior who has been set up against him, he does it—so the narrator tells us—in few words, *fohem wortum*. The hero is customarily concerned with action, not speech, and the dialogue begins with a straightforward question from Hildebrand to establish that his adversary is worthy of him in terms of family and reputation, although it is for us ironic when he asks who the other man's father was. The irony continues as a new theme is developed: that of knowledge, and that curiously hybrid word *chud*, 'known' now takes on some importance as the older man claims to know all men. Certainly he knows the father of this younger man, whom he addesses as *chind*, 'child', better than he thinks.

Hadubrand speaks (he is designated as 'Hildebrand's son', and throughout the dialogue the speaker is introduced with his patronymic, underlining at once the irony of the situation and the question of heredity and family), and his opening statement is extremely revealing. His name is Hadubrand, he tells us (and his adversary), his father's was Hildebrand. This is factual. The next part of what he has to say is reported: old, wise men from his people ('our people' in this context already implies 'not yours') who are now dead (a significant small addition) have told him that Hildebrand fled with Theoderic from the wrath of Odoaker. This fits with the pseudo-history of Dietrich/Theoderic. When Hildebrand fled, however, we are told that he left behind a young wife and a child, with no inheritance, and much attention has been paid to that passage:

> her furlaet in lante   luttila sitten,
> prut in pure   barn unwahsan,
> arbeo laosa . . . (lines 20–23)

[He left behind him in poverty a bride in the bower, with an ungrown child, deprived of inheritance.]

The bride is still in the bower, the marriage chamber, so that Hildebrand had no more sons after Hadubrand. The question of inheritance—whether it is true that the son inherited nothing, or will inherit nothing—is another matter to be stored up by the audience for the moment.[48] The final part of Hadubrand's opening speech represents his feelings and thoughts about his father, and this statement sums up the nature of the hero:

> her was eo folches at ente,   imo was eo fehta ti leop:
> chud was her   chonnem mannum.
> ni waniu ih iu lib habbe (lines 27–29)

[He was always at the forefront of battle and was always ready to fight. He was known to all men. I do not think that he is still alive.]

Hadubrand's words about his father's position in battle will—as we have already seen—be picked up by Hildebrand himself. Hadubrand is proud of the reputation of his well-known warrior father (although knowledge is ironical throughout the poem), but in a sense not proud enough. If he really *was* that prominent a warrior, he must by now be dead. But in the literary fiction, Hildebrand has one more heroic deed to carry out, and his decision to do so, his acquiescence to a cruel fate, is as important as the act itself.

Hildebrand now realises the extremity of the situation which he has to face. It is worth noting at this point that Hadubrand's views harden, as Hildebrand realises the extent to which he is trapped. The poem centres upon the older man, and it is his reactions with which are are concerned. He has been sent out as a champion to fight, and hence has a responsibility towards the silent army from which he has come; and yet his adversary turns out to be his only legitimate son. Those who could identify Hildebrand to his son *are* dead, and the son thinks that the father who left him without his inheritance must *be* dead.

It is at this point that Hildebrand attempts to remedy the situation by action, and in doing so makes a mistake. Commenting that the young man has never fought such a close relative—the statement is quite unambiguous—he offers him a gift, *bauga*, a twisted golden arm-ring, the kind of treasure demanded by the Vikings at Maldon,

---

48   For an exhaustive philological discussion of the point, see Ute Schwab, *Arbeo laosa* (Berne: Francke, 1972).

Coping with Necessity

at which Byrhtnoð was so scornful. This action is described by the narrator, and again every word counts:

> want her do ar arme   wuntana bauga
> cheisuringu gitan,   so imo se der chuning gap,
> Huneo truhtin . . . (lines 33–35)

[From his arm he took a ring made of twisted imperial gold, given to him by the king, Lord of the Huns.]

This is part of Hildebrand's property, property that should one day be inherited by Hadubrand. Yet it is clearly recognisable as coming from the Huns, so that instead of being seen as part of a gesture of conciliation, that torque is seen as confirmation that the man offering it is a Hun, which is what Hadubrand now takes him to be,[49] interpreting the offer as a trick and telling Hildebrand that gifts are to be received at spearpoint, an interesting parallel to the situation in the *Battle of Maldon*, where Byrhtnoð *offered* spears instead of the tribute demanded. Although the comparison between Byrhtnoð's rejection of the Viking demand and Hadubrand's of this gift has been made, it is not close, however, as the question of knowledge is crucial on this occasion, as it was not in *Maldon*.[50] Hadubrand even refers to his father now as an old Hun. What is more ironic, Hadubrand attributes Hildebrand's great age to his use of trickery of this kind, although both the gold arm-ring and the man's age itself offer in reality evidence of his prowess as a warrior.

---

49 Some critics have interpreted the entirely unambiguous reference to the king of the Huns as a reference to Theoderic; they need to go on and assume some kind of confusion on the part of the poet, of course, and such a process is not only unnecessarily tortuous, but also defeats a major point in the poem. See for example Herfried Münkler, *Das Blickfeld des Helden: Zur Darstellung des Römischen Reiches in der germanisch-deutschen Heldendichtung* (Göppingen: Kümmerle, 1983), p. 135. The earliest critics—such as Grimm—quite properly understood the words literally. Others see the reference as an unimportant detail: Lev Schücking, 'The Ideal of Kingship in *Beowulf*'. in Lewis E. Nicholson, *An Anthology of Beowulf Criticism* (Notre Dame: U. Notre Dame Press, 1963), p. 45. The point is, however, hardly 'colourless'.
50 Ralph W. V. Elliott, 'Byrhtnoth and Hildebrand: A Study in Epic Technique'. *Comparative Literature* 14 (1962), 53–70, esp. p. 58.

Hadubrand's already firm attitude hardens, however, and now, in expressing his complete disbelief that this is his father, he invokes a further set of unreachable witnesses: seafarers have told him that Hildebrand actually *is* dead, fallen in battle.

There is a certain amount of confusion in our somewhat battered text at this point,[51] but Hildebrand's reaction, at least, is clear. Cruel fate will now take its course, all the possible exits have been closed off, there are no witness available to explain things, to restore proper knowledge, and the attempt at reconciliation has failed. But there *are* witnesses to *this* encounter: the watching armies have seen and heard all. Hildebrand has no choice now but to fight, and it is at this point that he expresses his realisation that he must either kill or be killed by his (only) son. It is at this point, too, that we return to questions of inheritance and the battle-gear of the two men. Hildebrand comments first that he would indeed have to be a cowardly Hun (an ironic self-adopting of Hadubrand's assumption) not to fight, and reminds his adversary that should he win he may take his battle-gear. This would include in any case the gold torque already offered. Now this would be Hadubrand's in any case by right of inheritance on Hildebrand's death. The difference is that he is forced to earn it, just as Hildebrand himself is forced by circumstances to fight.[52]

This is not a battle poem—and certainly there is no glorying in battle here. Nor, indeed, is there any question of the hero actively seeking fame. What Hildebrand is doing is fighting because his position as Thedoeric's man and his reputation demands it: because

---

51 Lines 46–8, though assigned to Hildebrand, are probably misplaced, part of a speech in which Hadubrand denies that this obviously rich warrior who is now standing before him is—as he claims—an exile. There has never been any agreement on where the lines should go, however, or what is missing. The irony of following a line asserting that 'Hildebrand, the son of Heribrand is dead' with the formulaic opening 'Hildebrand, the son of Heribrand spoke . . .' is patent, however.

52 Recent articles stressing this element are Alain Renoir's 'The Armor of the *Hildebrandslied*'. *Neuphilologische Mitteilungen* 78 (1977), 389–95, and W. McDonald, 'Too Softly a Gift of Treasure'. *Euphorion* 78 (1984), 1–16. See also the brief paper by Kenneth J. Northcott, '*Das Hildebrandslied*: A Legal Process?' *Modern Language Review* 56 (1961), 342–8.

he has no choice. The battle-part of the work is brief, therefore, and clearly we do not have the ending. By the time the poem breaks off, however, the battle is in the later hand-to-hand stage, and we need spend little time on speculation as to how the battle *might* end. It is true that the men could kill each other or the son could kill the father. The so-called *Jüngeres Hildebrandslied*, the later German poem of Hildebrand, in which the wife is still alive and to whom the warriors return in the end is quite a different work and is irrelevant here. We do not even need the evidence of parallel tales of father-son conflicts, however, nor that of the so-called 'death-song' of Hildebrand at the end of the Icelandic *Asmundarssaga Kappabana* (where the Hildebrand figure talks about having killed his son), for the ending to be clear.[53] It is Hildebrand's fate as a hero not just to fight but to kill his son and thus his entire line. Only with this outcome does the poem make sense in logical terms. The details could never have been known had both men been killed, and if the son had been victorious his boast would have been simply that he had killed a cowardly Hun. Remember that there are no witnesses to the *reality* of the situation except Hildebrand himself, the only man who could have provided all the information for the poem as such.

Hadubrand could not inherit by deeds, and because of that he cannot inherit any other way. The Goethean concept of 'was du ererbt von deinen Vätern hast / Erwirb es, um es zu besitzen' [what you have inherited must be earned if you are to possess it] is realised in the fate of Hadubrand. He has at all events inherited in genetic terms his father's prowess in battle, else he would not have been chosen as a champion, but the armour and the gold arm-rings will still stay with Hildebrand, whose status as a hero now, however, will not rest upon the fact that he wins this battle, but rather on the fact that he has to bring himself to fight it at all. All Hildebrand will leave his

---

53 The *Jüngeres Hildebrandslied* and the Icelandic death-song are in Heinz Mettke, *Altdeutsche Texte* (Leipzig: Bibliographisches Institut, 1970), pp. 122–6. There is also a version of the death-song in Saxo Grammaticus and a parallel to the positive version of the *Later Hildebrandslied* in the Norse *Þidrekssaga*. The name of the son varies. Harms, *Kampf mit dem Freund*, pp. 23–9, discusses the *Later Hildebrandslied* in detail, devoting more space to it than to the original *Hildebrandslied*.

son is a memorial, the right song for both, since no blame attaches to Hadubrand, who has no reason to believe what this apparent Hun tells him. In the circular fictionality of the literary hero, the *Hildebrandslied* itself functions as a memorial to the son by showing how the father was trapped by *wewurt* into a single course of action.

The *Hildebrandslied* looks beyond the simple *res gestae*; the hero reacts and acts according to a set of inner principles which are partly determined by outside forces (duty to Theoderic, the view of the hero by others in and after his life) in an extreme situation. But in spite of its quasi-historical references, the *Hildebrandslied* is extra-historical, and it is also a literary product. The poem itself has a separate function as a memorial, as a demonstration and a confirmation that Hildebrand *did* act in a proper manner, worthy of himself, his ancestry (the poem refers also to *his* father, Heribrand), and indeed worthy of the son that he has to kill. Here the warrior-hero acts in accordance with the ideals of his state, even if that individual did not seek out the situation. It has been argued that since there is no acceptable ending to the work, it was left deliberately unfinished, so that the poem as we have it is, in a sense, complete, although in parallel versions the father indeed kills the son. Only intervention from some other source could stop the fight—as in the *Jüngeres Hildebrandslied*—but the political framework precludes that. Hildebrand has to win for Theoderic.

Is Hildebrand a tragic hero?[54] He comes closer than most, and he may be seen as the maker of his own doom in his ultimately misguided act of offering the ring to his son. Nor is there in this work any *overt* reference (as there frequently is) to the continuation of the hero's reputation in the song itself, and there is no Christian afterlife guaranteed for either man, the few references to God being little more than window-dressing. Certainly Hildebrand has been trapped by fate into a conflict of moral and political duties because of his own prowess as a warrior. But in spite of some attempts to find (incurred, though not, of course, necessarily deserved) guilt in the

54 In spite of this question, it is hard to support Heather Stuart's view in 'The *Hildebrandslied*: An Anti-Heroic Interpretation'. *German Life and Letters* NS 32 (1978/9), 1–9.

older man because he abandoned his young wife and child, there is no sense of *hubris* expressed in the poem. Hildebrand accepts fate almost in a concrete version of a Kantian view of freedom, the individual judgement that demonstrates awareness of an imperative, although it is in this case a duty to which he has no inclination. This is pre-enlightenment writing, and the imperative is politically determined as well as by an inner force, and the political-empirical basis is made concrete by the presence of the armies. It is necessary, however (perhaps we may even say in terms of teleological government), for Theoderic's forces to prevail, and Hildebrand, as Theoderich's right-hand man, has a feudal duty to ensure that they do. His ethics are the acceptance of that duty. Hadubrand, too, one assumes, would have had to applaud the immediate decision made by the older man to fight, given the development of the situation and the circumstances. In terms of freedom, then, the freedom visible in the hero—and presented in extreme form in Hildebrand—is that of a freedom to accept that one might have to do something which one would not choose to do. We might even move beyond Kant to a more clearly existentialist reading of the poem (or at least take it as far as Nietzsche) in indicating the ultimate effective isolation of the central figure,[55] since part of Hildebrand's entrapment lies in the complete impossibility of his asserting his individuality—in simple terms, of showing who he *is*—except through a specific individual action. That action is not capricious, but is shown in the poem to be inevitable and accepted by Hildebrand himself as the only way in which he can act. He cannot assert his individuality by saying; the only way he can demonstrate that he is the warrior he claims to be is by doing, that is, by acting as Theoderic's warrior, and accepting the inevitable, fighting as best he can. Even to fight to lose would destroy his identity, and the irony is that the only way in which he

---

55 For a lucid set of comments on freedom and the will in Kant (with references back to Aristotle), and in the existentialists, with special reference to Nietzsche, see Mary Warnock, *Existentialism* (London: OUP, 1970), pp. 4–22. On Kant's differentiation of actions for which there is no inclination in the *Grundlegung*, see David Ross, *Kant's Ethical Theory: A Commentary on the Grundlegung zur Metaphysik der Sitten* (Oxford: Clarendon, 1954), p. 14f.

can confirm his identity is by the essentially unnatural act of killing his son, and thus his own posterity. Only the poem remains.

Hildebrand will appear again at the end of the complex saga of the Nibelungen, but we may turn now to a very early, brief and somewhat unusual representative from that saga for a Germanic hero, this time a king, who once more carries out an act against inclination in a political context. The Edda poem known as the *Atlakviða* has been described as an *Urlied*, a primary version of that great cycle which in its later forms merges elements from Frankish, Burgundian and Hunnish history. The brief work, composed perhaps in the ninth century and included in the Codex Regius reflects two historical events: the fall of the Burgundians, and—more significantly—the sudden collapse of the hegemony of the Huns after Attila's death, reputedly of a haemorrhage on his wedding night with a German princess. Elsewhere his demise is attributed to drunkenness alone (a tradition Chaucer knew), but that drunkenness is here combined with an elaboration of the idea of his death in the marriage bed. The Attila figure himself is, in the *Atlakviða*, neither Germanic nor heroic, and at the centre is the Burgundian king Gunnarr. His death at the hands of Attila/Atli mirrors the historical fall of the Germanic Burgundians, of which nation *Nibelung* is probably a clan name, and who, led by a king Gundahari, fell first to the Romans under Ætius and then in 436 to the Huns, whom the Romans used as auxiliaries and with whom the Burgundians had already fought.[56] Elsewhere in literature Gunnarr/

56 Historical details are presented with clarity and supported by historical reference by Dronke, *The Poetic Edda*, i, 29–42, with (admirably cautious) comments of particular interest on the name Nibelung and the motif of the treasure. I have used Ursula Dronke's edition of this text, although her emendations sometimes differ from other editions and translations of the *Edda* (in the *Edda* edition of Finnur Jónsson the text is on pp. 385–97). The links between the *Atlakviða* and the Siegfried-Brünhilde-Gunther-Etzel complex as seen in the *Nibelungenlied*, for example, as explored in such detail by Andreas Heusler, *Nibelungensage und Nibelungenlied* (Dortmund: Ruhfus, 1920; 3rd edn 1929, with many reprints) are not relevant in this context, and for this reason a very early, indeed 'primitive' work has been chosen. Heusler discusses the work on pp. 23–6. See on the text Wolf, *Gestaltungskerne*, pp. 37–66.

Gundahari is treated less sympathetically than here, and Attila/Atli rather (although sometimes not a great deal) better,[57] but in the *Atlakviða* Gunnarr is a Germanic king, coping with a perceived situation, preserving himself and his people *as far as he can* against an alien force, that of the Huns, with whom his house is already uneasily intermarried. He falls, but the poet moves away from specific history to generality in linking his fall with the collapse of the Huns after Attila's death, historically nearly two decades later. The background of relationships is not explained in the work. We are simply shown how a messenger comes from Atli to Gunnarr, not demanding, but ostensibly inviting them to come and receive treasure at the court of the Huns. The message, delivered *kaldri roddo*, with a cold voice, is received by Gunnarr and Högni (the Hagen figure, here represented as his brother) in what is, as critics have frequently pointed out, a tense silence. Gunnarr states very clearly that they have no need of gifts from Atli, since their own treasures far surpass his; Högni, too, interprets a secret signal from Atli's wife, their sister Guðrun, that Atli plans treachery. Gunnarr decides, however, that they will go to the Hun court, and this decision is the most enigmatic feature of the work. To see this whole passage as a simple acceptance by Gunnarr of an unexplained fate, or even as an act of gratuitous vainglory, as has been done, begs too many questions.[58] Gunnarr's honour would not visibly be damaged by a refusal, unless it is simply because he is now allied to the Huns through marriage and a refusal would be insulting. As several critics have pointed out,[59] presumably he sees the invitation as a challenge. It is the first move in the projected further expansion of the Huns, a slightly more covert demand for tribute than those which we shall see Attila make in *Waltharius*. Gunnarr could have taken an armed

---

57 Dronke makes the point in her edition, and on Attila in literature, see Jennifer Williams, *Etzel der ríche* (Berne and Frankfurt/M.: Lang), 1981.
58 See Karl-Heinz Koch, 'Altes Sigurdlied und Altes Atlilied im Unterricht'. *Der Deutschunterricht* 8/1 (1956), 69–72. Koch's views on why Gunnarr sets off at all are unclear and his references to necessity are unconvincing.
59 As Carola Gottzmann, *Das alte Atlilied* (Heidelberg: Winter, 1973).

force with him—when he arrives at the castle of the Huns his sister rebukes him for not doing so, and he himself comments that it is too late to summon the Nibelungs—but then many more would have died. The Huns, indeed, had posted guards, expecting precisely such an approach. When first faced with the invitation, however, Gunnarr makes the decision to take it up quite alone— this is stressed in the poem—even in the face of Högni's perfectly well-substantiated reservations. He makes that decision 'sem konungr skyldi' [as a king ought], and also in a great spirit, with great courage, 'af móði storum' (strophe 9). His gesture, therefore, is approved by the poet, if not explained. The grandiose feeling of all this continues as he calls for drink, and then makes a defiant speech to the effect that the whole inheritance of the Nibelungs will be lost if he dies. The significance appears only later of his enigmatic statement that wolves will rule the Nibelung treasure. Although the word used for that treasure—*arfi Niflunga* (strophe 11)—is normal in Old Norse as with the Anglo-Saxon *yrfa* in this sense, it is literally the inheritance, *arfr*, of the Nibelungs. And the people weep when the few valiant men—*gunnhvata* [battle-bold] in strophe 12—leave the hall. As soon as the warriors arrive at Atli's court they are seized, although Högni defends himself to the extent of cutting down seven men and throwing another into the fire. This draws from the poet another generalised statement: 'svá skal froekn/ fiándom veriaz' (strophe 19) [thus a brave man should defend himself against enemies].[60] For the nature of the Germanic hero, however, the next few strophes are crucial. Gunnarr is now placed in a position of entrapment, but is offered (at least a potential) means of escape, through payment of tribute. Byrhtnoð, faced with such a question, gambled on a propaganda victory and refused, even if his historical master Æthelred eventually elected to pay. We shall see in the tale of Waltharius, too, how various nations *do* pay the tribute to the Huns. Gold, then,

---

60 The lines following these have been subjected to some emendations against the Codex Regius, and different readings have been offered; in this case Dronke's changes may not necessarily be the best; the strophic numbering also differs from edition to edition. Nevertheless, the objective statement stands.

is at the centre of the incident once again, and the brevity of the strophe concerned is striking. Where earlier we were given a complex picture of the Huns' hall and their defences, the bluntness of this strophe is remarkable, in the quick-fire *fornyrðislag* metre, the oldest of the Norse narrative metres, used elsewhere in the poem, too, to highlight statements of importance:

> Frágo frœknan
> ef fiör vildi
> Gotna Þióðann
> gulli kaupa. (strophe 20)

[They asked the brave man if he wanted to buy his life with gold.]

Gunnarr, then, here described as 'Lord of the Goths' (tribal designations vary somewhat), is trapped, and has now—regardless of why he chose to come in the first place—no way out. He can either pay tribute or die. However, what now becomes apparent is the true sense of his claim that if he does not return, no one will have the treasure of the Nibelungs, and now Gunnarr can act. When he demands first the heart of his brother Högni, the Huns attempt to trick him by bringing the heart of another less valiant warrior, the still-trembling heart of the cowardly Hialli, who is thus mocked *post-mortem*. The necessary absolute bravery (and indeed loyalty) of the Germanic hero, and its other side, the cowardice that we have seen in those who fled from Maldon, is thus demonstrated in this most graphic manner. Gunnarr recognises that this trembling heart cannot be Högni's, and the real heart is then brought. The whole incident is treated with literary parallelism: Hialli's heart is trembling, but trembled even more in the body; Högni's trembles hardly at all (we have been shown how bravely he died), but trembled even less in life. Now, however, Gunnarr has won: only two of them had known of the whereabouts of the Nibelung treasure, and now only Gunnarr survives. The Huns are therefore cheated of their prize; 'Rín skal ráða/ rógmálmi skatna' (strophe 27) [the Rhine shall rule the treasure, the metal that causes war]. We have seen the brave deaths of the warriors—how they died—but the *why* is equally important: their inherited treasure (in the form of *valbaugr* once again, rings of foreign, that is Roman imperial, gold) shall never come to the Huns. This may look at first sight rather like what some of the Victorians thought *should* have happened in Anglo-Saxon England, a refusal to pay the Danegeld regardless of the bloodbath that would then certainly have ensued. Indeed, Gunnarr has to die in the process, cast by Atli into a snake-pit, where he dies bravely, playing his harp to the last. Although this has been thought of as an unheroic death,[61] that it is indeed heroic is made clear by the objective statement of approval which it draws from the poet:

> Svá skal gulli
> froekn hringdrifi
> við fira halda. (strophe 32)

[This is the way a brave ring-giver ought to guard his own gold against other men.]

Gunnarr has—to the approval of the poet—shaped his own fate. Is this, however, just the necessary result of an act of bravado in coming to Atli's court in the first place, a pointless gesture of glory, the sort of thing that nineteenth-century imperialists wanted Æthelred to have done to the Danes? Once again, the real enigma of the work is why Gunnarr chose to make the decision to come at all, and with few men. We may recall that this is a decision applauded by the poet and which draws no hint of disapproval, not even as much as was aimed at Byrhtnoð for his decision to give quarter to the Vikings. The answer is that this is a *defeat* for Atli on his own ground and, what is more, his killing of Gunnarr leads directly (even if this telescopes actual historical events) to his own death at the hands of Gunnarr's sister Guðrun. First she kills their two sons and then gives the hearts to the warriors to eat (a reminiscence of the classical Medea motif); then she lures the drunken Atli to bed and kills him, after which she burns down the hall and dies with it. The Hun hegemony and Atli's hereditary line have been destroyed in this version. Gunnarr had gold, and

61 See Mowatt and Sacker, *The Nibelungenlied*, p. 144.

the Hun forces were strong and wanted to go further than just remain connected with him by marriage to his sister. Gunnar's final gamble, then, is on the treachery of the Huns, although he—like Högni—has every reason to suspect their motives in inviting him with his brother to their hall. He does not intend to pay tribute; rather he will die, because only this way can he make sure that he blocks all possibilities of the acquisition by the Huns of this treasure, which would increase their empire even more. By starving them of that extra gold—it is rightly and objectively dubbed *rógmálmi*, metal of strife—Gunnarr, though unable to preserve himself, has at least prevented the increase of the Huns. The rest of the Burgundians, of course, survive, in that Gunnar took only a small force with him.[62] The whole work pivots, though, on the lines I have quoted, and they are generalised by the poet: that this is how a ring-giver, a lord, should preserve gold against his enemies, from falling into the wrong hands. Whether or not Gunnarr could have foreseen the awful venegance exacted by Guðrun is a matter of speculation, but the collapse of the Huns—as indeed their hegemony did collapse, with amazing rapidity, on the death of the historical Attila—is the point of this work[63] Where the Greenland lay of Atli, the *Atlamál in Groenlenzko*, adapts the story and removes the historical details, and the German *Nibelungenlied* presents effectively the collapse of the Burgundians led by the at best ambiguous, and at worst ridiculous king Gunther, here Gunnarr's sacrifice is represented as the first blow against an alien force in the long term. Critics such as Ursula Dronke have examined closely the direct historical references to

---

62 On the stress in the work on the extreme concentration on the one hero, who is a king, dying for all his people, see von See, 'Held und Kollektiv'. pp. 11–13.

63 A glance at Colin McEvedy's *Penguin Atlas of Medieval History* (Harmondsworth: Penguin, 1961), pp. 16–22 illustrates the point very graphically indeed; simply by flicking through the earlier maps, the Hun empire grows to enormous proportions by 450, and then suddenly, in the next map (for 476), it is nowhere to be seen. See also Walter Goffart, 'The Map of the Barbarian Invasions', in *The Culture of Christendom: Essays in Medieval History in Commemoration of Denis T. Bethell*, ed. Marc A. Meyer (London: Hambledon, 1993), pp. 1–27.

Attila and to the Burgundians, but a more general comment on the Huns by the late Roman historian Ammianus Marcellinus gives us a picture of the Huns that Gunnarr presumably shared, and against which he was fighting:

> Per indutias infidi et inconstantes, ad omnem aurem incidentis spei novæ perquam mobiles, totum furori incitatissimo tribuentes. Inconsultorum animalium ritu, quid honestum inhonestumve sit, penitus ignorantes, flexiloqui et obscuri, nullius religionis vel superstitionis reverentia aliquando districti, auri cupidine immensa flagrantes . . .

> [If they call truces they are unreliable and do not keep faith, always ready to listen out for new possibilities that might crop up, giving way to blind fury too. Like dumb animals, they cannot distinguish between right and wrong, they are economical with the truth and like to be obscure; they have no respect for anyone's faith, and they are consumed with a massive desire for gold.][64]

'Auri cupidine immensa flagrantes' is precisely what Gunnarr had feared. The view of Attila changes fairly radically in other works—in fact sympathy for him seems to increase in inverse proportion to the vilification of Gundahari—but the lust for gold is there in *Waltharius* and in other works.

A final Old Norse poem, the *Völundarkviða* offers another approach to the trapped warrior. In this case the story is one of considerable antiquity, and the version in the *Elder Edda* may

---

64 Cited from the Loeb edition (though with my own translation) of *Ammianus Marcellinus*, ed. and trans. John C. Rolfe (Cambridge, Mass: Harvard UP, 1971f), iii, 386f. (= xxxi, 2, 11). See also C. D. Gordon, *The Age of Attila* (Ann Arbor: U. Michigan Press, 1960), p. 57, with other historical references; and Patrick Howarth, *Attila, King of the Huns* (London: Constable, 1994). On the Huns and Goths in general, see A. T. Hatto, 'The Secular Foe and the *Nibelungenlied*'. in *German Narrative Literature of the Twelfth and Thirteenth Centuries: Studies Presented to Roy Wisbey*, ed. Volker Honemann etc. (Tübingen: Niemeyer, 1994), pp. 157–71.

date back to a period roughly contemporary with that of the *Hildebrandslied*.[65] This time the historical background is of even greater obscurity, and the text is a veritable delight for antiquarians, containing as it does somewhat nebulous tales of mortals married to swan-maidens and a whole series of parallels with other cultures, most notably with the stories of Dædalos and indeed of the smith of the gods, Hephaistos. I do not propose to dwell on any of these aspects, nor indeed on the many versions of the tale from that in pictures on the Franks Casket to the *Þidrekssaga* and the Danish ballads, but wish rather to focus on the hero in this early work, Völundr himself.[66] Völundr is Wieland in German, Wayland in English, and we may begin with a more prosaic epitome of the first part of the Norse narrative: Völundr is the son of the Finnish king and a descendant of elves (he is even referred to as 'the lord of the elves'. but this merely indicates his special status). He is more greatly famed as a craftsman, a worker in metal, especially gold. His bride, the valkyrie Hervör the Wise, has left him and he lives alone in a forest. The Swedish king, Níðuðr sends a force of men to capture him, he is brought back and, so that he does not escape, he is hamstrung and kept on an island. The blows of fate suffered by Völundr and the trickery of Níðuðr

65 See G. Turville-Petre, *Origins of Icelandic Literature* (Oxford: Clarendon, 1953), p. 14, on the date and style. This text is cited from Jónsson, *Sæmundar-Edda*, pp. 141–53. See also Gustav Neckel, *Edda: Die Lieder des Codex Regius*, 4th edn rev. Hans Kuhn (Heidelberg: Winter, 1962). English translations again by Bellows, *The Poetic Edda*, and Terry, *Poems of the Vikings*. German translation by Genzmer, *Heldenlieder der Edda*.

66 On the different forms of the name, see George Gillespie, *A Catalogue of Persons Named in German Heroic Literature (700–1600)* (Oxford: Clarendon, 1973), pp. 141–3. The name is associated etymologically with manufacture, craftsmanship. On the name and all the different versions, see Robert Nedoma, *Die bildlichen und schriftlichen Denkmäler der Wielandsaga* (Göppingen: Kümmerle, 1988), with massive bibliography. Ker, *Epic and Romance*, links Völundr with Atli in the *Atlakvia*, but in fact Atli is far closer to the figure of Völundr's adversary, Níðuðr. See on the work as such Wolf, *Gestaltungskerne*, pp. 81–5, and more recently Paul Beekman Taylor, '*Völundarkviða*, *Þrymskviða* and the Function of Myth'. *Neophilologus* 78 (1994), 263–81.

are underscored in the first lines of an Anglo-Saxon poem, the marvellous elegy of *Deor*:[67]

> Welund him be wurman   wræces cunnade,
> anhydig eorl   earforþa dreag,
> hæfde him to gesiþþe   sorge 7 longaþ,
> wintercealde wræce,   wean oft onfond
> siþþan hine Niðhad on   nede legde,
> swoncre seonobende, on syllan monn.   (lines 1–6)

[Wayland knew about being an exile; the strong-minded warrior suffered agony and had sorrow and longing as his companions in his wintry exile, misery was often with him when Niðhad damaged the supple sinews and bound the better man.]

That last phrase—*syllan monn*—is crucial, and this is why Völundr has been taken at all. He is indeed a better, in fact a cleverer and more useful, man. The prose preamble to the *Edda* poem characterises him as such very simply:

> Hann var hagastr maðr, svá at menn viti, í fornum sögum

[He was the most skilful of all men, it says in the old stories.]

King Níðuðr has taken Völundr for two reasons. First, because he is, like Dædalos, very useful. Behind the whole question of his manufacture of gold rings lies his other skills: he is *homo faber*, man the maker, notably the maker of weapons, and his fame elsewhere in Germanic heroic poetry is associated very frequently with the making of swords. To take him prisoner is a political coup. But secondly he is master of a large amount of gold, and Níðuðr is concerned to have that *as well*. When the attack is made, Níðuðr and his men first find Völundr's hut empty. They might have taken the gold and fled, but instead they take one ring only, so that

---

67 *Deor*, ed. Kemp Malone (London: Methuen, 1933). Translation in Alexander, *Earliest English Poems*, pp. 43f. I have resolved yogh as *g* and wen as *w*.

Völundr imagines that his lost wife has returned. When he falls asleep he is taken, and thus Níðuðr has both gold and metal-worker. The somewhat enigmatic question by Níðuðr as to where the smith acquired the gold probably reflects the often self-justificatory question of rightful ownership that recurs in other Germanic heroic works. At all events, Níðuðr adds an insult to Völundr by giving one of the gold rings—the ring that has been associated with Völundr's missing wife—to his own daughter Böðvildr. The effect of the insult is perceived not by the king, however, but by his wife, and for the first time we have a decision made by a woman within the context of the heroic narrative. That decision, incidentally, is a political one, rather than, as critics have suggested, some kind of magic prescience of what will happen. Níðuðr's wife sees the hatred in Völundr's eyes when he sees the ring on Bödvildr's arm, and it is the queen who makes the decision to have him hamstrung and put on an island. To have him killed would be waste, but she is aware of the danger and causes the king to act accordingly. This is the lowest point for the hero, and he sums it up in an elegiac statement that is also the turning-point of the work, the set of circumstances that makes Völundr swear to take what revenge is still possible. When he does so, it is with an effectiveness which closes all doors of relief to his captor, Níðuðr:

> Sék Níðaði
> sverð á linda,
> Þats ek hvesta
> sem hagast kunnak
> ok ek herðak
> sem hœgst Þótti;
>
> . . .
>
> Nú berr Böðvildr
> brúðar minnar,
> bíðka Þess bót,
> bauga rauða.

and then:

> Sat né svaf ávalt
> ok sló hamri;

> vél gerði heldr
> hvatt Níðaði . . . (strophes 19–21)

[My own sword is shining at the belt of Níðuðr, the one my skill made and tempered . . . Böðvildr now bears what belonged to my bride, the red-gold ring. He sat and did not sleep, and swung his hammer, and plotted against Níðuðr.]

Völundr himself is speaking or thinking first of all, and it is the sword that is before his eyes. The fruits of his skill have been taken from him. So, too, the gold ring—the word *bauga* recurs here—that had belonged to his bride is now on the arm of Böðvildr and he cannot get it back. Therefore—the narrator tells us—he did not sleep, but worked out a plan against Níðuðr. Völundr becomes active again, and his first move is to trap and kill the two sons of the king—the destruction of the hereditary line is important again. These are driven by the lust for treasure, we are told, to the island where Völundr lives; this is the same initial motivation that caused Níðuðr to take his prisoner. Völundr reinforces this by showing the young men treasure, and promising to give them gold if they come back alone and tell no one. When they come, Völundr lets them look into the treasure chest, and as they do so he hacks off their heads. His revenge is, however, directed at Níðuðr, and having buried the bodies, he makes jewels out of their eyes, brooches from their teeth and cups from their skulls, set in silver. Although he does not know it yet, the king now has no male heirs. Meanwhile—the text is not entirely clear at this point—Böðvildr breaks the ring that has been mentioned as that belonging to Völundr's wife, and the one that lulled him into his sense of security before he was trapped. Völundr agrees to remake the ring, but this, too, is part of his revenge, although it is told very allusively in this version of the tale. He brings her beer, which is presumably drugged, and she falls asleep, after which—again we presume from what follows—he rapes her. Völundr is referred to later as her *friðill*, her lover, and she (even less plausibly, perhaps) as his bride, *brúðr*. At all events, she will bear his child:

> nú gengr Böðvildr
> barni aukin,
> eingadóttir
> ykkur beggja. (strophe 37)

[Now Böðvildr, your only daughter, is big with child.]

Völundr can now taunt the king with this as he escapes, which he does by making wings and flying from the island—this echoes the familiar Dædalos story. But the completeness of his revenge is what matters, and before he leaves, he extracts from Níðuðr a promise in exchange for information about the king's sons that he will not harm Böðvildr. The king swears this, and surprise has been expressed at the fact that—at the very end of the work—he honours his promise and is reconciled with Böðvildr, who has fled. But in fact he has no choice, and his recalling of his daughter is put laconically, as he instructs one of his trusted men to

> bið Böðvildi
> mey hina bráhvítu,
> gangi fagrvarið
> við föður rœða. (strophe 40)

[Bid the bright-eyed Böðvildr come, richly-dressed, to speak with her father.]

The king has to reconcile himself with his daughter and to the new set of facts. Now he has no choice but to accept: he must leave his kingdom to an heir, and both of his sons are dead. Böðvildr is his only daughter—we have been told—and the child she carries is therefore *his* only heir in the blood-line, even though the child is also Völundr's. Níðuðr therefore (and his wife—who presumably is beyond child-bearing age) must suffer this last element. The revenge, then, is complete, and the fate visited through the efforts of the king upon Völundr has been avenged completely on the king. The Anglo-Saxon *Deor*, which opened with the sufferings of Wayland, in fact strikes an interesting juxtaposition in that it goes on immediately to the suffering of Böðvildr—

Beadohilde in this text—and thus underlines the completeness of Völundr's revenge:

> Beadohilde ne wæs   hyre broÞra deaÞ
> on sefan swa sár   swa hyre sylfre Þing
> Þæt heo gearolice   ongieten hæfde
> Þæt heo eacen wæs;   æfre ne meahte
> Þriste geÞencan   hu ymb Þæt sceolde. (8–12)

[Beadohilda was not as grieved by her brothers' death as by her own fate when she realised that she was pregnant; *that* thought almost drove her mad.]

The Anglo-Saxon poem does not offer the resolution of the king's acceptance, and it is interesting that *Deor* compares Wayland and the girl, rather than the two adversaries, Wayland and the king. Insofar as the Norse text has a title it is *Frá Völundi ok Niðaði*, 'About Völundr and Níðuðr'.

How, then, does Völundr fit the pattern of the Germanic hero? Not necessarily in his special skills, although he does use those skills as others use their straightforward physical strength. Rather it is in his response to the blows of fate which remove him from one political context, and his reshaping of events to reestablish his own lineage in a new one. The fact that Hildebrand had to fight his own son is an unpredictable situation, but a set of circumstances which still have to be worked out within the framework of the given elements, the political force of which is embodied in those silent watchers, the two armies. In the last analysis, Hildebrand can only accept the situation, since he is subordinate to a code which he has accepted already in general terms. Gunnarr is a ruler rather than a vassal, and on his actions depend the fate of his nation; in this case we do not see all the workings out of circumstance, but he too accepts his fate. Although he has to die to do so, he prevents the victory of the Huns. Völundr, though captured and imprisoned, is able to salvage some of the situation, to get back in a sense some of what he has lost, if not for himself, then for the son who is to be born to Böðvildr. By closing off all alternative possibilities for Níðuðr by killing his sons and impregnating his daughter, Völundr has ensured that the rings and the sword will be returned to his child.

Swords and rings—power and gold, that is—are key themes in the *Hildebrandslied*, the *Atlakviða* and the *Völundarkviða*, just as they were in *Maldon* and they will be again in works like *Waltharius* or the *Nibelungenlied*. Herfried Münkler has voiced the ingenious idea that the disputed gold in works like these, or like *Waltharius*, for example, reflects the attempts on the part of the Roman Empire to set Germanic tribes against one another by payment, but although that referred to in the Hildebrandslied—*cheisuringu*—is indeed imperial, gold itself is a curse enough,[68] and the theme of inheritance in general terms is perhaps of greater importance in these works. Hildebrand cannot leave more than a memorial to his own son; although Völundr cannot rescue his own property for himself, he can nevertheless arrange things so that a child of his will inherit it, and this time it includes a kingdom. In the *Atlakviða* the inheritance—*arfr*—is a larger issue; it is the whole wealth of the Burgundians, the Nibelungs, and it is vital that it be kept away from an alien force of warriors who would use it to increase their own powers. Wolfgang Mohr's analysis of the *Atlakviða* (and he draws on Karl Müllenhoff's, made a long time earlier) is quite straightforward: 'The treasure of the Nibelungs is the symbol of Burgundian power. No, it is more than a symbol, it is a political reality. Wars were fought in the period of the folk-migrations about stores of treasure, and Atli's desire for it has a political aim. Whoever has the treasure has the quite unsymbolic power of being able to equip an army and to attract followers'.

All three heroes—Hildebrand, Gunnarr and Völundr—have their own inner motivation for their rather different actions, but that motivation always stems from the larger political context, which in its turn ensures that they must, if they wish to be true to themselves, behave in a certain manner. Indeed, in the three heroes a gradual move in the foreground *emphasis* may be visible from a personal ethical imperative to a more straightforward *Realpolitik*, even if the precise historical parallels in each case were already obscure when the poems were written down.

But all three works are still literary, and we may perhaps end on

---

68 Münkler, *Das Blickfeld des Helden*.

that point: the *Hildebrandslied*, the song of Hildebrand itself, is the hero's only inheritance and Völundr makes his own boast as he escapes from Níðuðr, so that *his* song is part of the poem. In the *Atlakviða*, though, we are left with a specific image: Gunnarr is quite literally trapped, cast into a snake-pit, but he remains defiant and meets death playing his harp. Wolfgang Mohr, once again, asks a relevant question here: 'What kind of song did Gunnarr sing?' and then links the scene with a description of the death in 533 of Gelimer, the unfortunate last king of the Vandals, who sang of his own downfall in a similar situation.[69] In the case of Gunnarr, the last part of the snake-pit strophe—'This is how a lord ought to guard his gold'—need not just be an authorial statement; it can also be the substance of Gunnarr's own song. What the dying king sings is a *Gunnarsdrápa*, the song of Gunnarr's heroic death. But on another narrative level that is only the song within the song. Gunnarr's act deprived Atli of his gold; but Gunnarr's acceptance of his own death would deprive the Hun king of his life, his posterity and his state. That, too, is part of Gunnarr's fame in the larger song that is the *Atlakviða* itself. Both are songs of victory.

---

69 Wolfgang Mohr, 'Geschichtserlebnis im altgermanischen Heldenliede' (augmented version of a paper first written in 1943), in *Zur germanisch-deutschen Heldensage*, ed. Karl Hauck (Darmstadt: WBG, 1965), pp. 82–101. See esp. pp. 92–4, with reference to Procopius' *Vandal Wars* and the fate of Gelimer. Translation of the quotation is mine. See on the harp motif John L. Flood, 'The Severed Heads: On the Deaths of Gunther and Hagen'. in *German Narrative Literature of the Twelfth and Thirteenth Centuries*, ed. Honemann etc., pp. 174–91. There are interesting general comments (but also with reference to Gunnarr) in Joseph Harris, 'Beowulf's Last Words'. *Speculum* 67 (1997), 1–32.

3

Youth, Age and Education

Beowulf, Ernst of Bavaria and
Heinrich of Kempten

Young heroes are sometimes (but not always) different from old
heroes. The apparent impetuousness that is sometimes ascribed
to Byrhtnoð, the old hero, is more usually found, perhaps, with
the young warrior. But young warriors go through a learning process
that can have its special problems, especially in the political sphere.
Before looking at the education of the young hero, however, let
me put in a reminder that my concern is with the Germanic hero
as such, rather than with the heroic epic. Accordingly, I have chosen
in spite of conventional literary compartmentalisation to illustrate
the problem with three works of rather different genres. The three
works cover a fairly long historical period—with material that is
not restricted by any means to the age of folk migrations, for
example, although the relationship to history is similarly distant in
each—and in each of them the behaviour of the hero is a little
different. Nevertheless the political lessons of the works are far more
similar than it might appear at first glance. In the first work, written
in the eighth century, the hero fights with dragons and monsters
and serves a wise king. In the second, from the twelfth century,
the hero, this time initially in dispute with the king, escapes and
fights with crane-heads, giants and flat-feet; in the third, a work
from the thirteenth century, the hero very nearly murders his king
(who is, admittedly, in this case somewhat less than wise), but
eventually does serve him, not by killing dragons and monsters, but

by fighting a more realistic group of Italian would-be assassins, having leapt naked from the bath to do so.

The first work—*Beowulf*—is firmly in the heroic world of the folk-migration period, and its style is formulaic. The second work, *Herzog Ernst*, is usually dubbed a minstrel epic, though informed debate on the term is impossible, since nobody really knows what it means. The third, Konrad von Würzburg's *Heinrich von Kempten*, is set ostensibly in a chivalric world. *Beowulf* is pre-chivalric by several centuries and the tale of Ernst—composed in the twelfth century—is also regarded as pre-courtly at least. Konrad's work was written at a time when the chivalry of the high middle ages had broken down, and indeed, he complains in his epilogue that chivalry is now in short supply. He sets his work, in spite of its chivalric trappings, in a presumed golden age, which, if it is historically identifiable at all, seems to be located in the tenth century, with historical referents that link with *Herzog Ernst* itself. All the works have, then, a similarly loose relationship to actual historical events, and they all have a general moral. That moral is the importance of the stability of the feudal state, and of coping with real and potential political chaos. All three show us, too, the old hero and the young hero, and more significantly the hero's learning process. The positive outcome seems to be of far greater importance than the notion of the 'intruder hero' as such, in spite of the emphasis placed on this by W. T. H. Jackson, for example.[70]

As Tolkien made so clear in his memorably titled and still so frequently quoted paper for the British Academy in 1936 *Beowulf: The Monsters and the Critics*,[71] that work has been inter-

---

70 In *The Hero and the King* Jackson occasionally seems concerned to make the hero fit his own thesis: while the notion of the intruder works with Siegfried (see p. 37) it does not work with others, like Beowulf, nor is Beowulf in old age radically different (see pp. 31–3). He does not consider Ernst or Heinrich. See also Maria Dobozy, *Full Circle: Kingship in the German Epic* (Göppingen: Kümmerle, 1985) on the question of conflict.

71 Reprinted in *An Anthology of Beowulf Criticism*, ed. Lewis E. Nicholson (Notre Dame: U. Notre Dame Press, 1963), pp. 51–103. Work on *Beowulf*—as Tolkien makes clear in the opening to this celebrated essay—is both varied in approach and very extensive indeed. The essay

preted in a great variety of ways, and in some of these interpretations we almost lose sight of the hero altogether as he disappears behind allegory or is argued out of existence. As far as current work is concerned, approaches to the poem continue to be heterogeneous. Recent studies include, for example, an entire volume of essays devoted (inconclusively) to *The Dating of Beowulf*; a number of investigations concentrating on the problem of Christianity in the poem (although folklore is perhaps beginning to take the upper hand again); and a study with the revealing title *The Condemnation of Heroism and the Tragedy of Beowulf,* which takes the work as a whole to be anti-militaristic and anti-heroic.[72] Whilst all these studies contain material of interest, one is able here to do little more than echo Tolkien's (admittedly somewhat backhanded) humility formula in offering any views at all in the face of those by such 'an heep of lerned men'. Clearly,

has been reprinted independently, and appears in extract in another useful anthology, *Beowulf*, ed. Joseph F. Tuso (New York: Norton, 1975). It is of interest that Tolkien's essay has remained of enormous influence, as have two small monographs, one by Dorothy Whitelock, *The Audience of Beowulf* (Oxford: Clarendon, 1951), and Kenneth Sisam, *The Structure of Beowulf* (Oxford; Clarendon, 1965). I would add Bruce Mitchell's 'Until the Dragon Comes . . .' in his collection of essays *On Old English* (Oxford: Blackwell, 1988), pp. 3–15 (and postscript, pp. 41–54). His review of a number of papers on the poem in the same volume, pp. 55–62, is very useful. See finally Arthur Gilchrist Brodeur, *The Art of Beowulf* (Berkeley and Los Angeles: U. California P., 1959), and with comparisons with other Germanic works, William W. Lawrence, *Beowulf and the Epic Tradition* (New York: Hafner, 1961).

72 *The Dating of Beowulf*, ed. Colin Chase (Toronto: U. Toronto Press, 1981); (for example:) Mary A. Parker, *Beowulf and Christianity* (New York: Lang, 1987); Fidel Fajardo-Acosta, *The Condemnation of Heroism in the Tragedy of Beowulf* (Lampeter: Mellen, 1989). All three works, incidentally, refer to political aspects of the poem. For overviews of scholarship, see Friedrich Schubel, *Probleme der Beowulf-Forschung* in the *Erträge der Forschung* series (Darmstadt: WBG, 1979); Douglas D. Short, *Beowulf Scholarship: An Annotated Bibliography* (New York: Garland, 1980), with an update 1979–90 by Robert J. Hasenfratz (New York: Garland, 1993); R. D. Fulk, *Interpretations of Beowulf* (Bloomington: Indiana UP, 1991); Eric Gerald Stanley, *In the Foreground: Beowulf* (Cambridge: Brewer, 1994).

too, Bruce Mitchell is right to insist that the dogmatic assertion 'that *this* is the meaning of *Beowulf*' is not to be tolerated. There seem, however, to be two very obvious points for discussion with the work—the monsters themselves, and the at first glance somewhat disjointed structure of a poem which moves from the deeds of a young warrior at Hroðgar's hall across a gap of fifty years to the last battle of that same hero, now a king, against another monster. The obvious answer to both problems is that the work is about Beowulf and the high points of interest in his career. It is true, however, that if the literary hero is relevant to the real world, then those monsters have to be interpreted in some fashion. Beowulf is as concerned as Sigurðr was about his reputation, too, but that reputation is valid always within a political framework. This seems to offer the best interpretation for all the monsters: they are a political threat, more specifically (and here is a major difference from the later texts I want to look at) an external threat to a stabilised society. They are the equivalent of the Vikings at Maldon.

Discussions of *Beowulf*, especially of the structure, tend to divide the work into two parts: Beowulf at the court of the Danes, and then the tale of Beowulf's last battle with the dragon. Beowulf himself, seen both as a young and as an old hero, links the two parts, but the structure is more complex than that.[73] In fact the very first part of the work is not concerned with Beowulf at all, and the presentation of Heorot, the centre of Hroðgar's empire, has an independent existence within the poem. It is presented first of all an ideal, and then we are shown how fragile political structures can be. We are shown first of all the development of a political society amongst the Danes based on hereditary kingship, beginning with Scyld Scēfing and passing to his successor and his successor's son. Futhermore, whilst discussing Scyld Scēfing's own son and heir, the poet gives us a programmatic picture of how an atheling,

---

73 Critics do, of course, also stress the unity of the work. John D. Niles, *Beowulf. The Poem and its Tradition* (Cambridge, Mass: Harvard UP, 1983) does not see the varied elements as a problem, but he does take the unifying feature as 'people and what holds them together'.

a young heir, should behave, and that picture looks on from youth to age. As ever, there are historical parallels, echoes of real history behind much of this. But the general political message is clearer with the literary Hroðgar than it might have been with a more accurate history of the Danes, Geats and Swedes.[74] Consider this general comment about the nature of the hero:

> Swā sceal geong guma   gōde gewyrcean,
> fromum feohgiftum   on fæder bearme,
> Þæt hyne on ylde   eft gewunigen
> wilgesiÞas,   Þonne wīg cume,
> lēode gelæsten;   lofdædum sceal
> in mægÞa gehwære   man geÞeon. (lines 20–25)[75]

[A young warrior must do good things, and give freely when with his father, so that when old age reaches him, friends will stand by him when he comes under attack. Praiseworthy deeds bring honour.]

This indeed happens with Beow, the son of Scyld, and then with his son, Hroðgar, under whose hand the social structure develops. Unlike Otto II in the *Modus Ottinc*, Hroðgar has (although in the context of the poem we perhaps ought to say: 'is shown as having in the past' since we never see him in action) achieved fame as a warrior king; he was given glory in battle—'Þā wæs Hrōðgare herespēd gyfen' (line 64)—he did not seek it as such. More to the point he constructs a great mead-hall, named Heorot, at the centre of what he rules:

---

74 See Ritchie Girvan, *Beowulf and the Seventh Century*, revised edn, with a chapter on Sutton Hoo by Rupert Bruce-Mitford (London: Methuen, 1971) for a survey of the historical elements. Recent full studies are those by J. A. Leake, *The Geats of Beowulf: A Study in the Geographical Mythology of the Middle Ages* (Madison: Wisconsin UP, 1967), and Sam Newton, *The Origins of Beowulf and the Pre-Viking Kingdom of East Anglia* (Woodbridge: Brewer, 1993).

75 Text cited from Klaeber, *Beowulf and the Fight at Finnsburg*; see also Wyatt's, Wrenn's and Swanton's editions, and the modern English version by Michael Alexander, plus the interesting recent edition by John Porter, *Beowulf* (Pinner: Anglo-Saxon Books, 1990).

þā wæs Hrōðgāre   herespēd gyfen,
wīges weorðmynd,   Þæt him his winemāgas
georne hyrdon,   oðð Þæt sēo geogoð gewēox,
magodriht micel . . .   . . . his wordes geweald
wīde hæfde. (lines 64–79)

[Hroðgar was given victory in arms, mastery in battle, so that
friends and kinsmen gladly obeyed him, and his group grew
to a great company . . . his influence ran over a wide area.]

A political unit has grown over the generations, and Hroðgar
becomes the acknowledged leader in his great hall, distributing
wealth (arm-rings again, *beaga*) and apparently secure. This small
empire is, however, *not* secure, and it comes under threat. While
we are not shown Hroðgar in battle, we are shown how the hall, the
centre of the political unit, comes under threat from evil. In fact
it is in the shape of a monster, Grendel, but the nature of that evil
is less relevant than the predicament of Hroðgar, unable now to
cope. We hear later that it is because he is now old and grey, *eald
ond unhār*, but his failure is still comprehensive. Not only does
Grendel kill his men, but his own society begins to break down,
as his own warriors even abandon their established Christianity and
begin to worship idols. The society requires help from elsewhere,
and it is into this society that Beowulf now comes.

A certain amount of care is needed with what is implied by the
term 'young' in the context of the hero. Beowulf is a young man
in the first part, or he would not be able to rule so long in his
own country. But *young* does not imply callow or untried, or even
lacking in reputation. The exploits in the first part of the work are
simply the first to be recorded in song, the first heroic exploits of
signal importance. These need to be exploits showing more than
human strength, but they are certainly not the first acts of the hero.
The surprise evinced by the unexpected prowess of an untried boy
is essentially a romance motif, rare in heroic poetry. The young
hero is not so young as to be without a reputation. Hadubrand,
still addressed as *chind*, 'child', is nevertheless already a champion
in his own right, and when in the German version of the tale of
the Nibelungen the young warrior Siegfried first appears at the

court of the Burgundians, Hagen knows all about him. Here, too, Beowulf does not arrive at Hroðgar's hall as an unknown to try his hand against Grendel. He is leading a group of men when he arrives in Denmark, and even before he states his name, the guard is impressed with his appearance—*ænlic ansyn*, 'most noble to behold'. In the court, too, one person at least has heard of him, the problematic Unferð, who—inspired by jealousy towards this apparently too confident warrior—accuses Beowulf of having lost a swimming contest undertaken (and this time Beowulf uses the term *cnihtwesende* himself) when Beowulf was a youth. Beowulf counters that he did, in fact, win the contest of which Unferð has heard, and goes on to insult his accuser in a speech that has its own resonance at the very end of the work:

> Þeah ðū Þīnum brōðrum   to banan wurde,
> hēafodmægum;   Þæs Þū in helle scealt
> werhðo drēogan . . . (lines 587–89)

[You have killed your brothers and your relatives, and you'll pay for that in hell.]

In the self-referential mode of the heroic epic the wrong song has already been sung about Unferð. We must not play down his importance, although there is a danger in too enthusiastic a reliance upon allegorisations, even those based on an interpretation of the name. A perfectly realistic interpretation of Unferð is possible. He is surely neither the embodiment of discord, nor a further aspect of the greater evil represented by Grendel—both views have been voiced in criticism[76]—but simply a member of Hroðgar's court

---

76 See W. F. Bolton, *Alcuin and Beowulf: An Eighth-Century View* (New Brunswick, NJ: Rutgers UP, 1978), p. 121f. René Derolez wonders, however, about the importance of the much discussed Unferð, noting the consistent variation in the spelling of the name in the manuscript: 'Hrothgar King of Denmark'. in *Multiple Worlds, Multiple Words: Essays in Honour of Irène Simon*, ed. H. Maes-Jelinek et al. (Liège: Department of English in the University of Liège, 1987), pp. 51–8. Sisam, *Structure*, pp. 40–3, makes interesting justificatory comments on Unferð. See most recently the (debatable) conclusions of Teresa Pàroli, 'Profilo dell'antieroe' in Pàroli, *Funzione dell'eroe*, pp. 273–321, esp. pp. 306–19.

who is jealous of this strong interloper. This is not an unusual state of affairs in literary presentations of the hero. Hagen is impressed when he sees, but also profoundly suspicious of Siegfried, who turns up and wins great favour at the Burgundian court. In another celebrated work that falls outside this study, the much vilified but very understandable (and also powerful) barons are equally suspicious of Tristan. The difference here is that Beowulf will save, rather than threaten, the society into which he has now come. Unferð has to be quashed, therefore, and Beowulf does so. When he himself comes to die, however, after the fight with the dragon, Beowulf declares (in a speech to which I shall return) that he cannot be charged with any crime like that of which he has accused Unferð:

> forðām mē wītan ne ðearf   Waldend fira
> morðorbealo māga . . . (lines 2741f)

'The ruler of men cannot charge me with killing kinsmen', says Beowulf, and his other acts have been honourable. The wrong songs will not be sung of him. Indeed, we have by this stage already heard—self-referentially within the epic—of one song being sung about deeds which we have even earlier heard in the song of Beowulf itself, that describing the death of Grendel.

Like Byrhtnoð at Maldon, Beowulf decides to fight Grendel on equal terms, and the glory is that much greater, the victory that much more visible when he does win, for all that critics have compared the two men in terms of excessive pride.[77] The comparison with Byrhtnoð at Maldon is revealing, in fact, and underscores the point that had Byrhtnoð defeated the Vikings on the terms given to them, the moral victory would have been that much greater. Thus with Beowulf. Byrhtnoð, furthermore, invoked the decision of God, taking it from a fateful decision (in the proper sense) to a divine judgement. Again Beowulf does the same:

> ond siÞðan wītig God

---

77 Jones, *Kings, Beasts and Heroes*, p. 13.

on swā hwæÞere hond   hālig Dryhten
mærðo dēme,   swā him gemet Þince.
(lines 685–87)

[And then all-knowing God, the holy Lord, will give the
upper hand to whomever he thinks right.]

The poet of *Maldon* is bound by history, and that battle was lost,
but here the literary hero Beowulf *does* defeat Grendel, and it is
as a result that a song is sung about the deed almost at once, a
simpler, but equally concise expression of the self-reflective *nature*
of heroic song than that embodied by the *Grípisspá*. Before the
second battle—with Grendel's mother—Beowulf puts into words
the warrior's need for good reputation in battle, and here it is seen
specifically as a way to conquer death. He has not sought out this
second evil, but it has come his way and he is now concerned to
rid Heorot of this second threat and ensure his own reputation
when he is dead. We may note here that unlike Sigurðr, Beowulf
is operating within a political context, even if the question of
reputation may be uppermost at this stage:

Ūre æghwylc sceal   ende gebīdan
worolde līfes;   wyrce sē Þe mōte
dōmes ær dēaÞe;   Þæt bið drihtguman
unlifgendum æfter   sēlest.
(lines 1386–89)

[We shall all leave the life of this world, so if we may, we
must get some reputation before death—this is appropriate
for a warrior when he is dead.]

Unferð generously passes his ancient sword to Beowulf and
is declared to have forgotten the earlier accusations; thereby
he redeems himself on one level, at least. And yet he is still
sharply dismissed by the poet: 'Þær hē dōme forlēas' (line 1470)
[there Unferð forefeited his reputation]. When we come to
the battle, too, while Beowulf's human bravery is stressed, it
is once again God who gave him the victory—'hālig God/

geweold wīgsigor' (line 1553f); the distinction will be far clearer later in the German *Ludwigslied* of how the hero does his best on earth, but it is up to God whether he gains the victory or not.

On this occasion Beowulf is given more than gifts; he is given a kind of *memento mori* sermon by Hroðgar, who is aware, and perfectly realistically, that age defeats every warrior. For all that, his kingdom has been defended by Beowulf, and he can leave a secure kingdom, whatever may happen in the more distant future. Hroðgar, moreover, has ruled the Danes for fifty years, and this provides the link between Beowulf's two sets of adventures. Beowulf's youthful acts established (rather than created) his reputation, and when he eventually takes over as king of the Geats he, like Hroðgar, rules for fifty years. In political terms this requires a mention, but not a description. What occupies the latter parts of the poem, however, is the transformation of the young hero into the old hero, of Beowulf into the equivalent of Hroðgar. There is no case for seeing the last fight, with the dragon, as some kind of long-distance revenge by Grendel (it has been done) or even to see the dragon's gold as cursed.[78] Certainly there are *apparently* cursed hoards of gold in heroic poetry, and not always associated with dragons: the gold of the Nibelungen, the gold taken with him by Waltharius when he flees the Huns. But in spite even of the fascinating idea (which can hardly apply to *Beowulf*, in fact) already noted by Herfried Münkler that the idea of cursed gold in heroic epics echoes the attempts of the Roman Empire to set Germanic tribes against one another by payment, gold itself is a curse enough.[79] Indeed, it does buy opposition, and it is linked with an opposition to Beowulf. What the final

---

78 A point made clearly by Raymond B. Tripp, 'Lifting the Curse on *Beowulf*'. *English Language Notes* 23, no. 2 (1985), 1–8.

79 Fajardo-Acosta speaks of 'the vengeance of the Grendels' in his *The Condemnation of Heroism*, although much of the argument in that book is unconvincing. On the Roman gold, see Münkler, *Das Blickfeld des Helden,* though Münkler does not refer to *Beowulf*. Gold is also an expression of human worth, of course: see Cherniss, *Ingeld and Christ,* pp. 79–101.

battle does is to give Beowulf a different type of testing, one against the odds. We have seen this already in the *Hildebrandslied*, where the father actually declared that the odds were against him, although he now faced dreadful alternatives. Beowulf similarly spells out the possibilities, and this time it is fate that will decide— not *wewurt* as in the *Hildebrandslied*—but certainly *wyrd*, its unmodified Anglo-Saxon equivalent.[80] Beowulf, like Hildebrand, is also described as the survivor of many battles. This one, however, he does not survive, although his courage is not in doubt, something thrown into relief by the fact that a group of his followers actually run away. One, however, does not, and his importance matches that of Ælfwine and the rest in *Maldon*. This is Wiglaf, who, like Ælfwine, recalls all that his lord, in this case Beowulf, has done for him. He reproaches the others in words, but most of all he does so by being there, the more so as he is a young warrior

> Þā wæs forma sīð   geongan cempan,
> Þæt hē gūðe ræs   mid his freodryhtne
> fremman sceolde. (lines 2625–27)

[It was the first time the young warrior had had to join battle beside his overlord.]

Beowulf voices in his dying speech—that in which he also expresses satisfaction that he has done nothing dishonourable—his own regret that he has no son to which he could pass his battle-gear, but he does pass it to Wiglaf, who is very clearly the hope for the future, regardless of whether in history the Geats were swallowed up by the Swedes or not, something of which the poet voices later.[81] There will be wars, but Beowulf kept the

---

80 Studies of this concept include Gerd Wolfgang Weber, *'Wyrd': Studien zum Schicksalsbegriff der altenglischen und altnordischen Literatur* (Bad Homburg: Gehlen, 1969).

81 Wiglaf's importance is stressed by Sisam, *Structure*, pp. 53–9. On the possibility of disaster after the death of Beowulf, see the intriguing suggestions of Roberta Frank in her 'Old Norse Memorial Euologies and the Ending of *Beowulf*'. *The Early Middle Ages: Acta* 6 (1982 for 1979), 1–20.

nation for fifty years, and he leaves behind him Wiglaf, a great barrow, a physical memorial, and finally the poem itself, which ends with another typically inward looking comment—the poet does not tell us about Beowulf, rather he tells us what the mourners said of him; once again, within the right sort of song the poet shows us the song being sung. There are no implications of excessiveness, surely, in that final word *lofgeornost*, 'most eager for praise.'

Nothing lasts. The Geat nation *was* subsumed by the Swedes. But during the period of the poem—in which two rulers, Hroðgar and Beowulf rule for fifty years apiece—the political balance was maintained, and the respective peoples lived, therefore, in happily uninteresting times. A similar political balancing act lies behind Konrad von Würzburg's *Heinrich von Kempten*, although the comparison may be a little unusual, and after that work (though Konrad himself does not say so—rather he complains that things are not what they were) an even large political entity fell into collapse.

Before we come to Konrad, however, let us move on only a century or so and bridge the gap by looking at Duke Ernst of Bavaria, the central figure of a work which has immediate points of contact with *Beowulf* in that the hero also goes abroad for an education, taking this time what amounts to a medieval grand tour, albeit somewhat against his will. One of the problems people have had with reading *Beowulf* has always been the presence of those monsters, and Tolkien's arguments against both the deconstruction (I use the word in an altogether different and even more sinister sense than it is now used in criticism) of the work to find various *ur*-levels through folklore, and also against an excess of allegorisation apply here too.

The story of Duke Ernst of Bavaria is known in a wide variety of versions in German and Latin from the twelfth to the fifteenth century, and echoed in Czech and Icelandic as well, but the version normally taken as the standard one is the earliest full text, known in German studies as *Herzog Ernst B*, and I shall concentrate on this version as well, whilst remaining aware that to include this material at all in the heroic context might cause the raising of critical eyebrows.[82] It is not that the version in question (admittedly a revision of an earlier A-text for which we have some fragments) was written probably during the Middle High German *Blütezeit*, contemporary with the Arthurian romances of Hartmann and with Wolfram's *Parzival*. After all, the heroic saga of the Nibelungen comes from this period, and the sole version to have survived of the epic of *Kudrun* underwent a revision of sorts when it was written down in the sixteenth century.

The real problem is one of genre; literary criticism has tended to see *Herzog Ernst* as little more than an adventure story. Indeed, the work is very much a kind of medieval equivalent to the modern science fiction novel, and if we compare the work with the relentless existentialism of the *Hildebrandslied*, say, then there are some odd things here. Duke Ernst, the central figure, having led an unsuccessful rebellion again the emperor and precipitated a civil war, goes on a journey in which he encounters a sticky sea and a magnetic mountain, and he meets people who have cranes' heads, or single eyes, or gigantic feet, or are giants or pygmies. On the other hand, while tales of the Germanic hero are usually based in reality, there is not infrequently at least a whiff of the miraculous. Beowulf's monsters are a case in point. Völundr is married to a swan-maiden and makes wings for himself (Duke Ernst takes to the air at one point, but does so in a far more logical fashion, at least for the twelfth century, by harnessing a griffin). There is magic about Siegfried, who has a cloak of invisibility, and who has killed dragons, and even in *Kudrun* the imminent rescue of the eponymous princess from captivity is announced to her by an angel disguised as a sea-bird. The real point, though, is that although *Herzog Ernst* need not be seen as an heroic epic, Duke Ernst himself is a Germanic hero eminently comparable with those already examined.

82 *Herzog Ernst, in der mittelhochdeutschen Fassung B*, ed., trs. Bernhard Sowinski (Stuttgart: Reclam, 1970). The fragments of the A-text are included in this useful edition. The older edition is that by Karl Bartsch, *Herzog Ernst* (Vienna: Braumüller, 1869). The title of a relevant study by Hans Simon-Pelanda is significant: *Schein, Realität und Utopie: Untersuchung zur Einheit eines Staatsromans (Herzog Ernst B)* (Frankfurt/M. etc.: Lang, 1984).

The tale as a whole moves from a real to what looks at first glance like a fantasy world, it is true, and there has been much concentration on this aspect of the work. Yet it is once again rooted in a distorted but recognisable historical context, and there is a clear political message, a point taken up, indeed, by some critics: Clemens Heselhaus referred to it over fifty years ago as 'one of the most political folk-poems that we possess'. and since then others have discussed the work from this point of view.[83] The fantasy adventures, moreover, fascinating as they may be, are subordinated to the political point, and indeed are integrated *into* the education of a ruler. *Herzog Ernst* is the story of a hero's education towards the proper fulfilment of his political role, and much of his education is carried out away from home; thus far I have used the term 'fantasy world' because we know, as twentieth-century watchers of television and readers of *National Geographic* magazine, that there is probably not really a race of people anywhere with cranes' heads. Whether the twelfth century was quite so sure is another matter entirely. Ernst comes into conflict with the political system in Germany, much as Heinrich von Kempten does rather later, but in this case he undergoes his adventures and indeed his political education abroad, and anything can happen there. 'Now that the earth possesses no more unexplored corners,' commented David Blamires in one of the few studies of the work in English, 'the voyage has been displaced to outer space, where the writers of science fiction pursue similar paths'.[84] Sometimes, indeed, they are predicated upon similar socio-political constructs: Asimov's *Foundation*-trilogy and even *Star Wars* owe more to Gibbon's *Decline and Fall* than meets the eye. The two elements of *Herzog Ernst*—a political struggle within a

83 Clemens Heselhaus, 'Die Herzog-Ernst-Dichtung'. *Deutsche Vierteljahresschrift* 20 (1942), 170–99; Heselhaus's views have been widely accepted. See Harms, *Kampf mit dem Freund*, pp. 89–95, and Uwe Mewes, *Studien zu König Rother, Herzog Ernst und Grauer Rock (Orendel)* (Frankfurt/M. and Berne: Lang, 1976), pp. 145–69. As Mewes notes, the work is of course a polyfunctional one; but it can still be viewed in this context.

84 David Blamires, *Herzog Ernst and the Otherworld Voyage* (Manchester: MUP, 1979); this and the following quotations are from his conclusion, pp. 75–7.

known and identifiable society, and a series of adventures—are closely integrated. David Blamires, again, has pointed out that 'the latter theme provides a means whereby the conflict between the son and stepfather can ultimately be resolved, although the motivation is ambiguous'. I am not sure that it is ambiguous, however, and I am less concerned with Blamires' interesting presentation of the adventure section as a version of the otherworld journey than with a view of it as a straightforward political education.[85]

As with *Beowulf*, there are structural questions with the saga of Ernst, and critics have discussed, again at length, the question of unity in the work. The first part of the work is based on an amalgam of two historical events. Otto the Great was in 953 in dispute with his son Liudolf, Duke of Swabia, which led to war and eventually to the siege of Regensburg. This is probably the basis for our tale, but the name Ernst and some other details have been taken over from a later Duke of Swabia who was in conflict with his stepfather, Konrad II. The literary Herzog Ernst is presented to us as a noble warrior, whose mother, Adelheid, marries the Emperor Otto, with whom Ernst at first gets on well, and rises rapidly to a position of great influence. His relationship however, arouses the jealousy of another nobleman, Henrich of the Pfalz, who manages to turn the emperor against Ernst. The B-poet slips in a standard explanation for the reader of why Heinrich does so—the devil advised him (650)—but this formulation is only a convenient dismissal, and the political basis for Heinrich's act is clear; Heinrich is as uneasy about this efficient Johnny-come-lately as Unferð is of Beowulf. The supposed interference by the devil removes any necessity for further explanation, and permits the continued foregrounding of the hero. At all events, Otto believes the slanders, most notably

85 The fact that this is—like many of the other tales of German heroes—a political story is implicitly acknowledged, oddly enough, in a satirical context in one of the few genuinely comic works to come from a writer in the former German Democratic Republic, Peter Hacks' play *Das Volksbuch vom Herzog Ernst*, in Peter Hacks, *Stücke* (Leipzig: Reclam, 1978), pp. 5–65, where the basic tale is used as an example of rigid feudalism and given some modern parallels. On the politics of the work in a medieval context, see Heselhaus once again.

that Ernst is a threat to the stability of the empire; more specifically, he believes Heinrich when he is told that Ernst is gathering the princes to his side, and so turns against him. Ernst thus becomes an enemy—through no direct fault of his own, except perhaps a deficiency in political acumen which might have let him out-politic Heinrich—and after an appeal by his mother has failed, he is besieged in Regensburg. His campaign lasts a number of years, and it is interesting that it is seen as a campaign not against the emperor, but as an 'urliuge gên dem rîche'—a feud against the empire itself. This point is repeated several times, and eventually Ernst realises that this can only lead to disaster. The point is spelt out programatically:

> swer lange urliuge wider daz rîche hât,
> ob er im ein wîle widerstât
> ze jungest muoz er an dem schaden stên
> (lines 1789–91)

[Anyone who engages in a feud against the empire, even if he manages to resist for a while, will still fall in the end.]

The most convenient edition of the text contains a translation into modern German which is accurate for the most part, but which tends to render *rîche*—the modern word *Reich*—as 'emperor'. Ernst, then, has come into conflict with the empire, and in a sense the lies of Henrich (who satisfactorily enough is killed by Ernst, diabolical or not) have proved to be self-fulfilling. For the sake of the stability of empire, Ernst needs to leave, and this takes us into the second part of the story, the travels—with a small group of followers—of the young hero.

It is tempting with this work simply to tell the story, and the importance of the purely narrative elements cannot be denied, signalled as they are usually by an introductory formula such as 'now there occurred an amazing thing'—the word *wunderlîch* recurs. The relevance of the adventure portion to Ernst as a hero, however, demands a playing down of this aspect of the marvellous. A couple of general points can be made about the adventures, in fact: by and large, as Ernst and his (dwindling) band get further away from the known world, the people that they encounter become stranger; and they do tend to fight for those who are more human-looking against those who are not. Thus they fight against (and fail to save a captive princess from) a race of crane-headed people in a lengthy incident near the start of their adventures. They are forced, too, to use human ingenuity to escape from the sticky sea and the magnetic mountain (on which sailors have perished), by sewing themselves up in cattle-skins and being carried away by griffins. In their efforts to avoiding becoming lunch for young griffins, however, they pass through an underground river and find *en route* the gemstone that will become the central jewel in the imperial crown,[86] a small but significant reminder of the fact that all these adventures of Ernst's are designed to help him become an integrated member of society within an ordered and preexistent empire. It is when Ernst takes service with the King of Arimaspî that the parallels with *Beowulf* become clear. True, the king is a cyclops, but this detail, *wunderlîch* as it is, is relatively soon forgotten; of greater importance is the mutual acceptance of Ernst and the king on the grounds of courageous appearance. Ernst then does service to the king by helping him to defeat those who are even more *wunderlîch*—sciapods, straight out of Pliny, but wielding what looks like a science-fiction ray-gun: *geschôz freislich* (line 4694) literally 'terrible weapons'. Ernst defeats them by strategy and bravery, however, and the battle is entirely human: all these creatures, too, share the endearingly human trait of aggressive expansionism:

> Der herzoge und sîne man
> kâmen sie frumelîchen an.
> sie sluogen und stâchen
> unz sie die schar durchbrâchen . . .
> (lines 4727–30)

[The duke and his men attacked them vigorously, cutting and thrusting until they broke through the line . . .]

86 See Percy Ernst Schramm, *Herrschaftszeichen und Staatssymbolik* (Stuttgart: Hiersemann, 1954–6 and 1978), II, 803–10, and Hans-Friedrich Rosenfeld, *Herzog Ernst und die alte Kaiserskrone* (Helsinki: Soc. Scient. Fennica, 1961).

For this, Ernst receives a dukedom from the cyclops king, and he then rewards his warriors. Ernst has taken up the same place in this parallel society that he had gained, but perhaps had not earned, in the society he had to leave. No longer Ernst the wanderer, he is again Duke Ernst. In this capacity, however, he now fights for the king against still more enemies of various kinds, again culled from the pages of Pliny, until he returns, via the Holy Land, to Germany, where the emperor recognises that Ernst has been treated unjustly and pardons him. In fact, this reconciliation is brought about by the empress, who gains the support of the princes. Ernst appears, too, as a penitent, just as Liudolf did before his father. He is restored to his former dignities, and thereafter plays an appropriate role in the state.

Beowulf travels abroad, is tested in the service of another king, and returns where he is eventually made king himself. Ernst operates within a more complex political system, that of an established empire that is clearly larger than the one centred upon Heorot. The travels of Ernst, however, are not those of a knight errant, but of an exile, who fought first to preserve his own reputation against slander, and then gave up the fight, having proved his strength and killed the slanderer, to preserve the stability of the state. His education abroad—in a land where he has to earn all his rights (including the title that he began with) though heroic deeds, defending and maintaining the stability of another noble king—fits him to return and be restored to a political system the stability of which is no longer threatened. Where songs are sung about Beowulf right away, however, here we are in a more literate society, and are told at the end of the story how the emperor had the whole tale written down, beginning with 'warumbe und wie er in vertreip', why and how he had driven Ernst out.

My third text is by Konrad von Würzburg, a writer of considerable conservatism, not a nobleman but a member of the middle class, a bourgeois who died in 1287. His works are varied and they are entertaining, but conservative political attitudes recur. And yet he is (as was once said of C. S. Lewis), not a dinosaur, but a *laudator temporis acti*. In his typical epilogue to *Heinrich von*

Kempten (the title I shall use) he gives a programmatic reason for telling his story. It is a tale of bravery and chivalry—*manheit* and *ritterschaft* are the German words used—both of which are, Konrad complains, in short supply nowadays. His narrative is set in the past, in the days, once more, of an emperor named Otto, and we have once again a literary distortion of tenth-century history. It is interesting, incidentally, that Konrad von Würzburg's work is known to us by two different titles referring either to the king or the hero: it is sometimes called *Otto mit dem Bart*—'Bearded Otto, the Emperor'—as well as *Heinrich von Kempten*, and both men are central to the work. There are overtones of the conflict between Otto I and Liudolf here again, in fact, but a closer candidate for an historical parallel to the emperor in the work this time is Otto II, who ruled from 973–83 and who was, if not actually damned, at least actually *praised* only faintly in the *Modus Ottinc*. He did attract the description 'the red', and the emperor in Konrad's work has red hair, a fine beard and a touchy temper. Otto II did also engage on a less than successful Italian campaign, which might be reflected in Konrad, but beyond that we cannot (and need not) progress much further in historical terms. Konrad's claim (also at the end of the work) to have read the story in Latin need not detain us either, since no actual source has been identified. This epigonal chivalric work has a similar relationship, then, to actual history to that in the earlier heroic writings. If Konrad sets his work not in the period of the folk migrations, however, but in what was for him an equally distant (and idealised) age, his theme applies nevertheless to the political chaos in Germany which would come in the latter part of the thirteenth century, as well as having general ethical applications. Kenneth Sisam commented—à propos of *Beowulf*—that 'personal devotion to one's lord distinguishes the Teutonic from the later feudal system, in which obligations tend to be limited or legally defined'.[87] This is true, of course, but the effect of obligation on the hero in the later period is simply enhanced by

---

87 Sisam, *The Structure of Beowulf*, p. 14.

this, and the inner feelings of that hero can be—indeed will be—much as before, only more so.

Ostensibly *Heinrich von Kempten*,[88] which Konrad wrote between 1261 and 1277 for a patron named Berthold von Thiersberg, is the tale of a knight who is a feudal vassal of the Abbot of Kempten in Swabia, a Benedictine monastery founded in 773 by the wife of Charlemagne, and as an imperial foundation, subject immediately to the German crown.[89] At an imperial diet in Bamberg, Heinrich quarrels with the emperor and is banished under pain of death. Later on he is forced by his feudal duty to the Abbot of Kempten to fight in an imperial army. Whilst taking a bath he sees the emperor attacked and, in spite of his personal feelings towards him, he lays hands on a shield and sword, and fights off the attack, naked as he stands. For this affirmation of loyalty he is pardoned by the emperor.

Unusual though it may be, the generally *heroic* nature of this event is fairly clear, and there are various elements of the earlier heroic code which merge, in any case, with the chivalric. Heinrich is compelled by the society of which he is part, and in which he has himself accepted benefits and responsibilities, to do as his overlord the abbot requires, however reluctant he might be himself. Here the conflict of duty is quite clear. His inner nature, too, makes him defend the emperor (and therefore the state) when he and therefore it are under threat. All this is subsumed under the heading *manheit*, which we might even translate as 'heroism'.

---

88 The standard edition is that edited by Eduard Schröder, *Kleinere Dichtungen Konrads von Würzburg*, vol. i (Berlin: Weidmann, 2nd edn, 1930). The text is cited here from the convenient edition with modern German translation in *Konrad von Würzburg*, trans. Heinz Rölleke (Stuttgart: Reclam, 1968), which is based on the Schröder edition. There is an English translation in J. W. Thomas, *The Best Novellas of Medieval Germany* (Columbia SC: Camden House, 1984), pp. 55–61. See in particular also the study of the text by Hartmut Kokott, *Konrad von Würzburg: Ein Autor zwischen Auftrag und Autonomie* (Stuttgart: Heinzel, 1989), pp. 93–107.

89 See John W. Bernhardt, *Itinerant Kingship and Monasteries in Early Medieval Germany, c. 936–1075* (Cambridge: CUP, 1993), on the importance of the royal monasteries.

There are throughout the work plenty of familiar designations—
helt, degen, 'warrior', 'thane'—as well as the later term *ritter,*
'knight'. Admittedly there is no overt emphasis on reputation,
although there are hints of it at least, as when the abbot stresses
that Heinrich is his best warrior. We are told, too, that Heinrich
has sons.

Heinrich von Kempten is not really a romance; there is no knight-
errantry, no quest, and there are no ladies present. On my bare
retelling, the work might be a straightforward picture of a Germanic
hero, carrying out a great deed that is put his way by fate, compelled
to do so by social pressures and by an inner acceptance, bravely,
perhaps almost in superhuman fashion—fighting naked against
odds—to defend his overlord. And yet it is not quite like that: the
two are estranged, and the reason for the original quarrel is of great
importance.

Heinrich is at an imperial celebration at Bamberg, and the work
opens when those assembled—a representative picture of the entire
feudal society—are ready for a feast. With great skill, Konrad
shows us a trivial incident which would hardly be described in
heroic or any other poetry at all, were it not for the fact that it
escalates. A squire, for whom Heinrich is responsible, breaks off
a small piece of bread and eats it before the meal has officially
started. The imperial chamberlain, noticing this, strikes the lad in
punishment for this infringement of good manners, knocks the
boy down and draws blood. Heinrich is responsible for the boy
and considers the punishment overly harsh, which perhaps it is,
but he therefore strikes at the chamberlain with too much force
and kills him. At this point Emperor Otto, of whose beard and
temper we have already heard, appears in the hall and sees the
fallen chamberlain. He demands to know the culprit, circumvent-
ing the *legal* process, but swearing vengeance 'by my beard'.
Heinrich is now threatened, and—fully aware of the significance
of the emperor's oath, which we have been told is always bind-
ing—he has no choice but to fight for his life. From that trivial
beginning the official imperial gathering, with all the estates represented, collapses into a mêlée. Social order is a fragile thing,
and Heinrich clearly went armed to the feast. Hroðgar's Heorot

was threatened by forces from outside, but the threat to this later
and more extended society is from within. It does not come from
any monsters or from the kindred of Cain, but rather from Adam's
inheritance, from man's inbuilt propensity to chaos and both from
the impetuousness of youth and the arrogance of age. Heinrich
ought perhaps to have tried to plead his case (which was after all
at least an arguable one), and Otto ought not to have sworn an
irrevocable oath before everyone that Heinrich's life was forefeit.
The results, however, are as threatening to the entire Holy Roman
Empire as Grendel's attacks were on the continued existence of
Hroðgar's hall. Moreover, since the enemy this time is from
within, we cannot expect an external saviour, a Beowulf, to come
and provide an answer.

Order *is* eventually resumed at Otto's gathering, but it is
precarious. First, however, the seriousness of the event is made
clear. Heinrich has only one way of defending himself, and that
is hardly in line with the supposed civilisation that the feudal
empire implies. He attacks the emperor directly and grabs him
by the beard, effectively holding his life hostage. From an opening
picture of the estates, a pageant of medieval order, we have a
hall with blood and the dead on the floor, and the emperor's life
at stake (and thus by implication the stability of the whole society)—and all from the most trivial of starting-points. In terms
of receptive timelessness, too, this is how wars begin. Although
the situations are not completely comparable, at least one historical
event in the complicated period of the disputed succession at the
beginning of Konrad's century was also a personal matter of private
revenge rather than of broader politics, namely the murder of
Philip of Swabia, the Hohenstaufen claimant to the throne, at
Bamberg in 1208. It is clear, then, in Konrad's work how pre-
cariously balanced the whole thing can be. Konrad's narrative is
exciting:

> hie mit der ûzerwelte man
> geswinde für den keiser spranc,
> er greif in bî dem barte lanc,
> und zuhte in über sînen tisch:
> ez wære fleisch oder visch

daz man dâ für in hæte brâht,
daz wart gevellet in ein bâht,
als er in bî dem barte dans . . .
. . .
diu krône wol gezieret . . .
viel nider in den palas.
. . .
[Heinrich] zuhte von der sîten
ein mezzer wol gewetzet,
daz hæte er im gesetzet
vil schiere an sîne kelen hin . . .
(lines 262–83)

[The fine warrior sprang at the emperor, grabbed him by
his long beard and pulled him across the table, and when
he got him by the beard he knocked to the floor all the
food that was there, be it fish or flesh . . . The bejewelled
imperial crown fell to the palace floor . . . Heinrich drew
a sharp dagger and soon had it pointing at the emperor's
throat.]

Heinrich (who once again clearly came armed to the feast) holds
the emperor, almost choking him, until he is granted safe passage.
The symbolism of the imperial crown knocked to the floor hardly
needs a comment, but Heinrich says quite specifically that if he is
not allowed to leave

ich stiche im ab den weisen
mit disem mezzer veste (line 315f.)

Der weise, the 'orphan stone' (the one found, incidentally, by
Herzog Ernst), is the chief jewel in the imperial crown, and
Heinrich's threat is that he will cut the crown from the emperor's
head with his sharp dagger. The threat is not aimed at the
emperor, but at the whole system. Heinrich is permitted to leave
safely, this time on a formal imperial oath, 'bî keiserlichen êren',
which is far more official than one sworn on the emperor's
beard. But Heinrich must take care not to let himself be seen
again.

Heinrich is banished, then, and order has been restored, but it is only by (in this case quite literally) a whisker. In a strictly courtly reading of the work, the whole incident is expository, providing a reason for Heinrich to be afraid of the emperor. But in broader political terms, the impetuous behaviour of the younger man (however justified) might have led to the death of the emperor and to civil war. If the chastising of a squire can lead to such a state of affairs, what would the effect of the death of an emperor be?

Heinrich, although now an exile, does not apparently harbour thoughts of long-term insurrection. Instead, he returns to Kempten, where he is a *ministerialis*, a feudal knight, and the years pass. In *Beowulf*, fifty years go by in an uneventful fashion until we reach the next point of interest. Here it is a period of ten years, after which Otto begins a campaign in Italy, probably an allusion to the Italian campaign by Otto II in 981–82, when he took Salerno, Bari and Tarento. During his Italian campaign Otto II was, however, ambushed and taken prisoner for a time, something which may lie behind not only the faint praise of the *Modus Ottinc* but also Konrad's fiction.[90] First, however, Otto calls for new forces, and the Abbot of Kempten, as an imperial title-holder, has to send his best men, and calls upon Heinrich. This faces Heinrich with a problem: he cannot meet the emperor, but he cannot refuse the demand if he wishes to continue to adhere to the social system of which he is part. First, he offers to send his two sons in his place. This the abbot refuses, partly with a threat which is itself not insignificant, reminding Heinrich of all he has had from him, and suggesting quite specifically that his fief could be given to others instead. This is something different from the earlier heroic work, with the stress on the legal aspects of feudalism to which Sisam referred. But in a sense it is only a realisation of the reciprocity that ought to have been observed by Byrhtnoð's followers in Maldon, and which his loyal friends mourned as having been forgotten. Equally, however, the abbot stresses with a clear statement that Heinrich is the equivalent, almost, of the chosen champion:

90   See Chris Wickham, *Early Medieval Italy* (Totowa, NJ: Barnes and Noble, 1981), p. 156.

sô nütze enist mir niemen
an dirre hineverte als ir . . . (line 482f)

'You are my most useful man'. says the abbot, 'on this military expedition'. Heinrich agrees to take part in the campaign, albeit with reluctance, because otherwise he will lose both his esteem, his reputation and his property. These still go together:

ê daz ich lâze ûz mîner hant
mîn lêhen und mîn êre
ê rîte ich und kêre
mit iu benamen in den tôt. (lines 498–501)

[I would rather ride with you even to my death, than throw away my reputation and my fief.]

This passage demonstrates very closely the relationship between external esteem, the reputation of the warrior (even at this later stage), and property. Konrad pays little attention to the campaign as such. Instead he takes us—surprisingly, but with a perhaps somewhat sly reference to his supposed Latin source—to a scene in which Heinrich is taking a bath. It is while he is doing so that he sees the emperor ambushed by men who are trying to kill him. Heinrich cannot watch this without acting, jumps naked from the bath, grabs a sword and shield and defends the emperor like 'ein ûzerwelter degen' (line 576), like a fine warrior, for Konrad an old-fashioned term clearly implying a hero. The description of the fighting, too, is in the heroic mode, with Heinrich either killing the attackers or putting them to flight. This act of individual courage balances and expiates Heinrich's earlier act. It is, furthermore, courage on the absolute level and in this act Heinrich demonstrates by his rescue of the emperor that he is committed to the stability of the state. Politically, too, the *status quo* survives because the emperor, for all his faults, is equated with the empire. Cases are rare in Germanic literature where an anointed king falls, although it does crop up in the disguise of fable in the terrifying and dark political satire of Heinrich der Glîchezâre's *Reinhart Fuchs*.[91]

___

91 Edited and translated by Karl-Heinz Göttert (Stuttgart: Reclam, 1976).

Heinrich von Kempten is not an heroic epic;[92] when a reconciliation with the emperor does come, Heinrich stresses once more that he has come on the campaign because if he had not, then he would have lost his lands. The inner compulsion and even the regard for his own reputation which was invoked before are not mentioned again, and the poet, Konrad, ends the whole work with his lament for times past. Nevertheless, what we have been shown are the possibilities implicit in any conflict between the hero and the king, a king who represents the stability of the state, however impetuous he himself might be. Konrad wrote near the time of the great interregnum in Germany and the period of civil unrest which was resolved only under the rule of the Habsburgs, but the political implications of the work are far more general. A warrior society, even one which has acquired a more extensive structure than that shown in earlier Germanic writings, can all too easily become unstable, and this underlines the paramount importance of loyalty. Critics have noted Beowulf's loyalty, for example, even to a temporary lord like Hroðgar, but Heinrich's loyalty is, like that of Ernst, ultimately not just to the feudal lords above him (the abbot, and above him the emperor) but to the whole political system. To be fair, Otto himself might, by his impetuous oath-swearing, be thought to have placed the structure of things into jeopardy, and he, too, learns a lesson: he has, after all, had to be rescued by a single naked warrior. True, there is no actual word of ignominy here, but the implied praise is not much less faint than it was in the *Modus Ottinc* where, we recall, the historical figure upon whom our emperor is probably based comes out of it simply as a man without a victory. His role here is ultimately that of a representative; he stands for the

---

92 See on the general point, however, the stylistic study by Wolfgang Monecke, *Studien zur epischen Technik Konrads von Würzburg* (Stuttgart: Metzler, 1968). Kokott, *Konrad von Würzburg: Ein Autor zwischen Auftrag und Autonomie*, pp. 93–105, notes the warrior elements in this challenging text, and urges a broad receptive base. There is a very detailed summary of research on the text (in which the comic elements are often stressed, for example) in Rüdiger Brant, *Konrad von Würzburg* (Darmstadt: WBG, 1987), pp. 117–22. It is not normally regarded as heroic in any way.

empire, for the system. Heinrich has, as a young man, shown his prowess as a warrior; he also shows loyalty in that the squire he defends is from his own home territory and in his care. But in doing so he nearly brings down the state. His great testing in later life, when he is placed into a situation in which he actually saves the state, also underlines for him the hierarchy of authority. That lesson is learned not only with the passing of time—we assume a maturing process during the ten years in which time Heinrich raises two sons and behaves well—but also by a testing *in extremis*. Konrad tells us, as briefly as the *Beowulf* poet mentions the fifty years of the hero's rule, that Heinrich 'sich schône gar betruoc' [behaved quite blamelessly] during the years away from court. We might put it more negatively: he caused no more trouble, did not develop his threat to the state. But banished by Otto from his sight, and hence from the greater political entity, he must still, like Ernst, earn the right to reenter. The difference between these three works, apart from that of political scale, is that the danger in the more extensive political world of *Herzog Ernst* and of Konrad's poem comes from within. In the world of *Beowulf*, the outside is larger, the threats more monstrous.

Beowulf exhibits all the innate self-awareness of the heroic poem, *Herzog Ernst* less so, even if the emperor does have it all written down. Konrad is a more conscious poet and actually tells us that this is the right sort of song with a definite moral, where the older heroic material was self-defining. The structural balance of Konrad's little work is simpler than that of *Beowulf* or *Herzog Ernst*, but if the events of Heinrich's youth and that of his maturity are carefully set to cancel one another out rather than to complement one another, that was true to an extent of Ernst as well, even if in Konrad's poem the first part of the education process is just time passing uneventfully, with not a monster or dragon in sight. However, the situations, the interesting parts, are all as extreme, and the message of each work is similar. The king needs the hero and the hero needs to mature. That the hero can, in learning his lesson, sometimes pose a threat, we shall see again in the Roland saga.

In *The Hero and the King*, W. H. T. Jackson took as his starting-point the fact that epics have social overtones, that they present 'some kind of model for behavior in a particular society'.[93] He concentrated too on the opposition in the 'decline or temporary weakness of a ruler who ws faced with a younger man bent on establishing a reputation'. I would wish—while broadening the range of the Germanic hero in literary terms to avoid the confines of the heroic epic—to place greater emphasis on the social aspect. Beowulf is concerned to establish a reputation, it is true, but the point is that he does so within the political context of Heorot. Ernst and Heinrich come into conflict with their rulers, but what they demonstrate is not the hero seeking reputation, but having to fight to maintain a reputation. And yet Beowulf has to do precisely this, in a way, against the taunts of Unferð. Actual conflict between the hero and king is present in the later works, but what overrides all is the question of social stability, and this seems to me to be the guiding structural element. Both the hero and the king are subordinate to the social order, and the question of reputation has a meaning only within the maintenance of that political structure. This is what the hero has to learn as a young man, and what he has to maintain as an old man.

---

93 See Jackson, *The Hero and the King*, preface, p. vii.

4

In the Hands of the Church

Waltharius the Visigoth and Louis
of the West Franks

When the Vikings sacked Northumbria and Lindisfarne at the end of the eighth century, Alcuin, who had left York for the court of Charlemagne, wrote letters to the King of Northumbria and to Bishop Higbald to voice the opinion that God was punishing the people for their decadence, and more specifically for sins such as thieving and fornication. Alcuin was also worried, however, about the entertainment enjoyed by the monks. 'Quid Hinieldus cum Christo?' asked Alcuin in a much-quoted and somewhat overplayed passage, what has Ingeld to do with Christ?[94] Heroic tales—and we know the story of Ingeld from *Beowulf*—were not spiritual reading. Alcuin's comment was not particularly original, and in fact little more than a formula; several centuries earlier, St Jerome had asked roughly the same thing about reading Virgil instead of the Bible, and a few centuries in the other direction, Martin Luther would ask it again, and would provide some rousing hymns as a counter to the popular songs of which he disapproved, but which were indeed popular.

It is not entirely clear precisely what Alcuin meant, nor whether his comment was much more than a rhetorical flourish, and to some extent the answer is that a lot of the written heroic material we have

94 In the *Monumenta Germaniae Historica, Epistolae Carolini Aevi* ii, ed. Ernst Dümmler (Berlin: MGH, 1895), p. 124.

was at least committed to writing by Christians. In the world of the Germanic hero, even a text as apparently distant from Christianity as the *Hildebrandslied* was still written down by monks, presumably because they thought it was worth recording, and it was also made respectable, perhaps, by the somewhat awkward additions of invocations at odd points in the text to *waltant got*, 'almighty God'. Their unmetrical position is often a giveaway, but at least Hildebrand, the warrior trapped by fate, sounds like a Christian. But there is a difference between heroic tales that were written down and those that were not, and perhaps Alcuin's disapproval was really aimed at a lost oral tradition. As far as written texts are concerned—and these, after all, are our solid material—Christianity is present in some respects in most cases, with the exception of the early Norse material.[95] Two very different works, however, can demonstrate some of the problems that the church had to face with the secular Germanic hero, and show how it tackled the point. Although both were written in or after the ninth century, one has as its subject the early period of Germanic tribal wanderings and the threat, once again, of the Huns, whilst the other is an absolutely contemporary work. In the first, the historical original of the hero in question is very obscure indeed—a Visigoth king of Toulouse, probably Christian, named Walja, who ruled for three years at the beginning of the fifth century, but who becomes the central figure of a Latin poem of nearly 1500 lines, the tale of *Waltharius*.[96] The second piece is most unusual in that its hero

---

95 With *Beowulf*, for example, approaches range from treating it as a completely Christian poem to the somewhat grudging comment of Jan de Vries that it seemed 'as if [the poet] wished to cast a Christian veil across the undoubtedly heathen theme': *Heroic Song and Heroic Legend*, trans. B. J. Timmer (London: OUP, 1963), p. 58f.

96 On the identification of our hero with the Visigoth Walja, see Henri Gregoire, 'Le *Waltharius* et Strasbourg'. *Bulletin de la faculté de lettres de Strasbourg* 14 (1936), 201–31, and Münkler, *Blickfeld des Helden*, pp 46–56. Already in 1892 Marion Dexter Learned had referred in her survey of the supposed Walther saga to a Visigoth Wallia, who was succeeded by Theoderic I of the Visigoths (not to be confused with the far more celebrated Theoderic—Dietrich—of the Ostrogoths): *The Saga of Walther of Aquitaine* (Baltimore: MLA, 1892, repr. Westport, Conn.: Greenwood, 1970). p. 160. Walja ruled from 415 to 418, while Theodoric, son-in-law of Alaric, the sacker of Rome and the first Visigoth ruler, ruled until 451.

(in the modern sense too) is a Frankish king whose deeds were praised in verse within months of the actual victory which the poem—the Old High German *Ludwigslied*—celebrates. What, then, have Waltharius the Visigoth and Louis of the West Franks to do with Christ? When I published a translation of the *Waltharius* I opened the introduction with a concise but I hope complete summary of all scholarship on the work. I hope, too, that the irony was as obvious as the fact that I was imitating fairly shamelessly Tolkien's celebrated summary of *Beowulf* criticism:[97]

> *Waltharius* was written in the early or late tenth century; it was written at the end or the middle of the ninth century; it was written in Carolingian times; it was written at the start of the eleventh century. It is anonymous; it is by Grimald of St Gallen; it is by Ekkehard I of St Gallen; it is by an unknown Frenchman; it is by an otherwise unknown monk called Gerald of St Gallen (of Strasbourg, of Toul, of Eichstätt, of somewhere else), who was German (French). It was written at St Gallen, Freising, Lorraine or somewhere else. Gerald's prologue is an integral author statement; it is quite separate and has nothing to do with the text. The prologue dedicates the work (the copy) to Bishop (or Archbishop) Erkambald of Strasbourg (of Eichstätt, of Mainz). It is in origin a Visigothic lay; it is an original work in Latin (though perhaps based on elements from known Germanic tales); it is a direct translation or adaptation of a Germanic epic. The Anglo-Saxon *Waldere* is earlier; it is based on *Waltharius*; it provides evidence of a Germanic Walther-saga; there is no Walther-saga.[98]

---

97 To be fair, Tolkien's approach has itself echoes of Carlyle's essay 'On History' of 1830.
98 Brian Murdoch, *Walthari* (Glasgow: SPIGS, 1989), p. 1. The Latin text is cited from the standard edition by Karl Strecker and Norbert Fickermann, *Poetae Latini Medii Aevi*, vi, part 1 (Hanover: Monumenta Germaniae Historica, 1951; repr. Munich., 1978), and there are useful notes in the edition by A. K. Bate, *Gæraldus, Waltharius* (Reading: University Medieval and Renaissance Latin Texts, 1978). The Strecker

Every one of the views I noted is put, usually very firmly indeed, in the secondary literature, and although some of the (still largely unresolved) issues may be ignored without damage to an appreciation of the text,[99] others *do* need a decision. That the work is German in origin is supported by plays on words in Latin which only work if a German basis is assumed, and certainly the material is Germanic. The poem is set in what we may I suppose call the classical period of heroic epic, that of the Germanic tribes, and the work has to do with Franks, Burgundians and Goths; however, the historical details relating to these tribes are even more distorted than usual, so that the work as such clearly belongs to a later period.[100] In our context too—the response of the church to the hero—it is appropriate to accept as integral the prologue to the work, which is ascribed to a certain Geraldus in those manuscripts in which it is found. Admittedly it is not in all the manuscripts, and not all editors of the text (including Strecker, the main editor) have printed it with the poem, especially those who do not believe that Geraldus was the author of the whole work. The question of authorship, and of Geraldus himself, on the other hand, need not detain us for long, since nothing else is known about him anyway, and very little

note 98 continued
edition does not contain Geraldus' prologue, however, and this is cited from Bate, who considers Geraldus to be the author and therefore includes it. The text is given with an English translation in Dennis M. Kratz, *Waltharius and Ruodlieb* (New York: Garland, 1984), and with a German translation by Karl Langosch, Ekkehard, *Waltharius* (Frankfurt. M.: Insel, 1987) and by Gregor Vogt-Spira, *Waltharius* (Stuttgart: Reclam, 1995). An earlier German translation is that by Felix Genzmer, *Das Waltharilied* (Stuttgart: Reclam, 1953). The Latin text is found with all the many (later) analogues, including those in Middle High German, Polish and Old Norse in Learned, *Saga of Walther*.

99 'Der Streit um das *Waltharius*-Epos geht weiter und läßt kein Ende absehen'. [the *Waltharius*-wars are still going on, and as yet there is no result in sight] are the somewhat despairing opening words in a paper by Rudolf Schieffer, 'Zu neuen Thesen über den *Waltharius*'. *Deutsches Archiv für die Erforschung des Mittelalters* 36 (1980), 193–201. See also Franz Brunhölzl, '*Waltharius* und kein Ende?'. in the *Festschrift für Paul Klopsch*, ed. Udo Kindermann etc. (Göppingen: Kümmerle, 1988), pp. 46–55.
100 See Bernd Schütte, 'Länder und Völker im *Waltharius*'. *Mittellateinisches Jahrbuch* 21 (1986), 70–74.

can be deduced, but the programmatic comments in that prologue are interesting. The prologue—twenty-two lines in a rather different verse form from the rest—opens with a straightforward prayer for the well-being of Erkambald (whose identity need once more not detain us), and an apologia for the work itself. Only towards the end is the theme actually introduced, and that negatively in the first instance. This work is not about God, but about the deeds of a young hero:

> non canit alma patris, resonat sed mira tironis
> nomine Waltharii, per proelia multa reuecti.

A *young* man, then—*tiro*—named Waltharius, who is much wounded in battle. Geraldus goes on, however, to give a reason for his writing the book:

> est mage ludendum, dominum quam sit rogandum
> perfectus longi vim stringit in arta diei.
> (Prologue, lines 17–20)

[The aim is to delight, rather than to instruct in religious terms, to shorten the long days.]

Waltharius, Geraldus seems to be telling us, really does have nothing to do with Christ, at least in the first instance. Significantly enough, the massive amount of secondary literature on the poem includes not only titles like 'Geralds *Waltharius*, das erste Heldenepos der Deutschen'. [the first German heroic epic], but also 'Walther—ein christlicher Held?' [a Christian hero?][101]

---

101 The first article is by Walter Stach, *Historische Zeitschrift* 168 (1943), 57–81; the latter article, by Ursula Ernst, resolves the question mark positively, *Mittellateinisches Jahrbuch* 21 (1986), pp. 79–83. A paper by Maria Lührs, 'Hiltgunt'. in the same journal, pp. 84–7 (a *Festschrift* number for Walther Bulst, with a selection on papers on *Waltharius*), reaches a similar conclusion on Waltharius's fiancée as a Christian figure. Of great interest in this context is an important paper by Dennis M. Kratz, 'Quid Waltharius Ruodliebque cum Christo'. in *The Epic in Medieval Society*, ed. Harald Scholler (Tübingen: Niemeyer, 1977), pp. 126–49, esp. pp. 126–37, although the elevation of the condemnation of avarice to the status of the central theme is perhaps overdone.

There are three aspects to this text, however. First, an historical one: the characters and the events may be linked once again with the Germanic history of the folk-migration period, but only ahistorically, and the poem gives us yet another version, for example, of that major event, the collapse of the dominance by the Huns, historically after the death of Attila. Here it is done in slightly comical, and far less violent, terms than was the case in the Norse *Atlakviða*. Secondly, we can observe, in the figure of Waltharius himself, the actions and development of a hero, and in a sense the generalised pragmatic political point is made in the same way as it is in *Beowulf*, insofar as what we are shown here is the interesting part of Waltharius's career. The fifty years of calm rule under Beowulf before the arrival of the dragon were afforded a couple of lines only, and here too the adventures of the young man occupy nearly all of the poem. But at the end, he comes to rule in Aquitaine, and we are told:

> post mortem obitumque parentis
> Ter denis populum rexit feliciter annis. (lines 1449f)

[After the death of his parents he ruled well for thirty years.]

This was ten times better than the historical king Walja. The literary Waltharius had, what is more—so the poet tells us in the concluding lines of the work—many other victories, but the recording of these are beyond the poet's *stilus retunsus*, his 'blunt pen'. Thirdly, however, we have to come back to the question of the church, and with this poem we have a curious intervention which ties in very well, however, with the political implications of the presentation of the hero, and with the important—but not described—period of many years of uninteresting times. The overall feel of *Waltharius*, whilst sometimes described as unsuccessful in literary terms, even as a travesty of heroic writing, is none the less politically of some interest, especially in comparison with works like the *Atlakviða*, which reflects the same initial historical structure, but does so in a very different manner.

The work begins with the Huns at the height of their powers in Europe, and we are shown in rapid succession three Germanic tribes, which, when under this threat from outside, realise that they have no alternative but to pay tribute and to send hostages. There is no question here of heroic stands against what is clearly a force of massive superiority, and the problem complex of *Maldon*, say, does not come into question. Indeed, the Huns under Attila did exercise a hegemony over many of the Germanic tribes, but here the tribes in question—the Franks, the Burgundians and the Visigoths of Aquitaine—have become confused with historical distance and later development, so that the apparently historical Huns (although the poet uses a variety of different and not always historically accurate names for them) may stand for any alien invading force. Here, too, the Franks are ruled by Gibicho and later Guntharius—both echoes of historical kings of the Burgundians. The unfortunate role normally played by literary equivalents of the Burgundian king Gundahari is reflected in the work to a certain extent, and his close associate is Hagen, as in other heroic works. But any actual historicity has been pushed far into the background and it is significant here as elsewhere that Hagen the adviser (like other advisers) is not really an historical figure at all. Brave attempts have been made to link him with historical figures in early Germanic history, it is true; but where Guntharius has a fairly well-documented equivalent, Hagen does not. The king is historical, a fixed entity; those who influence his actions (or fail to do so) in literary works are more fluid.

What remains in mind is the pattern of pragmatic politics in the work, such as the initial decisions of the counsellors of each tribe to negotiate with, rather than to fight against Attila. The three tribes send a large amount of tribute and each sends a hostage. The Franks send Hagano in place of the then king's son, Gunthari, who is too young; Aquitaine sends Waltharius, their prince, and the Burgundians send the king's only daughter, Hildigunda. Waltharius's relationship to the real King Walja is very much less relevant than his model role in the work as hostage, warrior and ruler. Hildigunda, who is betrothed to Waltharius, is quite unhistorical, and has been introduced to represent the Burgundians, presumably because the historical kings who ruled in Worms in the fourth century have been reassigned to the tribe that ruled there at the time the poem was written, the Franks.

The three hostages grow up at Attila's court and are treated with honour, although they are still hostages against the payment of tribute. The question of gold is again an extremely important one and will remain so throughout the work, coming to the fore once again when the old king of the Franks, Gibicho, dies, and is succeeded by his son Guntharius. Guntharius feels that he has made no agreement to pay tribute and it is cut off. Hagano, the Frankish hostage, now in danger of his life, at once flees, taking leave of his by now close friend Waltharius. There is no real historical parallel to this set of circumstances, but they represent the first crack in the Huns' power. Unable apparently to pursue Hagano—this is not explained—Attila decides to take measures to ensure the loyalty of Waltharius and Hildigunda, namely that they must be married to prominent Huns. Waltharius, by now an important military figure, decides that he, too, will flee, taking Hildigunda with him. There follows a celebrated scene in which Attila is invited to a feast and all his men are made drunk. In the *Atlakviða* this ended in a bloodbath as Gudrun took her revenge, but this time the Huns bow out of history in a less violent fashion. Two elements attach themselves customarily to the fall of Attila: his death on his wedding-night to a Germanic princess, and his drunkenness. Where in the *Atlakviða* the drunken Attila is murdered by his Germanic wife, here—and more degradingly—we have a famous, and specifically unheroic description of Attila's hangover, a stark contrast to the feast itself. On the night before, Attila drained at a draught a cup decorated with pictures of his ancestors' deeds; now he can only stagger out to try and find his host:

> Attila nempe manu caput amplexatus utraque
> Egreditur thalamo rex Walthariumque dolendo
> Advocat, ut proprium queretur forte dolorem.
> (lines 362–64)

[Attila, with his aching head held in his hands, came from his chamber, and in wretchedness called for Waltharius, so he could bemoan his sufferings.]

But Waltharius has gone, taking with him a large amount of treasure in the form, again, of gold arm-rings, *armillae*, a great war-horse, and Hildigunda. Nor, indeed, can Attila persuade any of his men, with promises of reward, to pursue him. The point of the unheroic description is clear, and cause and effect merge. Attila and the Huns are no longer a force to be reckoned with, although Waltharius and Hildigunda do not realise this.

The pair travel westwards from Attila's lands towards their home territory, and en route through the lands of the Franks, King Guntharius and his lieutenant, Waltharius's old friend and fellow hostage Hagano, become aware of them, or more specifically become aware of an armed man who seems to be carrying treasure. This is the core of the work in heroic terms, and various motifs interact with it. The focus is on the heroic behaviour or otherwise of Waltharius and Hagano—some manuscripts of the work even refer to it as the 'Book of the Two Friends, Waltharius and Hagano'—but also of Guntharius, whose motivation is of considerable interest.

When news comes to the Franks of the appearance of Waltharius in their territory, what is of immediate interest to the king is that he is clearly carrying gold from the Huns. Hagano, realising that this is Waltharius, asks the court to rejoice with him—'Congaudete mihi quaeso'—that his friend has also escaped. But Guntharius has other priorities. He uses the same words, substituting *iubeo*, 'I command', for Hagano's *quaeso*:

> Congaudete mihi iubeo, quia talia vixi!
> Gazam, quam Gibicho regi transmisit eoo,
> Nunc mihi cunctipotens huc in mea regna remisit.
> (lines 470–73)

[I command you to rejoice with me that I should see such a thing! The tribute treasure sent to Attila by Gibicho has been returned to my lands by the Almighty.]

Guntharius is king, so he can insist, and it is of interest first that he asserts an actual title to the treasure—this is his by rights, because it was paid by Gibicho—and then claims that God has returned it. Of course he goes too far: part of it belongs by rights to the Visigoths and the Burgundians, but it is on his land for the taking, if he can do so. The Emperor Frederick Barbarossa is supposed to have commented that even unsupported claims depended upon who held the club of Hercules.[102]

There are two problems, then: Hagano's, a conflict between feudal loyalty—the king's *iubeo* has been laid very firmly upon his *quaeso*—and friendship; and the question of might, right and possession. Guntharius commands a group of his warriors, including Hagano, to come with him to attack Waltharius, and Hagano reluctantly agrees. It is of additional interest to note that Hagano is the only one aware of Waltharius' fighting skills. The king demands his loyalty, but does not listen when Hagano makes a clear case—which is nothing to do with his own friendship, and is entirely pragmatic—for not attacking Waltharius. He does so very much in the role of subordinate—addressing Guntharius as *rex fortissimus*, 'strongest of kings', for example—but he makes it clear that he has seen Waltharius in battle and the others precisely have not. The Other World, he says, will soon welcome anyone who dares to attack Waltharius. The role of Hagano (and in other works, of the Hagen figure) as adviser to Guntharius is always a model: Guntharius does not listen to his adviser, and this contrasts with the first part of the poem, where the respective advisers of the Frankish, Burgundian and Visigoth kings advise (and are listened to) that resistance to the Huns would be impossible, and that they should pay tribute. We, of course, know that the Huns have refused to fight Waltharius.

It is the question of the gold which motivates Gutharius throughout, and he characterises it now as *furata*, 'stolen'. Waltharius and Hildigunda see an armed force coming against them, think first that these are the pursuing Huns, but realise that they are Franks. Waltharius realises, too, that he must fight to keep what he has. He takes up his stance as a warrior should at the entrance to a ravine, and the poet refers to him at this point as *heros*. The poet reminds us now, however, of our original question: what has Waltharius to do with Christ? In the twelve-line section Waltharius declares that no Frank shall live to boast of how he stole the treasure (which is now very much in the foreground). Waltharius also

102 J. B. Gillingham, *The Kingdom of Germany in the High Middle Ages, 900–1200* (London: Historical Association), p. 7.

expresses the thought that the one man in this force who worries him at all is Hagano. Having made his statement about the Franks, however, and only then, Waltharius falls to his knees and begs forgiveness (*veniam petit*) for having said this; and as far as his fear of Hagano is concerned, he hopes nevertheless to defeat him with—he says—God's help.

All of this seems a little *ad hoc* in its Christianity, but Waltharius is prepared to act both honourably and rationally as well regarding the gold, in order to avoid battle by treating if possible. Guntharius sends an envoy, Kamalo, who demands from Waltharius in his name the great war-horse, the treasure and Hildigunda (in that order); Waltharius first states, fairly mildly, that Guntharius has not yet gained the right of a conquerer, but then offers part of the treasure, a hundred arm-rings, in lieu of battle. Byrhtnoð had refused to offer tribute on the assumption that he might be victorious, but here the offer is an entirely reasonable one, and Hagano immediately advises the king to accept, stressing once more that Guntharius does not know Waltharius's prowess in battle. Indeed, he even becomes angry with his king, something which, interestingly, prompts the poet to add 'Si tamen in dominum licitum est irascier ullum' (line 632) [if it is ever appropriate to become angry with one's overlord.] Guntharius silences Hagano with an accusation of cowardice—a device we have seen in the *Hildebrandslied*—which forces him to agree to fight. When his offer is refused, a still calm Waltharius offers 200 gold rings—the increase in the bargaining is interesting— with somewhat harsher words about the Franks. When this too is refused, Waltharius, who is in possession both of the moral and actual high ground, engages in single combat with Guntharius' warriors, one after the other, since he is defending a position which permits only one warrior to attack at a time. One after another they fall, and Waltharius (rather oddly for a Christian) decapitates them once they are dead. In military terms, Waltharius was able to chose his location; others have it forced upon them, and Byrhtnoð, in a quite different situation, allows the enemy space.

The battles are varied and the individual warriors are presented with differentiation, but the outcome is always the same, and only once does an indication of the Christian basis to the work reassert itself. This, too, is linked with what we may see as an earlier aspect of the heroic ethos. One of the warriors sent against Waltharius is Patafridus, Hagano's nephew, his sister's son, and thus in Germanic terms a warrior to whom he is closely bound. That Waltharius kills Patafridus as he does all the rest gives a further impetus to Hagano when he, too, is forced to fight his old friend. However, before Patafridus joins battle, Hagano offers a kind of sermon against the sin of avarice, a splendid rhetorical piece beginning:

> O vortex mundi, fames insatiatus habendi,
> Gurges avaritiae, cunctorum fibra malorum! (lines 57f)

[O whirlpool of the world, insatiable greed! You maelstrom, avarice, root of every evil thing!]

The much-discussed passage, sometimes seen as the central theme, but also considered somewhat odd coming from Hagano, *does* remind us of what is at issue here in purely pragmatic terms. Waltharius is fighting for property that the Franks wish to take from him, even though he had offered an honourable way out. With twelve warriors against one, Guntharius clearly thinks, in spite of Hagano, that the gamble was worth while.

Eventually all the Franks are killed except Guntharius himself and Hagano. If there was an earlier Walther saga, perhaps this final battle was at the centre of it, with friend set against friend, although since there is no large-scale earlier evidence of such a saga, in spite of a great deal of later material, no valid comments can be made on the matter. The logic of the work we do have—that conflicts of loyalty force the two friends to fight— reminds us in some senses of the *Hildebrandslied*, but the situation is not really comparable with that work, or with other tales related to that of Hildebrand and Hadubrand, because the whole matter of recognition is absent. What is at issue here is more simply political loyalty. Hagano has to fight because of his allegiance to Guntharius, even though this has to be augmented somewhat by the accusation of cowardice earlier on, and by the death of Patafridus (which Hagano claims as his main reason for fighting, although he was well aware that Waltharius had no choice but to kill the younger man). A more interesting comparison might be with *Beowulf* and with *Maldon*; feudal loyalty demands that allies fight for their lord, although in the two Anglo-Saxon works some do not, even when the enemy is a completely external one. Here Waltharius is not Hagano's enemy and the national motivation is avarice, but Hagano *does* fight.

In the search for Germanic elements—by which is meant satisfyingly tragic and sometimes folkloristic or historical antecedents—in *Waltharius*, the fact is sometimes lost sight of that this is a (probably) tenth-century Latin work by a churchman. The relationship to history and the reflection even of the fall of the Burgundians under Gundahari is as irrelevant to the poet as it is to us, especially as they have somehow turned into Franks in any case. Whether the Visigoths were even much of a concept to the poet at all is debatable, and they have very little part to play in criticism of the poem, which is about the acquisition of gold and power. The poet is, for example, quite clear on the nature of Guntharius, whom Waltharius injures badly in the final battle. Hagano may not be able to get angry with his king, but the poet can describe him as a rabid dog, gnashing his teeth, or use adjectives like *superbus* to describe him.

The climax is the fight between Waltharius and Hagano, and it is noteworthy that even this is prefaced by a final attempt on the part of Waltharius to share the gold. Hagano refuses, and they fight. With the *Hildebrandslied* the logic of the work would fail if the watching armies were not there as witnesses. In this battle between friends, however, there are no watchers except the wounded King Guntharius and the woman, Hildigunda, and there is no victory by either side. Waltharius loses a hand, Hagano teeth and one eye and Guntharius has already lost a leg. These oddly specific mutilations are probably influenced by biblical references, the passage in Matthew, for example, which refers to the cutting off of a foot or a hand, or the putting out of an eye if they cause sin; but what is more important is that the fight now stops, and does so for logical, not theological reasons. The heroes, the poet tells us, are equal, and for them to fight on is pointless: each would kill the other, but exhaustion stops them:

quisnam hinc immunis abiret
Qua duo magnanimi heroes tam viribus aequi
Quam fervore animi steterant in fulmine belli?
(lines 1398–1400)

[Who could have left unharmed when two fierce heroes,
just as equal in their strength as fervour, stood and fought
in the thunder of war?]

All three surviving warriors—although Guntharius is in fact barely
alive—have been mutilated, and it is at this point that the poet
comments—and it is one of the most celebrated lines of the work—
on the reason behind it all: 'sic, sic armillas partiti sunt Avarenses'
(line 1404) [that is how the gold arm-rings of the Huns were divided
up.] Hildigunda treats the three wounded men, and a treaty is made
between them, one that could have been made earlier, but at least
is made (or perhaps renewed) at this point. The gold is shared and
Waltharius can return with Hildigunda to his home, and rule it for
thirty years.[103]

In the *Hildebrandslied*, however pointless the death of the individual and the termination of Hildebrand's line may be, there is
a continuation of the world after the poem that depends, to an
extent at least, on Hildebrand's decision to act: the forces of
Theoderic (Dietrich) prevail, as indeed they did in reality, even
if one warrior family has to be sacrificed to the greater good of
the state. At the end of *Waltharius*, however, there would be no
political advantage, and neither man would gain real glory. In any
case, the logic is that each would kill the other (the various later
versions in other languages are not consistent, however), leaving
Guntharius dying and Hildigunda unprotected. As it is, she is able
to bind up the wounds of the warriors.

Waltharius is a literary work by an ecclesiastic, but it has a political
moral. The religious voice of the poem speaks against avarice in

---

103 See Harms, *Kampf mit dem Freund*, pp. 29–33, on the battle. As a curiosity
of literary criticism, see too the medical essay referring to Hildigunda's
final task: W. Haberling, *Die Verwundetenfürsorge in den Heldenliedern des
Mittelalters* (Jena: Fischer, 1917).

particular, but one may wonder whether the poet is aware of the potential for word-play between *avaritia* and the treasure of the Avares, the name used normally for the Huns in the poem. The work presents us with a Germanic hero, Waltharius, who is forced to fight with his friend by political necessity as much as the fatal chance that he is discovered when passing through Frankish territory. But the church, whilst acknowledging the warrior ethos, and perhaps delighting in the description of fighting, remains pragmatic. There is no reason for a tragic ending here of the kind seen in the *Atlakviða* or even the *Hildebrandslied*. The Huns, whose great power was acknowledged when they were in the ascendancy, have lost that power, and with it their treasure, and there is neither need nor justification for these Germanic tribes to fight one another to the death. The moral of *Waltharius* and of that in some ways rather abrupt ending is that of political expediency. Fight if you have to —for defence, or because of your feudal loyalties, even, perhaps, for gold and increased power—but enough is enough, and when warriors are equally matched, a fight to the death is pointless. Whether there was a saga or not—and the Old Norse, Middle High German and Slav analogues are all later than our text—and how it ended, is irrelevant. Waltharius, Hagano and possibly even Guntharius are all heroes in that they are fighting with and for a political system, albeit with different motivations, but in the poem the Church steps in when it has to, and stops the fight at an appropriate point.

A poem celebrating another secular warrior and king, in this case one who is far more easy to identify historically,[104] offers a rather

104 Text in Steinmeyer, *Denkmäler*, no. 16 and Braune, *Lesebuch*, no. 36; with modern German translation in Schlosser, *Literatur*, pp. 274–7. English translation in Bostock, *A Handbook on Old High German*, pp. 239–41. We may dismiss the view, last voiced by Rosamond McKitterick, *The Carolingians and the Written Word* (Cambridge, CUP, 1989), pp. 232–5, that the subject of the *Ludwigslied* is actually Louis the Younger of the East Franks (Germany). That the king lost his father as a young man (the German king was forty when his father died), the division with Carloman only, and that he was away at the time of the raid are all decisive elements. McKitterick is interesting, however, on the political nature of the poem, although Saucourt was not—from the perspective of 881, only a 'minor success'.

different response on the part of the church to the Germanic hero as such from that seen in *Waltharius*. In this case, and very unusually, the hero is actually contemporary with the poem, and the events celebrated—which again may also be taken generally—are not drawn by the poet from this distant past, but are very recent happenings indeed. The celebration in song of Louis, king of the West Franks, and his victory at Saucourt in 881 was written within a year of the events upon which it is based, although whether, or the extent to which, this means that it can be taken as an historical document is a matter of debate. In spite of the great difference in historical perspective, the work may be at least roughly contemporary with *Waltharius*.

A saint may be a hero, and there has always been a clear overlap in vocabulary between the military and the holy, from St Paul's injunction to take up the whole armour of God down to more modern expressions of pious militarism, such as 'Onward, Christian Soldiers'. There has been much critical discussion of the supposed transformation of Christ into a Germanic warrior in the *Heliand*, a transformation which is, admittedly, sometimes somewhat exaggerated.[105] Although the heroism of the saint is usually one of hardships borne with fortitude, the vocabulary in early Germanic writings can coincide very strongly with that of the hero. Here is a famous example, some brief extracts from the first life of St Guthlac in the Exeter Book:

> . . . he mongum wearð
> bysen on Brytene   siþþan biorg gestah.
> Eadig oretta,   ondwiges heard,
> gyrede hine georne   mid gæstlicum
> wæpnum 7 wædum,   wong bletsade

---

105 See as a recent contribution in this much-discussed area G. Ronald Murphy, *The Saxon Saviour* (New York and Oxford: OUP, 1989), especially chapter 2. Murphy offers a concise survey of previous research, some of which sees the Christ of the *Heliand* as a Germanic lord, while other critics take the work to be more firmly fixed in Christian dogma than in the Germanic world. At all events, the question of how Germanic Christian poets handled actual Germanic heroes is rather different from that of whether or not they made Christ into a Germanic hero.

him to ætstælle   ærest aræde
Cristes rode;   Þær se cempa oferwon
frecnessa fela . . .
He [God] him sige sealde   7 snyttrucræft,
mundbyrd meahta,   Þonne mengu cwom
feonda færscytum   fæhðe ræran . . . (iii, 174–86)

[He (Guthlac) became an example to many in Britain when
he went into the hills. The blessed warrior, strong in
fighting, girded on his spiritual weapons and armour, blessed
the ground and then first of all raised the Cross of Christ
. . . God gave him victory and skill, and His protection,
when many enemies (or fiends, of course) came, firing
their arrows . . .]

There are clear echoes of St Paul here. But God gave Guthlac
the victory and he bears himself like a warrior:

Swa modgade   se wið mongum stod
awreðed weorðlice,   wuldres cempa
engla mægne.   Gewat eal Þonan
feonda mengu . . .
Swa sceal oretta   á in his mode
Gode compian . . . (iv, 323–45)

[He stood against many and bore himself worthily, the
glorious warrior, helped by the power of the angels. All the
demons—the enemies—fled . . . Thus should a warrior fight
for God in his heart . . .][106]

Many of the Germanic heroes operate in their poems within a
Christian context. In battle with the mother of Grendel, it is God,
the poet tells us, who causes Beowulf to win; the hero does his

---

106 Cited from *The Guthlac Poems of the Exeter Book*, ed. Jane Roberts
(Oxford: Clarendon, 1979). *Guthlac B* has similar generalised comments
on the nature of the (Christian) warrior towards the end. There is a
translation in R. K. Gordon, *Anglo-Saxon Poetry* (London: Dent, 1926;
rev. edn, 1954), pp. 256–79. The description of the saint as *wuldres cempa*,
'glorious warrior' is significant.

best on earth according to his own fate and inner compulsion; it is up to God whether he gains the victory or not. Of Beowulf's fight we are told, however, that 'God/ gewēold wīg-sigor' [God gave him the victory], and even if Byrhtnoð was not victorious at Maldon, his own invocation of God's judgement is, it will be recalled, a significant one:

God āna wāt   hwā Þære wælstōwe
wealdan mōte (lines 93f.)

[Only God knows who will win control of the battlefield.]

It is worth noting, by the way, that the participants are not told what the outcome of the battle will be, a kind of *actual* divine intervention that we shall not encounter until the Roland material.

The somewhat odd Old High German poem of the victory of Louis III over the Vikings in 881 provides one of the best examples of the specifically Christian hero, however, and the work has properly been compared with the *Battle of Maldon*. It is odd because it is in the wrong language. Albeit a Frank, the hero of the Old High German *Ludwigslied* can properly be regarded, by this stage in the ninth century, as a French king, and it is an historical accident only that has given us the poem in German, composed probably by an aristocratic monk from the Rhineland at the famous school of Hucbald of St-Amand in Picardy and preserved in a manuscript in which there is nothing else German at all, although there is a very early hagiographic poem in French. Louis III of the West Franks—the poem calls him Hluduig, the Latin title Hluduicus— became king at the age of sixteen or seventeen on the premature death of his father in 879, sharing responsibility with his brother Carloman. As might be expected, he had some difficulties establishing his rule, especially in the face of physical attack from counter-claimants like Boso, Duke of Provence, and political opposition from powerful and experienced men like Hincmar of Rheims. A further problem in the later ninth century was that of attacks by the Vikings on Francia in general, and the *Ludwigslied* is based, like the *Battle of Maldon*, on a single Viking raid, this time one in Picardy in 881, at which Louis and the West Franks were successful in beating off the Vikings.[107] The whole issue of the *Ludwigslied* as a piece of contemporary propaganda, specifically in support of the king against the Hincmar faction, has been very widely discussed, especially in recent scholarship, so that on this occasion we are faced, apparently, with a clear and practical political purpose to the work, although there are problems with this approach to the poem.[108] Louis is a contemporary hero in that the poem speaks of him as still being alive; at least, the German part of the poem does so—there is also a Latin part of the poem to which I shall return. However, Louis was killed within a year of his victory. One of the Annals—the otherwise entirely sympathetic set from St-Vaast—reports that 'because he was a young man' (*quia iuvenis erat*) he was chasing a girl as a joke (*iocando*) while on horseback, and in doing so rode against a doorway, causing internal injuries that killed him in 882, the year after the battle.[109] When the poem was written down in its final form, however, in the form, that is, in which we have it, it had become something rather different from a propaganda piece for the young king. It had become a memorial, and a Latin

107 Very few critics consider the poem as it stands in the manuscript, however—as a memorial piece, although this term has been applied specifically to *The Battle of Maldon*, for example, by Ute Schwab in Cooper, *Battle of Maldon*, pp. 63–85.

108 The most important studies (which overlap in some respects with each other) are those by Holger Homann, 'Das *Ludwigslied*: Dichtung im Dineste der Politik?'. in *Traditions and Transitions: Studies in Honor of Harold Jantz,* ed. Lieselotte E. Kurth et al. (Munich: Delp, 1972), pp. 17–28; Rudolf Schützeichel, 'Das Heil des Königs'. *Beiträge* (Tübingen) 94: Sonderheft (1972), 369–91; Paul Fouracre, 'The Context of the OHG *Ludwigslied*'. *Medium Aevum* 54 (1985), 87–103; and three papers in the collection *mit regulu bithuungan: Neue Arbeiten zur althochdeutschen Poesie und Sprache,* ed. John L. Flood and David N. Yeandle (Göppingen: Kümmerle, 1989), by Raimund Kemper (pp. 1–17), David Yeandle (pp. 18–80), and Paul Fouracre (pp. 81–93). That by Yeandle is especially full: he takes it as propaganda not only for Louis, but for the West Frankish line as such.

109 The passage is referred to by Janet L. Nelson in her translation of *The Annals of St-Bertin* (Manchester: MUP, 1991), p. 223. The other annals do not mention the fact, and the otherwise generally unsympathetic annals from St-Bertin, indeed, refer only to the king's eagerness to fight the Norsemen, from which he was prevented by illness.

superscript makes this clear. The point is usually overlooked in criticism that whatever its intent at the time when it was composed, it served as propaganda of this kind for less than a year at best, and possibly not at all.

Various monastic annals refer to the battle, many of them praise the action of the young king, and the victory was undoubtedly of some importance in the short term as a rare victory over the Vikings. The annals from St-Vaast, those of Fulda, and the *Chronicle* of Regino of Prüm in particular celebrate the victory as a major one, and only the *Annals of St-Bertin*—those written or adapted by Hincmar of Rheims—even modify this, stating that the king fled after the battle even though no one was pursuing him. According to the St-Vaast annals, Louis triumphed 'most gloriously' (*gloriossissime*) over the Vikings, while Regino (who does admittedly place the events in the wrong year, 883) speaks of how Louis defended the kingdom powerfully and in a manly fashion (*potenter et viriliter*) against the plague of heathens (*infestatio paganorum*). Admittedly, the St-Vaast annals do refer to a sudden rally by the Vikings, caused, the annalist says, by the smugness of the Franks who failed to praise God for their initial victory; but even he goes on to say that only the king's efforts save the situation. In those annals, too, as in the poem, the king is seen as being moved by the sufferings of his kingdom.[110]

The annals also give us further details that are of importance in evaluating the poem, such as the fact that just before the battle Louis was in the south of Francia assisting his brother Carloman to fight off Boso of Provence.[111] As the presentation of a

---

110 See Karl Leyser, 'Early Medieval Warfare'. in Cooper, *Battle of Maldon*, pp. 87–108, esp. p. 107.
111 On the annals and the history in the work, see Ruth Harvey, 'The Provenance of the Old High German *Ludwigslied*'. *Medium Aevum* 14 (1945), 1–20, and Elisabeth Berg, 'Das *Ludwigslied* und die Schlacht bei Saucourt'. *Rheinische Vierteljahrsblätter* 29 (1964), 175–99. These papers carry details of editions of the various annals, and for a translation of the St-Bertin text, see Nelson, *Annals of St-Bertin*, p. 222. I have used the very convenient collection of relevant historical texts appended to Claudia Händl, *Ludwigslied: Canto di Ludovico* (Alessandria: Edizione dell'Orso, 1990), pp. 153–64.

contemporary hero, within an historical context, but one placing all his actions into a clearly Christian framework, however, the Old High German poem is of very considerable interest. A recent paper by Paul Szarmach examining the generic context of the *Battle of Maldon* contrasts that poem with the *Ludwigslied* and with the Latin *Bella Parisiacae urbis* of Abbo of St-Germain, arriving at the conclusion that in the two continental poems 'the moral framework allows for supernatural intervention into human affairs either by the divinity or by the saints'.[112] This conclusion may require some clarification, although Sarmach is quite right to note that the Christian framework invests the battle with its significance. Whether it is an heroic poem or not will doubtless remain a matter of debate: there are already many articles, mostly in German, which attempt to establish the poem's genre, and it does not seem fruitful to try to add to them. It is a poem containing a hero, however, who is both Christian and Germanic—the terms are not mutually exclusive.[113]

The fifty-nine line *Ludwigslied* first of all shows us the youth of the king, establishing him as a servant of God. We are then shown the Vikings, who are here characterised even less fully than in the *Battle of Maldon*, but are described simply, as is sometimes the case elsewhere, as 'heathens'. The attacks on Francia are not even seen

---

112 Paul Szarmach, 'The (Sub-)Genre of the *Battle of Maldon*'. in Cooper, *Maldon*, pp. 43–61; see p. 47.

113 Discussions on the genre of the poem are rarely very fruitful. Indeed, the poem is placed under different headings in anthologies—including *Heldenlied* and *Preislied*—heroic poem or panegyric. See Friedrich Maurer, '*Hildebrandslied* und *Ludwigslied*: Die althochdeutschen Zeugen der hohen Gattungen der Wanderzeit'. *Der Deutschunterricht* 9 (1957), Heft 2, 5–15 (the subtitle is significant, since the *Ludwigslied* has also been seen almost as contemporary journalism); Max Wehrli, 'Gattungschichtliche Betrachtung zum *Ludwigslied*'. in *Philologia Deutsch: Festschrift . . . Walter Henzen*, ed. Werner Kohlschmidt and Paul Zinsli (Berne: Francke, 1965), pp. 9–20; H. Beck, 'Zur literaturgeschichtlichen Gattung des althochdeutschen *Ludwigsliedes*'. *Zeitschrift für deutsches Altertum* 163 (1974), 37–51. The last-named critic also produced some 'Gattungsgeschichtliche Betrachtungen': '*Waltharius*'. *Mittellateinisches Jahrbuch* 2 (1965), 63–73, stressing quite rightly its uniqueness as a literary monument.

in the German poem as an infestation. This is a contrast with the annals in general, which customarily stress the pagan Viking attacks on Christian installations, and sometimes, indeed, take Alcuin's line that their attacks represent a divine judgement. In the St-Vaast annals, for example, the Vikings are positively eager to sack the churches, and, indeed, actively thirsting for human blood.[114] More importantly, the Vikings are given a purpose here: they have been sent by God for two quite distinct reasons—to test the young king, and also to warn the Franks of their sins. The latter notion is the familiar one of the scourge of God, and is not really divine intervention in human affairs; rather it is an historical explanation of observed events in familiar theocentric terms. That the Viking raids were a punishment for sins was very widely assumed. Alcuin's letters on the sack of Lindisfarne name roughly the same sins as are mentioned in the *Ludwigslied*: thieving and immoral behaviour. The idea that God can use attacks of this kind as a punishment is familiar enough from the Old Testament onwards. That it should become part of the education of the young king is, however, less usual. The poet is showing us the king faced with hardship at a young age, the situation of *Waltharius* and many others. The brief poem makes that point very clearly indeed:

> Koron uuolda sin god
> Ob her arbeidi   So iung tholon mahti (lines 9f)

[God wished to test him to see whether he could bear hardship at such a young age.]

The stress on the king's youth may have been part of the propaganda for Louis in the confirming of his throne when the poem was composed; but it has to take on a more general validity after the king's death in the written version that we actually have. God is perceived as providing a pragmatic education for the hero. What the *Ludwigslied* does—with a remarkable consistency—is to

---

114 The 'cool spirit' of the annals towards the Viking raids claimed by J. M. Wallace-Hadrill in the 1974 Stenton Lecture is not always as evident as it might be: J. M. Wallace-Hadrill, *The Vikings in Francia* (University of Reading: The Stenton Lecture, 1974), p. 7. The whole lecture is of some interest in the present context.

place the hero king into a theocentric historical context.[115] The premises remain, the explanation is added.

The Vikings raids have the required effect in the first instance—the Franks are punished, and some repent and mend their ways, and once this is complete, then the testing of the king can begin. Louis, we are told, was away, but we are not told where, nor within the context is it important. Now, however, God asks Louis to return to help the Franks against the Vikings, and he agrees to do so. This is the sole instance of anything like direct intervention, something which was certainly intended as a propaganda point, with the king communicating directly with God. It is, however, little more than a concretisation of the desire by Louis to attack the Vikings, a desire that is mentioned, for example, in the St-Bertin annals. Once Louis has agreed to return and fight the Norsemen, God plays no further direct role, and it is again somewhat misleading to say, as Paul Szarmach does in his essay, that 'the divine and the human . . . work in concert to achieve the desired goal'. Such an interpretation comes close—though it is not the same—as the classic misinterpretation of the work which attacked its *Drahtpuppengesinnung*, the supposed 'puppet mentality' perceived in the work in 1923 by Andreas Heusler.[116] God may indeed know in advance the outcome of the battle, but Louis and his men very clearly do not. In fact the hero is now left, as it were, to his own devices, and there is no intervention at all beyond that impetus for the hero to take up arms. Louis does, it is true, claim to the Franks that God has sent him, but he makes clear that although he wishes for Christian men (*godes holdon*) to follow him in the pursuit of God's will (*godes uuillion*), he makes no promises. God may have intervened to send him into battle, but there is no further direct help, and certainly no indication of the outcome, and Louis is clear on this. Man's life

---

115 I have discussed the historical aspects of the work in 'Saucourt and the *Ludwigslied*: Some Observations on Medieval Historical Poetry'. *Revue belge de philologie et d'histoire* 55 (1977), 841–67. Wallace-Hadrill has some important comments on the interpretation of poems about the historical events of this period in his Stenton Lecture, however: *Vikings in Francia*, p. 6.

116 See Groseclose and Murdoch, *Die althochdeutschen poetischen Denkmäler*, p. 75f, on the point. Heusler's views were not widely accepted.

or death is up to Christ, but the sequence of brief statements typical of the style of the work is worth looking at in detail:

> Nu uuillih thaz mir uolgon   Alle godes holdon.
> Giskerit is thiu hieruuist   So lango so uuili Krist;
> Uuili her unsa hinauarth,   Thero habet her giuualt.
> (lines 36–38)

[I want all of those who are true to God to follow me. The length of a man's life is ordered by Christ, and if He wants us to die, then He has that power.]

The words spoken by Louis to his men recall those of Byrhtnoð before Maldon—that the length of man's life is up to God. Louis promises no victory, nor does he know even whether he will survive himself—he uses the phrase 'if I am spared' even in his agreement with God to fight the Vikings. The divine intervention, then, is strictly limited to an initial motivation.[117] Louis' behaviour from now on is that of the model warrior king, pursuing what J. M. Wallace-Hadrill (who took the term from the ninth century writer Smaragdus, a monk of St Michael's at Verdun) calls the *via regia*, the proper behaviour of a Germanic and Christian king.[118] He

---

117 This is very similar to two passages in the French *Chanson de Roland*, where Charlemagne is asked by God (via the Angel Gabriel) to set out, first to avenge Roland, and then at the very end to embark upon yet another battle for the Christians; he is not told whether he will be victorious or not. The divine messenger tells him that 'Li chrestien te recleiment e crient' [the Christians are crying out for your help], but by the end, Charlemagne is weary, although he knows he must fulfil his duty: 'Li emperere n'i volsist aler mie/ "Deus," dist li reis, "si penuse est ma vie" ' [the emperor is reluctant to set out. 'O Lord'. he says, 'how tiring is my life']: Hilka/Rohlfs, *Rolandslied*, lines 3998–4000.

118 J. M. Wallace-Hadrill, 'The *Via Regia* of the Carolingian Age'. in *Trends in Medieval Political Thought*, ed. Beryl Smalley (Oxford: Blackwell, 1965), pp. 22–41. Wallace-Hadrill discusses the links made between divine and human kingship, and the concept of the king *a deo coronatus*. His notes on Jonas of Orleans and his early ninth-century comments (831) on the distinction between the man and the office, as well as the king's moral attitude, are of interest in the light of the unfortunate circumstances of Louis's demise.

promises rewards for those who survive, or recompense to the families of those who fall, and then rides off eagerly—the motif hinted at even in the St-Bertin annals. The Vikings were characterised very briefly as *heidine man*, 'pagans, heathens' at the start of the poem, but now are simply *Northman*, 'Norsemen'. Battle is joined, with the Frankish warriors singing the *Kyrie*, asking liturgically that the Lord might have mercy upon them and stressing once again that they do not know that they will be victorious. This is not yet a crusade, in which death will be rewarded automatically with heaven. In the German *Rolandslied*, for example, the warriors cannot lose. Either they will win the battle or they will go to heaven, and it is significant that in that poem, their battle-song is the *Gloria*. Louis and his men are not so certain. All that Louis promises are rewards or recompense on earth. He fights under the same conditions as Byrhtnoð or Beowulf, aware that although he will fight as best he can, victory is up to God and the length of a man's life is determined by Christ. The ending of the poem is significant in its paratactic simplicity, dividing statements of general interpretation from simple description of the events:

> Gilobot si thiu godes kraft!   Hluduig uuarth sigihaft.
> Ioh allen heiligon thanc!   Sin uuarth ther sigikamf.
> (lines 55f)

[Praise be to God's power! Louis was victorious. Thanks be to the saints! His was the victory.]

The distinct second half-line in each case states that Louis won. The first half-line—a quite separate unit—thanks God and the saints that this should be the case, but there is no *direct* intervention on the part of God or the saints, and Louis' efforts as a hero are not diminished. This is true as well, in fact, of another rather odd literary reflection of the battle of Saucourt, a French one this time, in which Louis fights in single combat against Gormont— a corruption of Guthrum, a famous Viking who was not, as far as is known, present. In any case, in the fragmentary twelfth-century *Chanson de Geste* of *Gormont et Isembart* the opposition have all turned into Saracens. Louis joins battle with the Saracen king Gormont with the words 'Aïe, Deus, pere del ciel!' [God in heaven, help me], and he goes on to invoke the aid of specific saints, after which we are told that although Gormont hurls three spears at him,

> Deus le guari, par sa pitié,
> qu'il le l'at mie en charn tochié . . .[119]

[God protected him, so that none of them penetrated his flesh.]

Once again Louis does not know that this is going to happen, and there is no actual intervention, simply a comment on the poet's part that God has protected Louis.

The last lines of the German *Ludwigslied* are a straightforward praise of the king, who has behaved as a hero, with a standard panegyric conclusion commending his life to God's care. In fact, as we know, he died within about a year, but the song remains, and the version we have has a heading which is important in itself, even though not every editor has chosen to print it. It is in Latin, and is an indication that this is one of the right songs. The political importance of the work has been stressed as a propaganda piece bolstering the young king against the likes of Hincmar, who claimed directly to Louis 'ut nomine potius quam virtute regnetis' [that you are king more in name than in power]. But by the time it was written down in the St Amand manuscript, the king was already dead. Its actual political value in *contemporary* terms, therefore, was always limited, but the Latin title appended to it in the manuscript is in accord with the need of the hero and king for the right songs. That heading, moreover, is an instruction to the reader for the reception of the work, whatever it may have been conceived as in the first instance. The Old High German *Ludwigslied* is a memorial piece. It is a *rithmus teutonicus*, a German rhymed poem, inscribed to the blessed memory of King Louis, son of Louis, who was also a king—'de piae memoriae Hluduico rege filio Hluduici aeque regis'. Any question of disputed kingship is ruled out in this heading

---

119 *Gormont et Isembart*, ed. Alphonse Bayot, (3rd edn, Paris: Champion, 1931), lines 364 and 386f (Bayot's critical text). The origin of the work has been set as far back as about 1080: de Vries, *Heroic Song*, p. 36f.

even after his death, when there is no longer any propaganda value, through the reiterated hereditary justification.[120] Whatever the political intent of the poem when it was composed, the image of the hero has not changed. The church has placed the events described, the battle, into a much more consistent context and has assimilated the hero. The arguments in criticism of the work, especially in Germany, of whether the work is Germanic-heroic or Christian in essence are less than relevant. Such criticism has occasionally, in fact, gone somewhat too far in asserting the Germanic nature of the work. As late as 1954 reference was made to Louis fighting 'wie ein Berserker, ganz besessen von der Wut Wodans'. [like a berserker, possessed by the fury of Woden], which is by any standards a fairly spectacular piece of unsupported over-interpretation.[121] It can all be resolved with a compromise as simple as it is obvious: the work is Germanic *and* Christian, and it places the acts of an idealised Germanic warrior king into a Christian framework, a hero who fights for the state because this is what God wants him to do. 'Hilph minan liutin'. says God, help my people. But they are also the king's people.

Although perhaps propagandistic in conception, more attention needs to be paid with the *Ludwigslied* to the different *kind* of political validity that it acquired after the death of the king himself. Most studies of the work in a contemporary political context, and there are many, are predicated upon its position as a piece composed when the king was still alive, and hence aimed at the Frankish nobility, but that context was rendered irrelevant by the death of the king. The

---

120 Johannes Schilter's 1727 edition of Jean Mabillon's transcription of the *Ludwigslied* omits the heading, although the title page of the edition (referring to the work as an *epinikion*, a 'song of victory') uses the phrase *rhythmus Teutonicus*. It also gives (based on Regino of Prüm) the wrong year for the battle (883): *Thesaurus antiquitatum Teutonicarum* ii (Ulm: Bartholomaeus, 1727). It is interesting that some modern editions include the title, others do not. It is there in Heinz Mettke, *Älteste deutsche Dichtung und Prosa* (Leipzig: Reclam, 1976), p. 248f, and in Karl A. Wipf, *Althochdeutsche poetische Texte* (Stuttgart: Reclam, 1992), p. 156f. It is not present in Karl Wolfskehl and Friedrich von der Leyen, *Älteste deutsche Dichtungen* (Frankfurt/M.: Insel, new edn, 1964), p. 10f, nor Schlosser, *Althochdeutsche Literatur* p. 274f, though it *is* in Schlosser's notes.
121 See Groseclose and Murdoch, *Denkmäler*, p. 75.

Ludwigslied as we have it is a song to a dead hero contained in a Latin manuscript together with a French devotional piece dedicated to a saint. It has become a memorial poem recording an instance of appropriate (and hence more generally applicable) behaviour on the part of a Christian king placed into a Christian concept of history, a hero who has followed his duty as a king. If the *Battle of Maldon* is a memorial poem rather than an historical one as such, it is still a song to Byrhtnoð.[122] The *Ludwigslied* began as a propagandistic piece, perhaps, even as a piece of historical analysis (in that it both describes and explains what lies behind given events); but in the version we have—and it had its vicissitudes as a document—it has already become a memorial piece both explicitly in the title and implicitly in the picture it presents of a Christian hero.[123]

However, even the earlier and neither contemporary nor in any real sense historical story of *Waltharius* shows the church interested in, and accepting the hero and his code, ostensibly for entertainment; it does not even bat an eyelid at Waltharius's rather eccentric habit of decapitating his fallen enemies. But it uses the tale to demonstrate the need for political pragmatism and the avoidance of a taking a situation to its limits when this is possible. In the *Hildebrandslied*, the political construct of the whole demanded that the situation be followed through; in *Waltharius* various political elements establish the situation, but the poet is able to call a halt when no further expediency is being served.

Neither Waltharius nor Louis, we may note incidentally, is tragic. The key to the *Ludwigslied* is precisely that Louis was victorious, and this is because he did right and it was the will of God. With *Waltharius*, the key is more probably the ironic injunction to the audience to see 'how the gold of the Huns was shared', which functions as a warning and an admonition. Tragedy is narrowly, but very deliberately averted. Louis did not, in the event, live to

---

122 See Bessinger, '*Maldon* and the *Óláfsdrápa*'. p. 23, on 'incomplete historicity'. Dodwell, *Anglo-Saxon Art*, p. 134, takes *Maldon* as Byrhtnoð's memorial, as it is seen that way, of course, by Ute Schwab in her paper in the Cooper collection.

123 Paul Lefrancq, '*Rhythmus Teutonicus*' ou '*Ludwigslied*'? (Paris: Droz, 1945).

rule for many years, as requested of God in the standard formula found at the end of this poem as it is in Latin pieces of this and earlier periods as well. Even this, though, was anticipated in the poem itself in the view ascribed to Louis himself that God has control of our time on earth. This realised itself with his premature death in 882, but he remained a model hero king, celebrated in a memorial song about a victory of the kind so sorely missed by Otto II. But Louis, of course, was both real and contemporary, and his poet was bound by history. The poet of *Waltharius* had rather more scope, and the Visigoth hero, unlike his 'genuine' historical counterpart Walja, was spared to rule for thirty years.

5

Shifting Perspectives

Roland

P ride' and 'arrogance' are difficult, but frequently and inconclusively discussed, concepts in the examination of the Germanic
warrior or hero. So inconclusively in fact that one doubts whether
it is useful or fair to take either of those words at all to render
ofermod, for example, which was used of Byrhtnoð's attitude to the
Vikings at Maldon, or *übermuot*, which is applied by the poet to
the actions both of Siegfried and of Hagen in the German *Nibelungenlied*. Certainly to take such words in the original as an absolute
equivalent either of *hubris* in a tragic context or *superbia* in a Christian
one—or even both together—is dangerous at best. The former
innate flaw leads to a self-generated tragic fall; the latter leads quite
specifically to hell. Indeed, although there may be a cause-and-effect
sequence in the actions of a given warrior, which may in their turn
appear irresponsibly rash and which do sometimes lead to disaster,
the real interpretation of the action almost always needs to be placed
within a larger political context. It is perhaps even more dangerous
to make sweeping comparative comments, as when Gwyn Jones
declares Beowulf's unarmed attack on Grendel 'as excessive as
Byrhtnoð's at Maldon'.[124] He might indeed have added 'or as
Roland's at Roncesvalles'. as we shall see, the comparison between
Maldon and Roland's battle is often proposed. But this begs the
question of situational difference, and leaves open questions such

124 Jones, *Kings, Beasts and Heroes*, p. 13.

as whether the gamble taken was reasonable, and whom it would affect. The hero who is apparently dubbed arrogant by the poet need not necessarily be condemned objectively, and if we *are* going to condemn the hero's actions, then the situation must be examined carefully. The Germanic hero is motivated by his own perceived sense of necessity within a political context. Byrhtnoð's gesture to the Vikings in the *Battle of Maldon* poem is an individual military decision based upon a personal judgement of the immediate situation, and although in terms of the outcome it is as unfortunate as Hildebrand's decision to try and avoid a battle with his son by offering him a gift, there is no evidence that the poet thinks of it either as *hubris* or *superbia*: Byrhtnoð is surely not destined for hell. Heroes do make errors of judgement, of course, and in this lies their humanity, although in most cases the errors they make are what we may call reasonable ones. Actual—and culpable—arrogance can be observed often enough in situations where it is precisely *not* employed: of the Vikings and their demands; of red-bearded Otto, condemning a man without trial; of the loutish behaviour of Siegfried in the *Nibelungenlied* when he arrives at the court of Burgundy with twelve men and (in striking contrast to the arrival of Beowulf and his group at Heorot) threatens to overthrow the king. Few character judgements from outside can ever be absolute, and the individual hero might himself move from an impetuousness born of confidence in himself to a more deep-seated *amour propre*: the concepts of faith in oneself, self-confidence, over-confidence and egocentricity shade into one another, so that a hero may exaggerate his own perception of himself to the point where he becomes an anti-hero. This point would seem to come when a warrior becomes not a major figure in the state, but a liability, a danger from within. Sometimes the danger can be deflected, but not always. And if we have heroes, we may also have villains; sometimes it is difficult to distinguish between them.

One of the most problematic of the Germanic heroes in this respect is one whose tale is recorded in its first and best literary form in French, in the *Chanson de Roland*. Roland is at best ambiguous, although the problem is made more difficult still by the involvement of Christianity in his presentation in literature.[125] Otherwise his closest parallel is with Siegfried and his Norse forerunner Sigurðr, who in the Norse tales is self-centredly concerned with preserving his own personal reputation. But as we know from the *Grípisspá*, he does so in the face of a fate against which he is helpless. In German he is placed into a political context, but some elements of his Norse past still cling to him, and although apparently useful at first, his role at the Burgundian court turns out to be more like that of Grendel than Beowulf, since his real existence is *outside* the political unit and he is eventually the cause of its complete collapse. Roland, on the other hand, exists within and is part of a well-defined political framework: he is a general for a great emperor and warrior, Charlemagne. Yet in the *Chanson de Roland* he becomes a liability, so concerned that the wrongs songs are not sung about him that he causes the deaths of innumerable of his countrymen and damage to the state. Moreover, he does so without the remotest realistic chance of victory, and in this he again differs from Byrhtnoð.

And yet the *Chanson de Roland* presents Roland himself, at least on the surface, as a hero, so that with the familiar circularity of the heroic poem the *Chanson* might be seen as one of the right songs. We are told by William of Malmesbury (and later by Wace) that songs of the deeds of Roland were sung as military inspiration by another successful group of Germanic invaders, the Normans at Hastings; Duke William's forces were only a few generations away from Ganger-Hrolf and his Norse dukedom, centred on the town named after him, Rouen. We do not have any evidence of what kind of song the minstrel Taillefer actually sang to inspire the Conqueror's army. Looking more closely at the supposed hero Roland in the first great literary monument we *do* have, however, the Oxford *Chanson de Roland*, we may well wonder whether it is indeed one of the right songs.[126] Questions present

---

125 On the conflict between Christianity and heroism, though without reference to Roland, see Pàroli, 'Profilo dell'antieroe'.

126 For texts of the somewhat unprepossessing Oxford Roland (Bodleian Library MS Digby 23) see Chapter 1, note 16. This is generally accepted as the major version of the *Chanson*. Other French texts are edited by Wendelin Foerster, *Das altfranzösische Rolandslied* (Heilbronn: Henniger, 1883–86; repr. Amsterdam: Rodopi, 1971 [Châteauroux and Venice II] and Wiesbaden, Sändig, 1968 [Paris, Cambridge, Lyons]).

themselves about the motivation of the different potential heroes in the work, and whether or not they really merit the term 'hero' other than in its simplest sense of 'warrior' or 'particularly powerful warrior', especially if we define the hero as a warrior acting according to his own perception of duty within a given political context.

In both the *Chanson* and in the slightly later German version of the work, the *Rolandslied*, the reader is faced with a problem that will appear again more strongly in later works like the *Nibelungenlied*, namely the conflict between authorial comment and reader perception. Of the three main focuses of attention in the Roland saga as a whole, Charlemagne is beyond criticism; Roland, though he causes a military disaster, is invariably acclaimed as a hero. The third figure, Roland's stepfather Ganelon, is also a brave warrior, even though the *Chanson* adds on the first occasion we see him and before he has done anything at all that he 'did the treachery' and repeats this on a regular formulaic basis. Both he and Roland are sacrificed in effect (with all their men) to the greater good of the state, and though it is unlikely that we shall in fact be able to rehabilitate Ganelon, a closer consideration of his role—trying, if we can, to ignore that persistent tag 'ki la traïsun fist' that pursues us through literature beyond the immediate works—may throw light on the role of Roland as a hero.

The main question that presents itself is precisely: how does Roland compare with other Germanic heroes? More than any other, with the possible exception of Siegfried, he suffers from the overlap between the warrior fighting within and for a political system, and the uncritical (we might almost say schoolboy) adulation of what is really an aspect of the *miles gloriosus*. It is interesting that the two heroes that have aroused the greatest amount of emotion in recent times have been Siegfried, held up as a German ideal during the Third Reich, regardless of the fact that in literature he brings down an entire society, and Roland (claimed by the French *and* the Germans as a hero in the Second World War), who in the *Chanson* makes a military decision that is both unnecessary and indefensible, and brings about a disaster. Yet Charlemagne, Roland and Oliver have been bracketed together from the twelfth century onwards as champions of Christendom in art and literature alike,[127] and modern critics have reacted in a some-times extravagant manner. W. P. Ker in the 1890s informed us (less than coherently as far as his musical imagery is concerned), that 'Roland is ideal and universal; and the story of his defeat, of the blast of his horn, and the last stroke of Durendal, is a kind of funeral march or heroic symphony into which a meaning can be read for every new hero, to the end of the world'. Ker, in fact, considered that 'everything leads to the agony and heroic death of Roland . . . It is not as in the *Iliad* where different heroes have their day . . . Roland is absolute master of the *Song of Roland*. No other heroic poetry conveys the same effect of pre-eminent simplicity and grandeur'. A far more recent French critic, Pierre Le Gentil, prefaces his book on the *Chanson* with the assumption that 'even the most unsophisticated Frenchman remembers the wonderful scene of the hero's death with emotion'. Everything is simple if it is taken simply, but Ker can be countered on virtually all points: idealised is not the same as ideal, the story is far from simple, and it can be argued very well that not only is Charlemagne rather than Roland the absolute master of the *Chanson*, but that Roland is at the very best an ambiguous hero.[128]

The *Chanson de Roland* is not an historical work. The battle of Saucourt in 881 and that of Maldon in 991 are represented fairly accurately, if selectively, in their respective poems, but Roland's battle, at Roncesvalles in 778 is not treated accurately at all, and indeed, there is a change of enemy even more radical than that in *Gormont et Isembart*, where the opposing force did at least remain a pagan one. There is a description of the event—it cannot really be called a battle—on which the *Chanson* is based in the revision of the Carolingian imperial annals, the so-called Royal Annals for the

---

See the magnificent volumes by Rita Lejeune and Jacques Stiennon, *La légende de Roland dans l'art du moyen age* (Brussels: Arcade, 1966), translated as *The Legend of Roland in the Middle Ages* (London: Phaidon, 1971).

128 Ker, *Epic and Romance*, p. 295, and Pierre Le Gentil, *The Chanson de Roland*, trans. Frances F. Beer (Cambridge, Mass.: Harvard UP, 1969).

year 778,[129] but it is of greater interest to use as a starting-point some slightly later comments by Einhard, the biographer of Charlemagne, who drew on the annals when he discussed the battle in the ninth chapter of his *Vita Caroli*. Although the passage is too long to cite *in extenso*, some significant points may be picked out. According to Einhard, Charlemagne had been fighting the Saxons for a long time, vigorously and almost without a break, when he decided to make a sortie into Spain:

> Cum enim assiduo ac paene continuo cum Saxonibus
> bello certaretur . . . Hispaniam . . . agreditur . . .

This sortie was, moreover, brief but entirely successful, and he took every town and fortress that he attacked. He then returned with his army completely safely, *apart from one small incident*. The Royal Annals at least stress the depressing effect that this one unfortunate incident had on Charlemagne, but Einhard plays down its importance with the word *parumper*, 'to a small extent':

> salvo et incolomi exercitu revertitur; praeter quod in
> ipso Pyrinei iugo Wasconicam perfidiam parumper in
> redeundo contigit experiri.

> [he came back with his army safe and sound except for the
> fact that while actually in the Pyrenees he experienced to
> a small extent the treachery of the Basques.]

A group of Basques—Christians, that is, as opposed to the Moors in Spain—ambushed the last part of Charlemagne's army, the baggage train, killed the rearguard and plundered it, disappearing quickly

---

129 The *Royal Annals, Annales regni Francorum*, are ed. by Friedrich Kurze in the *Monumenta Germaniae Historica*, in the separate series of Scriptores rerum germanicarum in usum scholarum 6 (Berlin: MGH, 1895). There is a modern German translation with the text in the edition by Reinhold Rau, *Quellen zur Karolingischen Reichsgeschichte* i (Darmstadt: WBG, 1955); see pp. 36–9. The passage in question, which gives no names, is in the reworked version of the Annals, and was used by Einhard for his *Vita*. On Brittany and Roland see Julia M. H. Smith, *Province and Empire: Brittany and the Carolingians* (Cambridge: CUP, 1992), p. 58.

into the darkness before anyone could do anything about it. Einhard then adds:

> In quo proelio Eggihardus regiae mensae praepositus, Anshelmus comes palatii, et Hruodlandus Brittannici limitis praefectus cum aliis compluribus interficuntur.

Einhard tells us first that 'Eggihard, of Charlemagne's own retinue was killed, and so was an earl named Anshelm,' but then in third place he names as having been killed with them a *'praefectus*, overlord of the Bretons, named Roland'. These names are not in the Royal Annals. In the context of the Roland saga (a term we may indeed use in this case), however, Einhard's final comments are even more significant:

> Neque hoc factum ad praesens vindicari poterat, quia hostis re perpetrata ita dispersus est ut ne fama quidem remaneret ubinam gentium quaeri potuisset.[130]

[Nor could this be avenged right away, because the enemy scattered, leaving no indication of where they had gone.]

The incident which caused the death of the otherwise unknown Roland was a brief raid by treacherous handful of Christian Basques for the purpose of robbery, a detail in an otherwise successful campaign, but one that could not be (and never was) avenged because the perpetrators were simply never visible. The campaign itself was not always presented as a crusade, and the young Frankish king, Charles, who was incidentally not yet the great emperor Charlemagne, had in fact been negotiating with the Saracen leader Suleyman at Saragossa in a political attempt to make capital from the apparent discord amongst the Saracens in Spain at this time. Charlemagne also took some hostages at this time.[131]

---

130 H. W. Garrod and R. B. Mowat, *Einhard's Life of Charlemagne* (Oxford: Clarendon, 1915); translated by Lewis Thorpe, *Two Lives of Charlemagne* (Harmondsworth: Penguin, 1969). The passage is cited by Burgess in his introduction to his translation.

131 All the relevant material, including Arabic sources with translations, are gathered in the historiographic appendices to Ramón Menéndez Pidal, *La Chanson de Roland y el neotradicionalismo: orígines de la épica*

It might be expected that Carolingians annalists would deliberately play down what was, after all, a defeat, and it is possible that heroic songs developed fairly quickly around the incident. The anonymous life of Charlemagne's son, Louis the Pious, refers in an otherwise very brief account of the successful Spanish campaign nevertheless to the *infortunium,* the 'minor mishap' in which the rearguard was attacked, and then goes on to say that the names of the people involved will not be given, *quia vulgata sunt*—'because they are so well known'.[132] The various stages and materials providing evidence for the development of a saga, and the whole *question rolandienne,* to say nothing of French and German claims for possession of Roland himself as a national hero cannot be considered here (I hope to maintain neutrality by referring to the warriors as Franks), and concentration must be on the earliest literary text we have, on the *Chanson de Roland,* composed probably around the turn of the eleventh and twelfth century, and transmitted in the Oxford manuscript Digby 23. It is useful to compare it, even if we look at no other versions,[133]

Románica (Madrid: Espasa-Calpe, 1959), pp. 469–82. There is a French text, revised by René Louis and trans. I. -M. Cluzel, *La Chanson de Roland et la tradition épique de France* (Paris: Picard, 1960), see pp. 519–32. See also Georg Baesecke on 'Die Schlacht von Ronceval in Einharts Leben Karls des Grossen'. *Festschrift Paul Kluckhohn und Hermann Schneider* (Tübingen: Mohr, 1948), pp. 32–45 (comparing the Royal Annals with Einhard's text).

132 The anonymous *Vita Hludowici* is sometimes referred to as the work of the 'Astronomer'. The relevant passage is in the second section, Rau, *Quellen,* p. 262. That the incident should be mentioned at all in such a brief account in a work that is not even about Charlemagne is highly significant. The Astronomer also speaks of Charlemagne's efforts to liberate Spain from the 'most bitter yoke' of Saracen rule, p. 260.

133 Studies of the whole saga, often from a nationalist point of view, were made around the turn of the nineteenth and twentieth centuries. A German example is the dissertation (Marburg 1891) of Theodor Eicke, *Zur neueren Literaturgeschichte der Rolandssage in Deutschland und Frankreich* (Leipzig: Fock, 1891). Far better known is Joseph Bédier's *Les légendes épiques* (Paris: Champion 1908–13), and see also Maurice Delbouille, *Sur la genèse de la Chanson de Roland* (Brussels: Palais des Académies, 1954). Of the many later texts, such as the *Pseudo-Turpin,* the *Karl* of Der Stricker, the *Karlamagnussaga,* the *Volksbuch* and the rest I shall refer only to the Latin poem of Ganelon's treachery, the *Carmen de prodicione Guenonis.*

with the German adaptation by a priest called Konrad in about 1170, although we must bear in mind that that text, the *Rolandslied*, is very different indeed.[134]

As in so many heroic poems, history is transformed in the poetic reflections of the events, with a few elements retained. In the *Chanson* Roland, far from being simply the third Frank named as having fallen in a Basque ambush, dies on centre stage, defiantly and heroically, defending the Frankish rear against a massive army of Saracens. All that remains of the Basques is the word *perfidia*, as the poet expands the *idea* of treachery to provide a reason (interestingly an internal political one, again from another Christian) for why the rearguard was attacked in the first place. The ongoing struggle against the Saxons is transformed to a seven-year struggle against the Moors themselves, and most important of all, the final third of the French poem not only resolves the political theme and the treachery-motif, but shows us an act of vengeance that never happened, based once again on the successful incursion into Spain that actually *preceded* the disaster at Roncesvalles. Charlemagne—a figure who began, as it were, to grow in stature and indeed age almost immediately after his actual death (he is 200 years old in the *Chanson*) fights, as the great emperor that he in fact was not at the time, and defeats a Saracen emir, after which the initial treachery, too, is punished. The rearrangement of history seems to focus attention on Roland, but in spite of that rearrangement

---

134 Text cited from Hilka/Rohlfs, *Das altfranzösische Rolandslied* (but see Whitehead, *Chanson de Roland*); the edition cited here numbers the *laisses* in the most sensible fashion (avoiding for example, 125a), but line numbers are given here in addition. The German *Roland* cited is *Das Rolandslied des Pfaffen Konrad*, ed. Carl Wesle, 2nd edn by Peter Wapnewski (Tübingen: Niemeyer, 1967). Text with modern German translation by Dieter Kartschoke (Frankfurt/M.: Fischer, 1970; now Stuttgart: Reclam, 1994). English translation: J. W. Thomas, *Priest Konrad's Song of Roland* (Columbia, SC: Camden House, 1994). The *Song of Ganelon's Treachery* is cited from Gaston Paris, 'Le *Carmen de prodicione Guenonis*'. *Romania* 11 (1882), 45–518; English trans. by Arthur Livingston, 'The *Carmen de prodicione Guenonis*'. *Romanic Review* 2 (1911), 61–79. For a good survey of all but the most recent secondary literature on the *Chanson* and other texts, see Joseph J. Duggan, *A Guide to Studies of the Chanson de Roland* (London: Grant and Cutler, 1976).

and the idealisation of the warriors and their emperor (in both the French and the German version, though in different ways) a political plot is constructed around the fragments of history which remain. There is a temptation to compare the literary Roland as a hero in the Roncesvalles poems with Byrhtnoð and with Louis of the West Franks, because all are presented as fighting against expressly pagan enemies. Such comparisons must be made with great caution, however, because there are differences beyond the simple distance from actual events which allow us to speak of historical poetry with more justification in the cases of *Maldon* and the *Ludwigslied*. In particular, critics have linked the literary versions of Maldon and Roncesvalles, usually (if not always justifiably) by comparing the supposed arrogance of the protagonists.[135] This again needs closer attention. The starting question, however, with the *Chanson de Roland*, is one that has proved to be significant elsewhere—with *Beowulf*, *Herzog Ernst* and other texts: that of an apparently disjointed structure. The work falls into three parts. Charlemagne's dealings with the Saracen King Marsilie and the embassy of Ganelon, which leads to the latter's treachery and the death of Roland; then the fight with the Emir Baligant and the vengeance of the Franks; and finally the trial and death of Ganelon. We do not have the temporal gaps that seem to have caused such difficulty with *Beowulf*, or the geographical ones as in *Herzog Ernst*, but still the episodes are discrete ones. Although a case can be made for seeing Roland as linking the three sections, he is dead and buried by the end of the second part. The most important element overall is Charlemagne's efforts to maintain order over potentially unruly vassals, so that his larger military efforts on behalf of the state can be carried out. Pierre Le Gentil has claimed that the *Chanson* is not a 'Chanson de Charlemagne', but other critics have

135 Ker, *Epic and Romance*, p. 64, links the two works by noting that both involve a battle in which a captain causes disaster by pride and self-reliance 'by refusing to take fair advantage of the enemy'. In military terms the two events are not really similar, however; even had Roland sounded his horn earlier the day might well not have been saved. Nor, indeed, can one term both acts—as he does—'tragic errors or transgressions' that bring on 'the crash and ruin at the end of the day'.

stressed the dominant role of the emperor. The problem is not quite the same with the German *Rolandslied*, which states clearly at the start that this is a tale of 'eineme turlichem man . . . daz ist Karl der cheiser' (lines 9–11) [a beloved man, Charles the emperor], and critics have seen it more regularly as a *Staatsroman*. In a doctoral thesis in 1949 Gabriele Glatz commented of the *Rolandslied* that 'aus dem französischen *Rolandslied* [ist] ein deutsches *Karlslied* geworden,' but I am tempted to paraphrase Oscar Wilde on Browning and translate her comment as 'the German *Rolandslied* is a *Chanson de Roland* about Charlemagne', and add 'and so is the *Chanson de Roland*.'[136]

At the opening of the work, Charlemagne has been fighting in Spain for seven years, and the weariness of the soldiers is stressed. Only Saragossa holds out as a Saracen stronghold under King

136 Le Gentil, *Chanson de Roland*, p. 97; but see Eugene Vance, *Reading the Song of Roland* (Englewood Cliffs, NJ: Prentice-Hall, 1970), p. 14. Gabriele Glatz, *Die Eigenart des Pfaffen Konrad in der Gestaltung seines christlichen Heldenbildes* (Diss. Freiburg/Br, 1949) is cited with agreement by Karl-Ernst Geith, *Carolus Magnus* (Berne and Munich: Francke, 1977), p. 89 (see pp. 84–124 in general). Konrad's opening is noted by George Fenwick Jones, *The Ethos of the Song of Roland* (Baltimore: Johns Hopkins Press, 1963), p. 165. On the assessment overall of the *Rolandslied*, see Marianne Ott-Meimberg, *Kreuzzugsepos oder Staatsroman* (Zurich and Munich: Artemis, 1980), and more recently Jeffrey Ashcroft, '*Honor imperii—des riches ere:* The Idea of Empire in Konrad's *Rolandslied*'. in *German Narrative Literature of the Twelfth and Thirteenth Centuries*, ed. Volker Honemann etc. (Tübingen: Niemeyer, 1994), pp. 139–56. On the political implications of both works, see for example Rudolf Köster, *Karl der Große als politische Gestalt in der Dichtung des deutschen Mittelalters* (Hamburg: Wachholtz, 1939); Robert Folz, *Le souvenir et la légende de Charlemagne dans l'empire germanique médiévale* (Paris: Belles Lettres, 1950); Eberhard Nellmann, *Die Reichsidee in deutschen Dichtungen der Salier- und frühen Stauferzeit* (Berlin: Schmidt, 1963); Erich Köhler, '*Conseil des barons' und 'jugement des barons'* (Heidelberg: Winter, 1968); Ingo Nöther, *Die geistlichen Grundgedanken im Rolandslied und in der Kaiserchronik* (Hamburg: Lüdke, 1970); Petra Canisius-Loppnow, *Recht und Religion im Rolandslied* (Frankfurt/M. etc.: Lang, 1992); and Peter Haidu, *The Subject of Violence: The Song of Roland and the Birth of the State* (Bloomington: Indiana UP, 1993). The last-named is somewhat over-complicated in style but asks interesting questions, wondering whether flight from the battle would have been cowardice, for example.

Marsilie. Having taken counsel with his advisers,[137] he decides to sends an envoy to Charlemagne and, although Marsilie is routinely vilified by the poet, his initial strategy is understandable and clear in political terms. His plan is to promise Charlemagne tribute and send hostages as surety. Charlemagne will then leave with his army, but no tribute will be sent. The hostages will be sacrificed, but in terms of *Realpolitik*, Marsilie's chief adviser and envoy, Blancandrin feels that this is acceptable as the lesser evil:

> Asez est melz qu'il i perdent les chefs
> Que nous perduns l'onur ne la deintét,
> Ne nus seiuns cunduiz a mendeier. *(laisse 3, lines 44–6)*

[Better that they lose their heads that we lose our honour and our lands, and we are reduced to poverty.]

We should recall here the way in which the Franks and the others actually do buy off Attila in *Waltharius* by tribute and hostages, and indeed the breaking of the tribute treaty by Guntharius, which places the Frankish hostage, Hagen, in great danger. In Konrad's German version, the equivalent figure, Blanscandiz, is even more subtle, planning even to rescue the hostages by a raid, once the Christian forces, safely out of Spain, have divided up and returned to their own territories. Konrad, however, makes him actively diabolical, and here as elsewhere the good and bad divisions are far clearer.

The offer is made to Charlemagne in council, a group which includes Roland and also Ganelon, who is identified immediately as the traitor, the one 'ki la traïsun fist', and at once a crucial point is made, namely that Marsilie has in the past proved himself untrustworthy. Once before, he appeared to sue for peace and then

---

137 The crucial role played by Marsilion's adviser, Blancandrin, is stressed by Pierre Le Gentil, *The Chanson de Roland*, p. 78. It is incorrect, however, to imply, as Jackson, *Hero and King*, p. 57, seems to do, that Blancandrin alone has the ear of Marsilion, whilst Charlemagne actually holds a council. *Laisse* 4 (line 61) concludes with the general agreement of the Saracens to Blancandrin's plan, which they have clearly heard. The poet sees both political set-ups as parallel.

murdered the two envoys sent by the Franks, Basan and Basile. This is used as an argument by Roland for not accepting the offer; he prefaces his argument with a statement, however, apparently stressing his own valour, but in fact reminding the others—who are significantly silent—that the war has been going on for seven years already and that he, Roland, is prepared to besiege Saragossa for ever if need be. Charlemagne is as silent as the rest, and it is Ganelon, already stigmatised by the poet, who argues *mult fierement* (which we need not, however, see as an improper pride) to accept. It is notable that there is little further debate. His argument for accepting is endorsed by another warrior, who is praised by the poet, in contrast with what was said of Ganelon, and there is general agreement. In fact, the ebullient Roland was correct in his reading of the situation, but equally no real blame attaches yet to Ganelon, who simply voices the general weariness at the length of the war; a further protracted siege could go on for a very long time. Several of the later speeches by warriors other than Ganelon reiterate the point that the war has been going on for too long. Once again the German text has Ganelon more specifically anti-Roland, though what he says of him there is perhaps not without some truth: 'mennisken blutes en wart er nie sat' (line 1129), he says: 'he is never tired of bloodshed'.

This brief argument on external policy is followed in the Oxford *Roland*, however, by a far longer internal one: who is to go to Marsilie as an ambassador on what will clearly be a dangerous and delicate mission?[138] We recall what happened to the envoys Basile and Basan. Naimon (Neimes), Duke of Bavaria, the last speaker,

---

138 Le Gentil, *Chanson de Roland*, p. 80, seems to think, rather oddly, that the mission is not dangerous, although he is aware of the fate of Basan and Basile. Erich Auerbach, however, considers that, but for the treachery, Ganelon would have died (as Ganelon himself thinks): 'Roland against Ganelon' in *Mimesis*, trans. Willard Trask (New York: Doubleday, 1953), pp. 83–107. See also Emmanuel J. Mickel, *Ganelon, Treason and the Chanson de Roland* (University Park and London: Pennsylvania State UP, 1989). On aspects of the conflict, see the important paper by Hans-Erich Keller, 'Changes in Old French Epic Poetry and Changes in the Taste of the Audience'. in *Epic in Medieval Society*, ed. Scholler, pp. 150–77, esp. p. 162.

volunteers and is rejected, and then Roland offers. This is at once countered, not by Charles but by Roland's friend Oliver, who says—almost certainly correctly, but ironically in view of what happens later—that Roland will do it badly:

> Vostre curages est mult pesmes et fiers
> Jo me crendreie que vos vos meslisez
> (*laisse* 18, lines 256f)

'You are too impetuous and too haughty' says Oliver—*fiers*, the word used of Ganelon too, incidentally—'and I'm sure you will get into some quarrel'. Indeed, Charles rejects every one of the group of twelve warriors around Roland, presumably on the same grounds: none would be suitable for such a delicate mission. It is at this point that Roland suggests his stepfather Ganelon, and the use of the designation *mis parastre* points already, as Auerbach makes clear in his justly famous analysis of the scene, 'Roland against Ganelon'. to a conflict. Stepfathers and stepsons frequently quarrel, so that this is a fairly readily acceptable reflection of reality, but we are not really prepared for Ganelon's reaction. Perhaps Ganelon has in mind the fate of Basile and Basan, to whom he refers later; certainly his fear is stressed in the German text, and in the *Chanson* he makes clear later on that he expects not to return from this embassy. But his first response in the *Chanson* is to flare up in majestic anger, fling back his cloak and swear that he will have his revenge on Roland, who promptly volunteers to go in his place, implying—by now a familiar motif in works of this kind—that Ganelon is afraid to go. This Ganelon rejects, agreeing that he will do whatever Charles commands. Roland's next act is surely unforgivable, however: he laughs at Ganelon, and this can only increase the anger of his stepfather. It is noteworthy that related versions of the story have edited out this feature. The German text—which simplifies the pictures both of Roland and of Ganelon—sets a perfectly reasonable Roland against a fearful Ganelon, and the feeling of immense tension between the two men, and the mockery by Roland, is absent. That work in any case emphasises Roland as a man of God, while Ganelon is associated consistently with Judas and with the devil.[139] In another version, the difficult and somewhat flowery Latin *Carmen de prodicione Guenonis*, the *Song of Ganelon's Treachery*, written rather later than the *Chanson*, it is spelt out that Roland nominates Ganelon out of love and not out of hatred, but that the latter takes it as hatred.[140]

Ganelon agrees to the embassy, but reminds us that he is himself very close to the imperial family. His wife is Charlemagne's sister (and the mother of Roland by her first husband), and—we are told—he has a son who will one day be a warrior. This may be the source of earlier conflict between Roland and Ganelon, a family dispute, and Ganelon is at pains to mention that he bequeathes all his lands to his own son and not to Roland. Once again the German version by Konrad develops this and clarifies it, having Ganelon accuse Roland of wishing to push aside the son, Baldwin. The German text is interesting on this point, when Ganelon tells Charlemagne:

> uirliuse ich den lib
> so nímt Rolant
> al min erbe zu siner hant.
> er uirstoezet dinir swester sun . . .
> (lines 1445–48)

[If I am killed, Roland will take all I leave behind for himself, and he will dispossess your sister's son.]

The literary Roland is also Charlemagne's sister's son, and in the clarified German text he firmly and expressly denies any such intent, referring to Baldwin as his brother. Indeed, he says quite specifically 'sines erbes en gere ich nit' (line 1477), [I don't want his inheritance.]

---

139 This is done both expressly and through the symbolism: see my paper, 'The Treachery of Ganelon in Konrad's *Rolandslied*'. *Euphorion* 67 (1973), 372–7. For other discusses of the presentation of Ganelon in this light, see Herbert Backes, *Bibel und ars praedicandi im Rolandslied des Pfaffen Konrad* (Berlin: Schmidt, 1966), p. 102; Horst Richter, *Kommentar zum Rolandslied des Pfaffen Konrad*, vol. i (Berne and Frankfurt/M.: Lang, 1972), p. 297, and Ott-Meimberg, *Kreuzzugsepos*, p. 205. The religious dimension and the political one exist side-by-side, of course.

140 *Carmen de prodicione*, line 41: the line is difficult, however. See the comments by Livingston in his translation, p. 63 n. 2.

In both versions Ganelon again curses Roland when he takes the emblems of office as an ambassador, but the glove falls as he takes it. Whether or not this indicates fear (the German text stresses Ganelon's fearfulness, but that is not the same as cowardice), the Franks take it as an omen. For all that, Ganelon sets off on the embassy boldly, but his departure is not without significance: an uncle bids him farewell, and a number of knights—*tant chevaler*—offer him words of support and, more specifically, criticism of Roland:

> Li quens Rollanz nel se deüst penser,
> Quë estrait estes de mult grant parentéd
> (*laisse* 27, lines 355f)

[The earl Roland had no right to think of this, and you are of a very noble lineage.]

This sounds very much like a faction speaking, and Ganelon again stresses that if he dies—as he is sure that he will—these men should accept Baldwin, the son (and by implication not Roland), as their *seigneur*, something which is absent from the German.

In this mood, Ganelon is naturally receptive when Blancandrin, who very quickly finds out about his hatred of Roland, plays upon this and with him forges a plot that will remove him. When Ganelon delivers the actual reply of Charlemagne—increased demands and baptism of the Saracens—Marsilie is predictably angry, and Ganelon's response is that of a hero, but things do not come to a fight, and when Ganelon reiterates the demands, he adds the plan that he has devised to destroy Roland. Charles, claims Ganelon, will not weary of fighting while Roland, his nephew, is still alive—'cum vivet sis niés' (*laisse* 14, line 544), varied as 'cum vivet Rollant' in the next *laisse* (42, 557). In fact the death of Roland will prompt the return of the *already* weary Franks to take their revenge. Whether Ganelon believes this himself is a matter of debate, but he is determined only upon one thing, and that is to remove Roland, and he arranges therefore that Marsilie will attack the rearguard, which he will ensure is led by Roland. He swears—as an act of quite literal faithlessness—on the holy relics in his sword. In none of his dealings does he criticise Charlemagne. Again, those later texts which simplify the motivation by vilifying Ganelon and boosting the image of Roland lay greater emphasis, for example, on the fact that Ganelon is offered gifts by Marsilie. In the *Carmen de prodicione* Ganelon is made drunk by Marsilie, and that Latin text also inserts a little homily against avarice which reminds us of that in *Waltharius*.

After Ganelon's return and favourable report, the Franks prepare to withdraw their forces, and a debate is held as to who will command the rearguard. This is clearly a dangerous task, and Ganelon at once names his stepson—using the term specifically again—and this causes a reaction of extreme anger from Roland, who curses (again using the term and underscoring the relationship) his stepfather.[141] In his anger (which is far less prominent in the German text) he is most concerned, as Ganelon doubtless intended, to avoid even the suspicion of cowardice, and Ganelon has therefore trapped Roland by using his own concern for reputation. Roland is quite specifically eager that no one will be able to accuse *him* of dropping the symbol of office. Once again it is Naimon who has to make clear that Roland is so angry that Charles has no choice but to appoint him. This is no sign of weakness. Charles is presumably well aware of the inner conflict and cannot risk allowing any disturbance during a military campaign which is at this point precarious in any case. He tries to leave Roland with half of the army, but Roland refuses, and this refusal, too, has led critics to make too close a connexion between the *Chanson* and the *Battle of Maldon*. Here, for example, is an unacceptably glib statement from a paper written in 1973: 'The heroic gesture of Byrhtnoð in allowing the Vikings onto land parallels well the gesture of Roland in refusing to take half of the army when it is offered, electing rather to retain a smaller force: both outcomes are tragic'.[142] In my own defence—since unfortunately I was the critic concerned—the remark was parenthetical rather than central, but for all that it will not do. Byrhtnoð allows the Vikings across in

---

141 Jackson, *Hero and King*, sees the work as a series of confrontations, p. 56. See also Auerbach's paper.

142 Murdoch, 'Saucourt and the *Ludwigslied*'. p. 862 n. 68. I hope that my comment does not detract from the rest of the paper.

the hope of defeating them. Roland is concerned only with his own reputation, particularly vis-à-vis Ganelon, and his continued refusal to accept or call for more help even when the numbers are actually *seen* to be overwhelming is a gross military error, even if Roland genuinely thought that he might win at first.

Charlemagne's reaction is of interest. He guesses (and this is reinforced in dreams) what will happen, but Roland promises him quite specifically that all *will* be well:

> Passez les porz trestut soürement
> Ja mar crendrez nul hume a mun vivant.
> (*laisse* 63, lines 790f)

> [You may go through the mountain passes with complete confidence, fearing no man while I am alive.]

This further traps Charlemagne, who can now hardly call Roland's own expression of valour into doubt, in spite of the irony of that last self-centred statement.

The *laisse* in which we move towards the battle—which is clearly going to be against overwhelming odds, as we are shown huge numbers of Saracens—ends with a couplet the first line of which is probably the most famous in the work: 'Paien unt tort et crestiëns unt dreit' [Pagans are wrong and Christians are right], but the second of which expresses Roland's own private determination: he has already warned his warriors to fight so that the wrong songs are not sung about them afterwards, and now he declares of himself: 'Malvaise essample n'en serat ja de mei' (*laisse* 79, lines 1015f), 'No-one shall tell a bad story about me'. Nor, indeed, will he permit his close friend Oliver to criticise Ganelon, and even though Oliver asks him three times to do so, he refuses to sound his great horn and summon the bulk of the army to their aid. His reasons are again all to do with reputation: he would dishonour his ancestry—Ælfwine and Wiglaf said the same kind of thing in Anglo-Saxon,[143] but so does Ganelon's supporter Pinabel later on in this work—and his country, but above all he

---

143 Jones, *Ethos*, p. 122.

would lose his reputation at home. Oliver points out that there is very little chance of victory, but although God and His angels are invoked as the patrons of *la dulce France*, it is still Roland himself who is at the centre:

> Ne placet Damne deu ne ses sainz ne ses angles
> Que ja pur mei perdet sa valur France.
>
> (*laisse* 86, lines 1089f)

[God, His saints and angels forbid that *France* should lose its reputation because of *me*]

The emphases in the translation are mine, of course, but the whole passage pivots upon that *pur mei*, and Roland's quite literally egocentric view of the situation is clear. There is a stark contrast with the *Ludwigslied*, where God and the saints are thanked separately by the poet for the victory, rather than being invoked as custodians of the national honour; and also with *Maldon*, where we have a far more pragmatic refusal that a country—*Æþelredes eard*, which is not viewed in the same terms as *la dulce France*—should pay tribute without a fight.

The question of whether Roland and his men actually could win is an interesting one. In the *Chanson*, Oliver points out repeatedly that the Saracen force is the largest ever seen, and that no shame would attach to Roland were he to sound his horn, while Roland responds primarily in terms of reputation. It is made clear in other works, however—such as the Latin *Song of Ganelon's Treachery*—that Roland actually *does* think that he can defeat the Saracens. In a sense this is an even greater arrogance, as Roland leads his men onwards, 'haut reputans hostes posse nocere sibi' (line 224), [not imagining that the enemy could harm him.] He has already promised his men victory, although in the Latin work this is not resolved, as it is in the *Rolandslied*, into a situation where the soldiers are effectively promised victory whether they win or lose, worldly glory or a heavenly crown.

Although overruled, Oliver continues as the voice of wisdom (another of the more celebrated lines in the work states briefly that Roland is bold and Oliver is wise, although it is usually seen as a complementary balance rather than as a contrast), and he repeats several times the accusation:

Vostre olifan suner vos nel deignastes;
Fust i li reis, n'i oüssum damage. *(laisse* 87, lines 1101f)

[You did not deign to sound your horn; if the king came,
there would be no harm.]

It is easy, especially in accord with expectations about medieval
epics, to see heroic determination in Roland's refusal even to seek
help. Perhaps it is less easy—though the poet does help us, through
the eyes of Oliver—to see Roland as a disaster, a hero gone too
far, sacrificing at least a part of the state to his own egocentricity
and to his private feud with his stepfather, a feud so private that
he will not even allow Oliver to comment on Ganelon. The
unhistorical Oliver is of some importance, providing a kind of
commentary on Roland's activities for the audience. Just as the final
vengeance is something which *ought* to have happened, but which
historically did not, Oliver is a voice of reason who *ought* perhaps
to have been there to curb Roland, but was not. At all events
Oliver is almost unique in heroic literature in that he offers direct
criticism to the central figure. No one criticises Byrhtnoð's decision,
but Oliver is critical of Roland almost from the start.[144]

It is at this point, we may say, that the church steps in (to an
even greater extent than in other works) and Roland is exculpated.
Unlike the situation in the *Ludwigslied*, where an earthly reward
was promised to the survivors or to their kindred, and where the
ultimate fate of the warriors was left up to God, here the warrior
archbishop Turpin makes clear that the Franks cannot really lose:

Se vos murez, esterez seinz martirs,
Sieges avrez el greignor pareïs. *(laisse* 89, lines 1134f)

[If you do die, you will be martyrs and have a place in
paradise.]

---

144 See Elliott, 'Byhtnoth and Hildebrand'. p. 59. Oliver is sometimes taken
as a somewhat shadowy addition (see Vance, *Song of Roland*, p. 14, and
Le Gentil, *Chanson de Roland*, p. 110) but Jackson, *Hero and King*, p. 64,
points out that Oliver represents the view that power must be subordinated to the general good.

This is the familiar principle of the crusades, attested in such passages as the following from the anonymous history of the First Crusade referring to an attack by the Turks in March 1098:

> Fueruntque in illa die martirizati ex nostris militibus seu peditibus plus quam mille, qui, ut credimus, in celum ascenderunt et candidati stolam martirii receperunt . . .[145]

[And by the grace of God our men defeated them. On that day more than a thousand of our soldiers were martyred and—such is our belief—went to heaven and received the white robe of a holy martyr.]

Konrad's German version of the Roland saga, in any case far more concerned with conversion and the religious aspects, takes this point far further than the *Chanson*, and has the Frankish warriors virtually seeking death in battle, after Charlemagne has promised them at the very start that they will receive a martyr's crown if they fall. Probably the greatest difference between the two texts, in fact, is the loss of Oliver's threefold request to sound the horn. In Konrad he asks once, but is told that things are now in God's hands, and after that he can ask no more. In Konrad, however, God has already promised Charlemagne the overall victory, and intervenes directly to give strength to the outnumbered Franks at Roncesvalles, even though they are going to lose in military terms. Roncesvalles becomes, then, almost a rush towards martyrdom, something which baffles the pagans completely; they exclaim in amazement that the Franks are not leaving the battlefield, but are actively seeking death—'den tot sie suchent' (line 6416). The warriors go into their last battle singing the *Gloria*, therefore, an interesting contrast with the *Ludwigslied*, in which

---

145 From the *Gesta Francorum et aliorum Hierosolimitanorum*: text with French translation by Louis Bréhier, *Histoire anonyme de la première croisade* (Paris: Champion, 1924), p. 88 (*Narratio septima*). See H. V. Routh, *God, Man and Epic Poetry* (Cambridge: CUP. 1927; repr. New York: Greenwood, 1968), ii, 114. Later writing on the battle of Dorylaeum in 1097 refers to a pair fighting 'like Roland and Oliver': Jones, *Ethos*, p. 94.

the warriors, less confident of a heavenly crown, sang the *Kyrie*.[146] This specifically crusading ethos (in Konrad in particular, but also in the *Chanson*) is quite different from that seen in the *Ludwigslied* or in *Maldon*, although they, too, concern battles against pagans. The defeat of Roland is historical; his passion (complete with darkness at noon and then an ascension) is an answer. It is interesting that even in military terms the battle's outcome (which was hopeless from the start) should be presented in the literary work, the *Chanson*, as having been very close indeed, when that point is *not* made in the poem of Maldon, in spite of what is said in the chronicles. Such chronicle evidence as there is says pretty well the opposite of Roncesvalles, but then, this is not the real raid of Roncesvalles in any respect. Right to the end of the battle, however, Roland is still expressing concern that the wrong songs are not sung about him, but he says too—prophetically this time—that Charlemagne will exact venegance. More important, however, is the last-minute quarrel between Roland and Oliver. For two proverbially close friends—medieval records showing brothers baptised Roland and Oliver are frequent enough to be used as an indicator of the date and popularity of the literary transformation of the débâcle at Roncesvalles—there is tension between them which is first seen in Oliver's comments rejecting Roland as possible ambassador, and which lasts throughout the work. Now, although Turpin does ostensibly reconcile the pair, Oliver's comments on Roland's heroics—and I use the word intentionally—are telling:

> Mielz valt mesure que ne fait estultie
> Franceis sunt morz par vostre legerie . . .
> Vostre proëcce, Rolland, mar la veïmes
> (*laisse* 130, lines 1725–31)

[Clear thinking is better than stupidity, and a lot of Franks have died because of your foolhardiness . . . your prowess, Roland, is a liability.]

146 Murdoch, 'Saucourt and the *Ludwigslied*'. p. 864.

While the text does not have Oliver make an accusation of arrogance as such, the sense could hardly be clearer, and at all events it is far more specific than Byrhtnoð and that single reference to *ofermod*, the more so as here it is a companion rather than the poet who makes the point.

The horn is sounded at the last, but Ganelon prevents Charlemagne from responding at once, reminding him that Roland has already taken one city (Pamplona, in fact) against his orders. Only when the horn is blown again does Charlemagne have Ganelon arrested and order the Franks to return, by which time Roland has died in that valiant final stand which, according to Pierre Le Gentil, regularly causes such emotion, and has been taken directly to paradise by Gabriel. The effect on the Franks now is to want to avenge Roland and the others at Roncesvalles. There is a difference once more between the *Chanson* and the German text, however, in that in the latter we have a reiterated desire to avenge Roland which is much like the repeated references to Byrhtnoð in *Maldon*, but which is not quite matched in the French version. 'Gedencke an Rolandes tot' (line 7784), says Charlemagne in the German, and then later 'rechet Rolanden' (line 8580), 'Remember the death of Roland! Avenge Roland!' Although in the *Chanson* Charlemagne clearly mourns Roland, his invocation is generalised:

> Vengez vos filz, voz freres et voz heirs
> Qu'en Rencesvals furent morz l'altre seir!
> (*laisse* 245, lines 3411f)

[Avenge your sons, brothers and heirs, who fell at Roncesvalles.]

This is a far broader view of the effect of the battle, although the German text does summarise the whole situation with a reference to Christ's words in John 12:24: 'granum frumenti cadens in terram mortuum fuerit . . . si autem mortuum fuerit, multum fructum adfert' [a grain of wheat must fall into the ground and die . . . but if it dies, then it yields rich fruit.] Christ, in effect, is allowed to sum up the (non-historical) effect of the battle of Roncesvalles and the death of Roland.

The final battle between the Franks and the Saracens under their new leader, the Emir Baligant, climaxes in the *Chanson* with the pitched combat between the two leaders themselves. In the fight, Charles is nearly unhorsed, but first the poet tells us that God does not want him to be defeated, and then Gabriel urges him directly to fight on. There is a contrast with the German text again, however, in that Konrad adds to the heavenly encouragement the information that Charles will actually win:

> wes sparstu den man?
> diu urtail ist uber in getan:
> uerfluochet ist al sin tail.
> got git dir daz hail;
> dine uiante geligent unter dinin fuzen. (lines 8545–49)

[Why are you letting him go? He has already been condemned and he is damned. God will give you the victory, and your enemies will lie beneath your feet.]

The German text shows divine intervention, but in the *Chanson* the king is merely urged by heaven to do his best, just as Louis was ordered back to Francia in the *Ludwigslied*. There is a distinction between the treatment of Charlemagne and Roland in both versions of the tale of Roncesvalles, however; Roland is not urged on directly by God, but—unlike Charlemagne—is taken to heaven and out, in one sense, of the heroic realm.

The concluding section of the *Chanson* is devoted to Ganelon and to a new political situation, and it is by no means an appendage to the story of Roncesvalles, but part of Charlemagne's political problem. Ganelon is tried for treason, and states his case with great clarity. He has always served the emperor, he says, but Roland wished to kill him, and for that he took his own vengeance. This he does not see as treason:

> Serveie [l'empereur] par feid et par amur;
> Rollant sis niés me coillit en haür,
> Si me jugat a mort et a dulur . . .
> Vengét m'en sui, mais n'i ad traïsun.
> (*laisse* 272, lines 3770–77)

[I served (Charlemagne) with loyalty and with love; his nephew, Roland came to hate me, and wanted misery and death for me . . . I took vengeance, but did not commit treason.]

Personal vengeance and the well-being of the state are clearly in conflict here, but the situation is now a political one centring upon Charles. Ganelon has declared his innocence of the specific charge, and he is supported by a very powerful clan led by Pinabel. Roland, so far from being a rallying point, is dead, something which the Franks use as an argument for *not* punishing Ganelon. Only one unprepossessing warrior, Thierry, is prepared to fight Pinabel in a trial by combat, and even he first tries to treat with Pinabel, who refuses in the name of his family. Only when Thierry is victorious do the Franks accept Ganelon's guilt, and his entire faction is hanged after Ganelon has been very publicly torn to pieces.[147] In Konrad, as might be expected, he is consigned thereafter to hell.

We do not know in the French text the real cause of the friction between Roland and Ganelon, although the explanation offered in the German version is part of the author's determination to focus the images of both men as plainly good or plainly bad. In French, the clearest distinction of this kind is between Christians and pagans. In dealing with the Saracens, Ganelon clearly *has* acted treasonably, because his act of private revenge has caused great losses to the Franks, whether or not this needs to be taken further and be seen as a betrayal of Christendom that makes him 'worse than Judas'. But Roland has acted just as excessively, refusing by caprice either to take the additional forces or to summon Charlemagne, and he has caused as much damage. The hero can take risks, but they must be reasonable risks. Roland's defeat was inevitable, but the inevitability was not fated, since it could have been avoided without loss of honour at various points. However, once the whole incident has passed, Charlemagne is a victor in

---

147 See Robert Bartless, *Trial by Fire and Water: The Medieval Judicial Ordeal* (Oxford: Clarendon, 1986), pp. 103–26, on this kind of trial by combat, also with reference to Ganelon.

several ways. A major source of potential discord in the upper echelons—indeed in his immediate family—has been removed. Oliver's comments about the dangers of Roland's heroism, too, remind us of the question: is the *Chanson* one of the right songs that Roland was so concerned about? Neither Roland nor Ganelon, though brave, is anything more than egocentric. Roland overreaches himself by defying the laws of military logic (as Oliver points out) and there is no real justification for his failure to carry out the task to which he was appointed. The Christian gloss on this act, the agony and canonisation of Roland, is artificial. Politically, Roland's failure to sound his horn, and his exaggerated fear about his own reputation, has caused nothing but damage to Charlemagne, even if it has had a beneficial effect in the political short term. The Franks were tired of the long war, and the death of a popular hero proves a valuable initial rallying-point, just as Byrhtnoð's was. Beyond that, however, Roland compares badly with other heroes. His only real similarity with Byrhtnoð—an experienced man who has made military decisions in the past and who takes a calculated risk at Maldon—is this role after death. Charlemagne recognised the danger for the rear-guard, but Roland insisted on placing himself into the situation; Byrhtnoð had to face the Vikings anyway. Younger warriors and vassals, like Beowulf at the court of Hroðgar, or Ernst at that of the king of Arimaspî, even Heinrich von Kempten in his later years defending the emperor, all save the state by acts of heroism. Roland's act of self-imposed heroism actually damages the state.

The problems of Roland as a hero would be echoed in a slightly different light in a later literary work, in Kleist's *Prinz Friedrich von Homburg* in the nineteenth century, in which the eponymous hero goes into battle in defiance of an order, and is in fact victorious. The Great Elector, however, is forced to condemn him to death for insubordination, and the Prince himself comes to accept that he must subordinate even an unexpressed wish for gratuitous personal glory for the good of the state. Roland does not himself realise this political point, but Oliver does.

Ganelon, too, acts out of a spirit of individuality alone, not concerned in this case for reputation directly, but concerned to rid himself at any costs of a stepson who clearly puts him in the shade, or who has actively tried to damage him. The basis of their quarrel is unclear in the *Chanson*, and although we may guess (with Konrad's help) at the cause, perhaps it does not really matter what that basis is. It is enough that it is there. And once Roland has gone, Ganelon is fairly confident that he can ride out the storm, and he comes very close to doing so. The barons, it must be recalled, are on his side at most points in the *Chanson*, and support him at the end.[148] Only by divine intervention (or by natural justice—call it what we will) at this point is Charlemagne rid of a dangerous faction.

Charlemagne has enemies within as well as outside; the Saracens are the real enemy, but inside his own realm, indeed, within his own *comitatus*, is another enemy: not the over-eager Roland, nor the treacherous Ganelon, but the feud between them, which could escalate at any time. When we step away from the presentation of the battle of Roncesvalles to look at it in perspective, even within the *Chanson*, it becomes once more only an incident—admittedly a highlighted one—within the context of a longer war, which now culminates in a quite unhistorical major battle, between two great religious ideologies, climaxing with the single combat between the almost equally matched leaders, Charlemagne and the Emir. Charlemagne is victorious and he fulfils his own aims, continuing to do what he thinks right in spite of his weariness. In the *Chanson* this is realised, perhaps, as what the angel tells him, although in contradistinction to Konrad's version, in the *Chanson* the angel does not tell him the outcome. The *Chanson de Roland* shows us an incident from the life of the hero Charlemagne both as a military commander and as a ruler; he asserts his military strength by taking revenge for the fallen at Roncesvalles, using them as a spur to the weary Franks to fight on. His subsequent victory, which uses the dead Roland, limits the damage caused by the already escalating

---

148 Jackson, *Hero and King*, p. 70. In the case of Tristan, who is also opposed by a manipulative power-bloc of barons, the latter are silenced by a divine judgement, albeit a dubious one, and in the long run they are victorious. Tristan has, admittedly, both saved the state (from Morholt) *and* damaged it (by his relationship with the queen).

feud between Roland and Ganelon. By the end, both sides of that feud have gone.

Has the Roland of the *Chanson* really ensured that the right songs are sung about him, and (in the circularity of the heroic epic) is it itself one of those songs? In a sense it is: Roland goes to heaven after falling bravely in battle. But Oliver's modifying words remain in the mind, and so does the feeling that the battle was not really necessary, and that behind it all is a feud between the stepfather and his stepson. The search for arrogance as such is probably a red herring in the evaluation of the heroes unless we define it precisely as an exaggeration, a lack of *mesure* which leads into *estultie*. Roland is usually thought of as a hero, and indeed he may actually fit the pattern in works written after the *Chanson*, or in lost oral ones from an earlier period, but whether he is really a hero in anything but the very simplest sense of a brave warrior in the political context of the *Chanson de Roland* is quite another matter.

Roland is—if I may be allowed the term—not particularly historical, certainly not as a real relative of Charlemagne, any more than is Ganelon, a figure linked loosely with an obscure, anachronistic and not in fact very recalcitrant bishop called Wanilo of Sens. As usual with heroic literature, some of the other figures of the *Chanson* (though not Oliver) have quasi-historical parallels spread over a wide period of time, but the ahistoricity of the work (provided we do not get too involved in games of identification) focusses the mind on the general political impression. Germanic, Frankish and crusading elements may all themselves cause shifts in perspective in the consideration of the hero, but the constants of balance and necessity remain. Charlemagne, the true hero of the *Chanson*, may be weary at the end of the poem, but this is not caused only by the war in Spain. He has emerged, too, from a complex and personally painful political struggle involving factions very close to his own family and therefore throne. By the end of the *Chanson* he is rid, however, of Ganelon 'ki la traïsun fist' and his entire group of supporters, who worked against the state. Less happily for Charlemagne in personal terms, Roland, too, has gone (and with him *his* group of powerful followers), although here his act of *estultie*—Oliver's word, not mine—has at least had the political effect in the long term of acting as a spur for the Franks to return and complete the campaign. Martyrs are useful. The removal of Ganelon's faction balances the removal of Roland's, although it is better to be be a saint and martyr than a traitor. But we might still be inclined to paraphrase Alcuin and ask: 'quid Hruodlandus cum imperio'? What in real terms has Roland actually achieved?

6

Damage and Damage Limitation

The Nibelungs, Hilde and Kudrun

It is probably foolhardy to try to tackle in the space of a single chapter the question of the hero in two very large works. The two great heroic poems of the classical medieval period in German, the *Nibelungenlied* and *Kudrun*, balance each other, however, in various quite different ways.[149] One obvious point is that the

149 Editions are as follows: the text of the *Nibelungenlied* is cited from *Das Nibelungenlied*, ed. Karl Bartsch, 15th edn by Helmut de Boor (Wiesbaden: Brockhaus, 1959; 21st edn by R. Wisniewski, 1979). Modern German translations include that by Helmut Brackert (Frankfurt/ M.: Fischer, 1970) and English translations are by D. G. Mowatt, *The Nibelungenlied* (London: Dent, 1962), and A. T. Hatto, *The Nibelungenlied* (Harmondsworth: Penguin, 1965). The poem's 'sequel', *Diu Klage* can be found in *Der Nibelunge Noth und Die Klage*, ed. Karl Lachmann, 6th edn by Ulrich Pretzel (Berlin; de Gruyter, 1960); there is an English translation by Winder McConnell, *The Lament of the Nibelungen* (Columbia, SC: Camden House, 1994). I am indebted to Winder McConnell for letting me read his translation in draft and for keeping me in touch with his researches into the heroic epic in general. *Kudrun* is cited from *Kudrun*, ed. Karl Bartsch, rev. edn by Karl Stackmann (Wiesbaden: Brockhaus, 1980). A convenient German translation is that by Karl Simrock, rev. Friedrich Neumann, *Kudrun (Gudrun)* (Stuttgart: Reclam, 1958), and there are recent English translations by Brian Murdoch, *Kudrun* (London: Dent, 1987); by Marion E. Gibbs and Sidney M. Johnson, *Kudrun* (New York: Garland, 1992); and by Winder McConnell, *Kudrun* (Columbia SC: Camden House, 1992). There is an edition and modern German prose version of both major texts by Werner Hoffmann, *Das Nibelungenlied/ Kudrun* (Darmstadt: WBG, 1972).

Nibelungenlied is extremely well known, even outside German studies, while *Kudrun* is not. Although in 1967 Werner Hoffmann devoted a full chapter in what was then one of the few full-scale analyses of *Kudrun* to the relationship of the two works, contrasting them, and concluding that the supposed (but not terribly well attested) tragic ideal in earlier heroic poetry had given way in *Kudrun* to 'Annäherungen, Ausgleichungen, Kompromisse' [rapprochements, balances and compromises], the later work still appears in a secondary position. Broader studies of the heroic epic have always had a tendency to mention it without any analysis.[150] The general view still obtains that *Kudrun* is inferior to the *Nibelungenlied*, probably because of the questionable notion that heroic poetry, or at least the best heroic poetry, ought to end tragically. Certainly in pragmatic political terms the ending of the *Nibelungenlied* portrays chaos and disaster on a massive scale. So firmly was a tragic ending felt to be an heroic ideal, however, that when in 1910 Ernst Hardt wrote a play based on the positive *Kudrun*, he actually (and in literary terms somewhat unusually) deliberately provided it with a *un*happy-end, in which the eponymous princess is stabbed and dies.[151] Possibly he had failed to notice that the positive ending of the medieval *Kudrun* is achieved only after a great deal of bloodshed.

Although recent criticism, beginning perhaps with Magdalene Weege's 1953 Mainz dissertation, but well represented by scholars such as Winder McConnell in the USA, has quite properly been

---

150 Werner Hoffmann, *Kudrun: Ein Beitrag zur Deutung der Nach-Nibelungischen Heldendichtung* (Stuttgart: Metzler, 1967), p. 288. Barbara Siebert, *Rezeption und Produktion: Bezugssysteme in der Kudrun* (Göppingen: Kümmerle, 1988), stresses also that *Kudrun* provides an 'answer' to the *Nibelungenlied* in many respects. As far as general works are concerned, Jan de Vries, for example, in his *Heroic Song and Heroic Legend*, mentions *Kudrun* several times, but never discusses it at all, although he analyses the *Nibelungenlied* in detail. This situation is hardly unusual in general studies of the heroic epic, even those interested in the role of women.

151 Ernst Hardt, *Gudrun* (Leipzig: Insel, 1912). Somewhat later, the right-wing poet Will Vesper took the tale of Kudrun's imprisonment and escape as a parallel for the defeat and rebirth of Germany after the First World War: *Die Gudrunsage* (Oldenburg i. O.: Stalling, 1925).

at pains to move *Kudrun* out of the shade of the better-known *Nibelungenlied* (where it remained even in the hands of some of its most partisan interpreters) by insisting on the avoidance of any comparison with the earlier work, the fact remains that in terms of the hero and his role, *Kudrun* may still profitably be contrasted with the poem of the Nibelungen and need by no means be seen as inferior.[152] Where the *Nibelungenlied* ends in disaster and the collapse of a state, *Kudrun* ends in reconciliation and the extension of empire.

Where the foreground is occupied in the *Nibelungenlied* by the great warriors, most notably Sîvrît (for whom we may use the more familiar name Siegfried, which will also help distinguish him from a character in *Kudrun*) and Hagen, *Kudrun* places the women—Hilde of Ireland, Hilde of Denmark and her daughter, Kudrun—very firmly in the foreground. Indeed, the work has been referred to as a *Frauenroman*, a 'women's novel'. Admittedly, even in the *Nibelungenlied* the importance of the dark queen, Kriemhild, is such that at least one manuscript refers to the work as 'The Book of Kriemhild'.[153] But the question is only one of emphasis, and the foregrounding of one set of figures does not exclude the others completely. In *Kudrun*, Hilde and Kudrun are not heroes, although they are part of the heroic world, a world which itself reflects political reality. Rather, they are used to reflect the code of the hero, and indeed to modify it where necessary. Putting it very simply, the *Nibelungenlied* shows us a dynasty that failed; in *Kudrun*, a ruling dynasty goes from strength to strength in spite of setbacks. In spite of no fewer than three recent translations of *Kudrun*, it is still a relatively unfamiliar work, however, and this will, perhaps, justify spending more time on it here than on the *Nibelungenlied*.[154]

---

152 Winder McConnell, *The Epic of Kudrun* (Göppingen: Kümmerle, 1988), p. 1. Magdalena Weege's dissertation, *Das Kudrunepos: eine Dichtung des Hochmittelalters* (Lemgo, 1953), is not always easy to find.

153 It was first published as *Chriemhilden Rache*, 'Kriemhild's Revenge', although she undergoes a curiously positive metamorphosis in the later poem of lament, *Diu Klage*.

154 The W. Krogmann-U. Pretzel bibliography of the *Nibelungenlied* and the *Klage*, which first appeared in 1960, has been updated several times. As an indication of the extent of the material, Winder McConnell produced 'Some Comments on Recent Criticism' in *Res Publica Litterarum* 13

The historical backgrounds of both works lie once again in the period of the folk migrations, but they are as usual of little importance as reflections of historical events. The pictures of Gunther (Gundahari of the Burgundians once again) and of Siegfried (reflecting an obscure Frankish king) or even of Attila, are hardly historical, although the *Nibelungenlied* does reflect in its final catastrophe the effective eclipse of the Burgundian state and, to an extent anyway, the fall of the Huns. With *Kudrun*, the actual historical elements are even more remote. We can point, à propos of King Hetel in the work, to the island of Hiddensee—etymologically Hetel's island—in the Baltic, but we cannot really go much beyond that. Both works may be viewed as political models, however, showing us the warrior hero within, affected by, and dependent upon his feudal political context which at the same time defines his role *as* a hero. If there is a message shared by the two works, it is the need once again to cope with political chaos and the need for constant control, with the warning rider that damage cannot always be contained. The last point concerns above all and perhaps rather oddly the best-known figure of all, Siegfried, who falls, even more than Roland, outside the background-determined definition of a hero; whilst generally thought of as a hero, indeed almost the archetypal hero-figure, his acts lead to disaster. The danger inherent in Siegfried was indicated already in the *Grípisspá*, although the point of that work was the focus on the individual, and he himself was satisfied that his private honour would be unimpaired

note 154 continued
(1990), 155–78, offering a useful survey of the major studies which appeared in 1987 alone, admittedly something of a bumper year. Slightly earlier was Lutz Mackensen, *Die Nibelungen* (Stuttgart: Hauswedell, 1984), for example. All kinds of areas of Nibelungen studies (such as the whole question of the reception of the work, in which scholars such as Otfried Ehrismann have produced fascinating material) have to be left out of consideration here, of course. The work itself does, however, continue to attract an excessively nationalistic-Germanic approach. On the background to the saga and the analogues, the standard work is Andreas Heusler's 1920 study, *Nibelungensage und Nibelungenlied* (Dortmund: Ruhfus, 6th edn, 1965); and see more recently, Hermann Reichert, *Nibelungenlied und Nibelungensage* (Vienna and Cologne: Böhlau, 1985); and Theodore M. Andersson, *A Preface to the Nibelungenlied* (Stanford: Stanford UP, 1987).

however much he might suffer in a life mapped out by fate. In the *Nibelungenlied* we are shown the workings out of his acts within a structured context in which they serve as the seeds of chaos. In *Kudrun* we are shown equally fierce and sometimes as individualistic warriors, most notably Hagen the Wild and Wate of Stormland, plus two younger men, Hartwig and Hartmuot, and any of these could precipitate disaster were they not controlled. Yet to speak of 'control' is to invoke the wrong concept; 'balance' might be more appropriate.

The *Nibelungenlied* is based on the same material as we have encountered in Norse texts, and it combines the tales of Sigurðr and his relationship with Brünhild and with the Burgundian princess (here named Kriemhild), with the story of the fall of the Burgundians and the death of their king, Gunther, accompanied by his closest ally, Hagen. The associated tale of the fall of the Huns after Attila's marriage to a Germanic princess, so closely integrated in the *Atlakviða*, is only hinted at, and Attila himself—Etzel in German—survives, although his sons do not. This combination on a broad scale of various different narrative strands has led once again to discussions of the unity of the work. The problem of how to relate the first part of the work, leading up to the marriages of Siegfried and Gunther, to the second, the fall of the Burgundians—sex in the former, violence in the latter—can be dealt with in various ways, one of which is to take the work as a warning that alliances implied by the marriages do not always work. An additional problem with the *Nibelungenlied* is that, unusually amongst all the texts so far considered (and *Kudrun* as well), there is in this case a broad manuscript tradition which shows considerable variation at different points.[155]

So far we have seen the hero subordinated eventually to the state, his actions foregrounded, but determined by the demands of stability and political order; the message of the *Nibelungenlied* is that the hero

---

155 Discussed in the editions, and demonstrated in the massive volume edited by Michael Batts, *Das Nibelungenlied: Paralleldruck der Handschriften A, B und C nebst Lesarten der übrigen Handschriften* (Tübingen: Niemeyer, 1971). See for a comparison of the effect of so many manuscripts (approaching forty, including fragments) with the position with medieval German romances, Kees H. R. Borghart, *Das Nibelungenlied* (Amsterdam: Ro-dopi, 1977).

as an individual can be—if he asserts that individuality fully—a political threat. There is a gradation from Byrhtnoð, who loses a military gamble, to Roland, who places too much emphasis on his own prowess, possibly for the wrong reasons, but who, like Byrhtnoð, serves as a rallying point after death; and then to Siegfried, whose acts when living are often questionable, and whose role after death as the object of Kriemhild's obsession is to cause yet more damage. In spite of the assurances made to Sigurðr in the quite different Norse *Grípisspá* (where fate is the only context), it is highly questionable whether the German *Nibelungenlied* is one of the right songs for Siegfried. There is nothing inexorable about the situation here. Nor does it help, in fact, to draw a contrast—as Carola Gottzman has done, for example—between the hereditary king and what she calls the *Idoneus*, the warrior individual who bases everything on his special strengths. The Latin word *idoneus* means 'fitting, suitable' and Siegfried is, simply, not suitable for kingship; nor, indeed, is the hereditary principle seriously questioned in this work or in *Kudrun*.[156] Much attention has been paid to the message of the poem, with predictably varied conclusions. If there is a message to the *Nibelungenlied*, it may be a warning against the wrong kind of alliance. In the work, it can be argued that the real hero is Hagen (again a much discussed proposition, with—it must be said—fairly frequent decisions made in entirely the other direction), who attempts, but fails to preserve order and balance in a state into which a strong and assertive, indeed threatening individual has been introduced. Far from pursuing a course laid down by fate—as Sigurðr must do in, or rather after, the *Grípisspá*—the German Siegfried is far closer in essence to an outside

---

156 Carola L. Gottzmann, *Heldendichtung des 13. Jahrhunderts* (Frankfurt/M.: Lang, 1987). Few critics deny the political import of the *Nibelungenlied*, of course: see Hugo Bekker, 'Kingship in the *Nibelungenlied*'. *Germanic Review* 41 (1966), 251–63, and Heinz Rupp, 'Das *Nibelungenlied*—eine politische Dichtung'. *Wirkendes Wort* 35 (1985), 166–76. On the hereditary principle and its acceptance from Plato to Machiavelli, see R. M. Hare, *Plato* (Oxford and New York: OUP, 1982), p. 59. On the avoidability of disaster and the role of Siegfried, see Mowatt and Sacker, *Nibelungenlied*, p. 9. Jackson's views on the conflict between the hero and the king are also relevant here.

force like Grendel, and if this goes too far, then it is at least appropriate to see him as an extremely dangerous liaison.

Siegfried turns up at the court of the Burgundians ostensibly in pursuit of marriage to Princess Kriemhild. It is worth recalling that Siegfried's father and mother have already warned him against this liaison, mentioning Hagen in particular. This is Siegfried's first act of self-assertion, and if his parents refer to the *übermüete* [arrogance] of Hagen, then Siegfried's *own* arrogance is implicit in insisting on this venture. Before he is even fully in view at Worms, the Burgundian court, Hagen shows himself as the one who knows about Siegfried, and gives a fairly concise synopsis of the background that *we* know from the Norse texts: the fight with dragons, the invincibility and the massive amount of treasure. This means that Siegfried is rich and strong, and Hagen's advice is that Siegfried would be a useful ally, but must be handled with care, something which proves to be sound counsel, as Siegfried's first act is to threaten Gunther. In the name of his own reputation he opens with a direct and deliberate statement of aggression which is entirely political, effectively staking a claim for all of Gunther's territory:

> ez enmüge von dinen ellen   din lant den fride han
> ich wil es alles walten,   und ouch diu erbe mîn,
> erwirbest daz mit sterke,   diu sulen dir untertænec sîn.
> (strophe 113)

[If you cannot give stability to your lands by your power, then I shall take them over; and if *you* are strong enough, you can take *my* inheritance.]

Gunther offers diplomacy against this (continued and unprovoked) arrogance, until eventually Siegfried is calmed down, ostensibly by thoughts of the princess that he had come to woo. Marriage *can* be an alternative to war—we shall see this as a guiding principle in *Kudrun*—but although Siegfried had this in mind when he set out, he appears to have forgotten it when he arrives at Worms. The Burgundians, Gunther's brother Gernot in particular, demand restraint from Hagen, and eventually Siegfried is admitted, somewhat uneasily, to Gunther's court. The prospect of marriage to Kriemhild is then kept in abeyance until Gunther's territory is threatened by a Saxon invasion, and on the counsel of Hagen Siegfried is enlisted to help in a defence which (we are told) would otherwise be impossible to maintain.

There is no doubt that the now proposed marriage to Kriemhild is strictly political,[157] and an alliance is indeed set up, but before Siegfried can marry Kriemhild, he has to agree to assist Gunther in his wooing of another princess, Brünhilt. The story is well known and not of signal relevance here. With the aid of a cloak of invisibility, Brünhilt is conquered by Siegfried on Gunther's behalf (and significantly Siegfried has to bring in a force of men at one point in case of danger). Gunther passes Siegfried off as his vassal, and whatever the assurances of Gripir might have been for the Norse Sigurðr, the German Siegfried's position is compromised by his acquiescence in a dishonourable situation. This is compounded by the celebrated scene on Gunther's wedding night, when his advances are spurned by the vigorous Brünhild until Siegfried, again invisible, subdues her on his behalf, again foolishly taking a ring and a belt from her.

Once married to Kriemhild, Siegfried retires to his own country, but he leaves the impression with the in any case disgruntled Brünhilt that he is a vassal to Gunther, something which she brings into play in demanding of Gunther that Siegfried and his wife be brought back to the court, ostensibly for a feast. Hagen, when this is mooted, considers the great wealth that Siegfried has to hand—the Nibelungen treasure—and in political terms the situation is not dissimilar to that in *Waltharius*. In that work Guntharius at least laid a claim to the ownership of the treasure that had some element of truth in it, whilst here the vassal idea, however spurious, might provide a justification for the Burgundian side in what will now become a

---

157 Mowatt and Sacker, *Nibelungenlied*, p. 54, speak of Kriemhild as a 'marketable commodity'. Nor need we really believe the view that Siegfried is motivated entirely by love of the up to then virtually invisible Kriemhild, though critics from Carlyle onwards have maintained that this is the case. See also Neil Thomas, 'The Testimony of Saxo Grammaticus and the Interpretation of the *Nibelungenlied*'. *Oxford German Studies* 20/21 (1991/2), 7–17. On Siegfried's supposedly subordinate role, see Mary Fleet, 'Siegfried as Gunther's Vassal'. *Oxford German Studies* 14 (1983), 1–7.

conflict. A dangerous situation soon arises. The question of who is subordinate to whom is raised by Brünhilt as a question of precedence in entering the cathedral, and Kriemhild is provoked into revealing the details of Gunther's wedding night, proving it by possession of the ring and belt—and indeed by wearing the latter. Worse, she hurls at Brünhilt the question 'Wie möhte mannes kebse werden immer küniges wîp' (strophe 839, 4)—how can a vassal's concubine—and the word is technical in respect of status as well as simply insulting—be a king's wife? Personal conflict at this level leads to broader political conflict, although the personal side is apparently resolved between Gunther and Siegfried after the latter swears that he did no more than subdue Gunther's wife for him.

An alliance now forms, however, between Hagen and Brünhilt, after the latter appeals to him for vengeance. The motivation of Gunther's queen may be insult, or an inverted love for Siegfried, but Hagen's motivation is once again very clearly political.[158] He sees Siegfried expressly as a cuckoo in the nest—'suln wir gouche ziehen'. he asks (strophe 867, 1), 'are we supposed to bring up this cuckoo here'? Significantly, it is made clear that others are less than content with Siegfried's continued presence—'dô waren in unmuote genuoge Guntheres man' (strophe 871, 4) [plenty of Gunther's men were unhappy].

In a work with strong individual characters, it is important to keep an eye on the background. That last comment is not highlighted, but it is especially important in the case of the *Nibelungenlied* to recall that author's apparent partisanship (which may be formulaic or deliberately ironic) for individual figures may be misleading in evaluating the true nature of a given situation. Thus in the French *Tristan* of Beroul the eponymous hero is dazzling and the barons

---

158 As made clear by D. G. Mowatt in his important paper 'Studies Towards and Interpretation of the *Nibelungenlied*'. *German Life and Letters* NS 14 (1960/1), 257–70, although the *gouch*-comment is probably to be taken literally. Mowatt's paper again, significantly, echoes Tolkien on *Beowulf*, and is is worth noting that the collective *Wege der Forschung* volume edited by Heinz Rupp, *Nibelungenlied und Kudrun* (Darmstadt: WBG, 1976) contains German versions of this and other papers by Mowatt, Sacker, King and other English-language critics.

are characterised throughout as wicked. But they threaten to withdraw their support of the king if Tristan, the interloper, is not removed, and as such make manifest the fact that their interest is a controlling one. Hagen is not alone in his antagonism to Siegfried, although it is he who now plans and carries out his murder. His motivation may be loyalty to Brünhilt, or to the state as a whole; it may even be desire for the wealth controlled by Siegfried. But that he is not alone in his antagonism is very important indeed. Nor, in fact, are Siegfried's final acts in the work—and at the Burgundian court—particularly praiseworthy or heroic, as he lets loose a bear to disrupt a hunting party.

The death of Siegfried provides a turning-point and a new political situation. Kriemhild is widowed, antagonistic to Hagen, alone and virtually trapped at her brother's court, and in charge of a large amount of wealth, the Nibelungen treasure. Hagen's counsel now is one of reconciliation: it would be useful to the Burgundians to be in the favour of the widowed Kriemhild, and again he is explicit. The potentially dangerous Siegfried, the over-individualistic cuckoo in the nest has been removed, but gold equals power:

> Dô sprach der helt von Tronege 'möht ir daz tragen an
> daz ir iuwer swester   ze vriunde möhtet hân
> sô kœme ze disen landen   daz Nibelunges golt.
> des möht ir vil gewinnen,   würd' uns diu köneginne holt.'
> (strophe 1107)

[Hagen of Tronje said: 'if you could restore friendship with your sister, the Nibelung gold would come here to Burgundy, so that we should have much to gain by friendship with the queen.']

Forgiveness is granted by Kriemhild to the brothers, but not to Hagen, and she returns to their court. The treasure is brought there too, amongst it a gold rod (*rüetelîn*, strophe 1124, 1) which could make one, we are told, master of the world. Gold can indeed afford mastery, and Kriemhild now begins to attract warriors to her. This again alarms Hagen, since she is clearly using the treasure to buy power *within* their land; for this reason he again—with the connivance, though not the assistance, of the brothers—removes it and hides it in the Rhine.

Kriemhild, trapped and deprived of the treasure, can now do nothing but wait, harbouring resentment, now the sole representative of what appeared for a while to be developing as a Siegfried faction within the court. There is no question now of the dead Siegfried becoming a positive rallying-point for others; he was an outsider at this court anyway. Kriemhild may be moved by the desire for revenge, but her treasure *is* restorable, at least potentially, and this becomes part of her obsession. Kriemhild therefore agrees to a marriage proposal from the king of the Huns, Attila, won over by the promise from Rüdeger, Attila's ally, that revenge could be taken on her enemies.

Hagen has removed Siegfried, of whom he was dubious at the start, and also the treasure as a threat to the Burgundian stability. Now he alone opposes this new alliance with Attila, aware that there is potential here for disaster. The character of Hagen has been the subject of much debate, and he has been seen both as a loyal statesman and an unscrupulous, even an amoral *Realpolitiker*, but there is no doubt about his position throughout the work as the warrior who attempts throughout to keep the forces of chaos and instability at bay.[159] This time he is not listened to. The Burgundian brothers plead first Kriemhild's happiness, then the fact that they will never visit the Hunnish court and so will be safe, and finally that they do not wish to be traitors.

159 See for example K. C. King, 'A Reply'. *Modern Language Review* 57 (1962), 541–50. Some literary analyses are very anti-Hagen, such as Hugo Bekker, *The Nibelungenlied: A Literary Analysis* (Toronto and Buffalo: UTP, 1971), esp. pp. 118–48, and more recently Pàroli, 'Profilo dell'antieroe'. pp. 288–301, who takes him as an amoral figure and who refers to other relevant studies representing both sides of the argument. Hagen's importance, in the *Nibelungenlied* as in the (mostly earlier) analogues, is affirmed by the extensive studies by J. Stout, *und ouch hagene* (Groningen: Wolters, 1963), and Olivier Gouchet, *Hagen von Tronje: étude du personnage* (Göppingen: Kümmerle, 1981). Gouchet divides the primary texts studied into those sympathetic or neutral to Hagen, and those which treat him negatively, notably the *Nibelungenlied* and the *Klage*. Just how valid an assessment via this kind of comparison is, is disputable, but Gouchet does make clear the point of discrepancy between authorial statement and reader perception.

The last statement is thoroughly hypocritical, of course, and the second is forgotten when after some years the Burgundians are indeed invited to Attila's court. Again Hagen counsels against this, but is overruled, although this time he is again not the only one to do so.[160] The encounter with the Huns is uneasy from the start. In spite of a further alliance by marriage on the way—the betrothal of one of the Burgundian brothers to the daughter of Rüdeger, one of Attila's allies—Kriemhild's desire for revenge is apparent from the moment the Burgundians arrive at the Hun court. Hagen's reluctance to go there at all was confirmed, in fact, by the prophecies of some water-sprites along the route; on realising already at that point that they are fated not to return, Hagen literally breaks up the boat that could take them. The arrival is uneasy and antagonistic, and Kriemhild confronts Hagen (who by way of provocation is wearing Siegfried's sword) directly as soon as she sees him. Eventually open warfare develops and the Burgundians are killed, with the final scene recalling the *Atlakviða* with the roles of Högni and Gunnar reversed. The real focus, however, is the treasure once again. It has been argued that the motif of Kriemhild's revenge for Siegfried has overtaken that of the treasure, and that Kriemhild's demands are illogical, but this is surely not the case: the treasure is real. Kriemhild cannot regain Siegfried, but she *can*, at least in theory, still regain the treasure.[161] Although the Burgundians have been defeated and he faces certain death, Hagen is concerned at the last to defy Kriemhild, personally, perhaps, but also because she has now become part of the Huns. He swears that will not reveal where the treasure is until Gunther is dead and, when the king has indeed been killed, Hagen declares his final defiance: now no one can betray the secret. Kriemhild kills him and is slain herself by Attila's close associate, Hildebrand, but his words as he does so are significant:

---

160 See Helmut de Boor, 'Rumoldes rat'. *Zeitschrift für deutsches Altertum* 61 (1924), 1–11.

161 Otfrid Ehrismann offers a compromise on the matter by conflating the demands for Siegfried and the treasure, *Nibelungenlied: Epoche—Werk—Wirkung* (Munich: Beck, 1987), p. 174, although McConnell considers that this is a point that is unlikely to be resolved: 'Recent Cricitism'. p. 161.

swie er mich selben bræchte   in angestlîche nôt,
idoch sô wil ich rechen   des küenen Tronegæres tôt.
(strophe 2375, 4)

[Although he put me in great peril, I want nevertheless to avenge the brave hero Hagen of Tronje.]

Hildebrand is echoing in fact the words of his own master, Attila, who has just described Hagen as 'der aller beste degen, der ie kom ze sturme oder ie schilt getruoc!' [The finest warrior who ever entered battle or bore a shield.] The outsiders Attila and Hildebrand affirm at the last the major importance of Hagen, who has tried to maintain order in a warrior society, but has failed.

Diu Klage, 'The Lament', the so-called sequel to the poem, which is found with it in many of the manuscripts, is not a great work, and we need spend little time on it. Not only does it describe in over 4000 lines the aftermath of the final battle, however, but it also seeks some kind of justification for the slaughter. Its most significant point is that Kriemhild's actions are justified as the embodiment of loyalty, whilst those of Hagen—characterised as *der grimme*, the grim or savage man—are presented as consistently malicious. His arrogance is seen by another character (as indeed by critics as well)[162] as the root of all the carnage, in a passage which is expressed with a general point:

mînen herren hân ich verlorn
niwan von Hagenen über muot,
diu dicke grôzen schaden tuot (lines 4028–30)

[I have lost my lords only because of Hagen's arrogance, which so often leads to disaster.]

The word *übermuot* (or its equivalent) recurs in heroic writing, with shades of meaning from over-eagerness to actual *hubris*; however, the presentation of Hagen is consistent in *Diu Klage*, and Hildebrand actually expresses his regret at killing Kriemhild,

162 See J. K. Bostock, 'The Message of the *Nibelungenlied*'. *Modern Language Review* 55 (1960), 200–12, esp. p. 207f.

commenting too that everything is to be blamed on Hagen—it is all 'von Hagenen schulden' (line 1253). In the *Nibelungenlied* itself, of course, Kriemhild was a she-devil, and Hildebrand was appalled at the death of a warrior like Hagen.

Some of the questions which have preoccupied *Kudrun* studies—the historical and literary analogues, the genre of the work, and its unity—need not concern us here. The work as we have it exists in a single manuscript, rather than the three dozen or so of the *Nibelungenlied*. It was written down in an antiquarian collection in the first years of the sixteenth century, although the composition of this version was probably in the thirteenth. Given that the historical parallels to the events of the text are far earlier, we have already a variety of potential dates for the work, at which reception questions could be raised. *Kudrun* indicates as clearly as *Waltharius*, though in a different way, how difficult it is to place a date on a medieval work at all. It is set in an heroic world—I have stated elsewhere that it is essentially a Viking world—and the heroes are comparable with those of the *Nibelungenlied*, especially in their political context. Only the foregrounding of the women is unusual, but these women are unlike the politically passive ladies of some medieval romance.[163] Rather they call to mind some of the comments of Tacitus about German women. Chapter 18 of the *Germania* is a good starting point for a consideration of *Kudrun*:

> ne se mulier extra virtutum cogitationes extraque
> bellorum casus putet, ipsis incipientis matrimonii
> auspiciis admonetur venire se laborum periculorumque
> sociam, idem in pace, idem in proelio passuram
> ausuramque . . .
>
> [Nor may a woman think that the heroic virtues or the
> fortunes of war have nothing to do with her, and she is

163 But not in all. See Petra Kellermann-Haaf, *Frau und Politik im Mittelalter* (Göppingen: Kümmerle, 1986), p. 337. On the Viking aspects, see my translation, and also Ingeborg Schröbler, *Wikingische und spielmännische Elemente im zweiten Teil des Gudrunliedes* (Halle/S.: Niemeyer, 1934).

reminded when she marries that she is now going to be the man's close associate in toils and dangers, in peace and war.]

Tacitus had already described how flagging Germanic armies had been restored when the women pleaded with the men to make sure that they were not sent into slavery. However much his real concern might have been to offer a contrast with contemporary Roman habits, Tacitus certainly presents Germanic women as chaste, monogamous, much honoured, and the partners of the men in all areas, fulfilling different tasks, it is true, but equal in status to the men.[164] This vision of women, and indeed the question of slavery, has strong after-echoes in *Kudrun*. We need to bear in mind, again, that both of our poems deal with a specific class, which is why the modern—and in any case highly imprecise—term *Frauenroman*, 'women's novel' is a dangerous one. In the case of *Kudrun* we need to refine it to mean something like 'a narrative (not a romance) in the foreground of which are ladies of the highest nobility in a medieval (or perhaps early medieval) warrior society'.[165] One is even tempted, since German lends itself so nicely to such formulations, towards something like *Herrscherinepos* (if we need to define the work that closely), a 'queen-epic'. Even there we miss the development of the role and perception of the queen from the Carolingian period onwards from that of *consors regni*, 'partner in the *kingdom*', a formula which was widely used in the Ottonian period in Germany, for example,—to a subordinated role as the wife of a ruler.[166] The equal partnership of the wife in Germanic

164 Tacitus, *Germania* 18; see also 8. *Cornelii Taciti opera minora*, ed. Henry Furneaux and J. G. C. Anderson (Oxford: Clarendon, 1900; repr. 1939). There is an English translation by H. Mattingly, *Tacitus on Britain and Germany* (Harmondsworth: Penguin, 1948).
165 The term was used first for the work in the 1950s, but developed in a monograph with a significant title by Theodor Nolte, *Das Kudrunepos— ein Frauenroman* (Tübingen: Niemeyer, 1985). Although the latter term is probably better avoided (as embracing potentially writings by for and about women), Nolte's study is of considerable interest.
166 The development of the *consors regni* formula has been traced by Thilo Vogelsang, *Die Frau als Herrscherin im hohen Mittelalter* (Göttingen: Musterschmidt, 1954). Vogelsang uses the useful term *Mitkaisertum*, 'partnership in imperial rule', in this context.

society (concubinage is a separate issue), with parallel powers but a different role, was known far later than Tacitus, most notably in the Norse world. Similarly, the role of the wife left in charge in the absence (sometimes permanent, and always potentially so) of her Viking husband in Old Norse has been discussed.[167] These issues are also relevant to *Kudrun*.

The familiar problem of textual unity has also received a great deal of attention in *Kudrun*, in which we focus upon different events with disparate amounts of time between them. In fact the story has three high points: the tale of Hagen the Wild, King of Ireland; the wooing of his daughter Hilde and her marriage to Hetel, King of the Hegelingen, in Northern Germany; and the betrothal, abduction, and rescue of Hilde's daughter, Kudrun. Although the three stories may indeed have had a separate existence at some stage, as we have the work, they do form a perfectly coherent whole, offering us a surprisingly clear political picture of the dynamic development of a ruling dynasty over a span of several generations. The narrative concentrates again on the interesting parts of this development. If in this case some of the fallow periods are less happy than those implied in *Beowulf* or *Waltharius*, the conclusion to the work shows how political chaos—though not bloodshed—can be avoided. Indeed, a further element seen in other works appears in a new guise. Where the education of the hero, in adversity, can prepare him for rule, or to take a proper place in society, here it is a woman, Kudrun herself, who undergoes the suffering that will lead her to take up in the end her position and, we assume, assist her husband wisely thereafter. There seems little sense in dismembering the work entirely, even if the folklorist approach insists that Kudrun's grandfather is a reflection of the Viking kings of Ireland, that she herself has close parallels in the tale of Cinderella, and that her abduction is really just a reduplication of the wooing of her mother. Kudrun, this approach implies, should not really be in *Kudrun* at all. Apart from a few narrative anomalies—one of the minor characters

---

167 See for example Barbara E. Crawford, 'Marriage and the Status of Women in Norse Society'. in *Marriage and Property*, ed. Elizabeth Craik (Aberdeen: AUP, 1984; repr. 1991), pp. 71–88.

manages to keep her youth and beauty for three generations—the epic works admirably as it is, and we do not need to cut up a healthy patient to find out whether or not he is alive. Nor should we worry about the central figure's name, Kudrun, which is linguistically a mixture of north and south German forms. There are plenty of Gudruns in heroic literature, but only one Kudrun. The early sixteenth-century Ambras manuscript, the only one in which the text survives, is quite specific: 'This book'. it says, 'is about Kudrun'. The unity of the work depends upon the dynastic development from a warrior king through his forceful daughter to his equally strong grand-daughter, Kudrun herself, who is mistaken for a pawn, but who reveals herself at the end of the work as a queen.

The work begins in Ireland, although the Germanic names do indeed indicate perhaps the Viking kingdom set up there in the ninth century, and it opens significantly with the death of a king who is in fact Kudrun's great-great-grandfather. There is an emphasis on the line of hereditary nobility, and indeed on the need for appropriate marriages from the very beginning of the work. The first focus is upon the young Hagen, however, Prince of Ireland, who is carried off by a griffin to a remote island. However magical this might seem, his survival, encounter with and rescue of three princesses, and then his return home, fighting single-handedly the sailors who have rescued them but who now want to use them as hostages, all depend on strength and wit. There is, it is true, a hint of magic here in that the young man kills and drinks the blood of an unknown creature about which the poet is both vague and brief, noting only that it is like a *gabilûn*. The nature of the beast is irrelevant, but it is more significant that Hagen does not on drinking the blood become invincible (with the compulsory danger-point shared by Achilles, Siegfried and indeed Superman) or invisible. What we are told is rather more realistic—'dô gewan er vil der krefte/ er hête manigen gedanc' (strophe 101, 4) [he gained much strength and began to acquire wisdom.] This is a condensed form of the motif of the hero gaining a practical education. Hagen's development on the island, to which he is snatched away just at the point where (as we are told) he is already wanting to get away from the charge of his mother's women, and during which he also acquires responsibility for the three princesses (one of whom he later marries), is a different version of and a new motivation for the education motif. Hagen indeed learns survival, and also acquires the formulaic epithet *der wilde Hagene*, Hagen the Wild, the Savage. The second focus of the work is on Hagen's daughter. Having returned to Ireland, established himself as high king, married and fathered the Princess Hilde, we are shown not only his firm maintenance of law and order but his attitude to his daughter's suitors. His rule is described in detail and is worth looking at as a little political vignette:

> Dô begunde rihten   her Hagene in Irlant,
> swaz er unbillîches   an den liuten vant,
> des muosten si engelten   von im harte sêre,
> inner einem jâre   enthoubet er ahtzig oder mêre.
>
> Nu schuof er herverte   in sîner vînde lant
> durch die armen wolter   füeren deheinen brant.
> swâ ir mit übermüete   deheiner wart erfunden,
> dem brach er die bürge   und rach sich mit den tiefen
>   verchwunden (strophe 194f)

[And so Hagen began his rule in Ireland. When he found crimes had been committed, he made the wrongdoers pay for it very severely—within a year he beheaded more than eighty people. Then he set out against his enemies. He did not set fire to the villages because of the poor people, but if anyone was arrogant, he razed his castle and inflicted deep wounds on him.]

Because of all this, Hagen acquires the new title of 'devil-king', but the point is his establishment of firm rule, and we may presume that he only needed to kill eighty in the *first* year. It is naturally important to him than his daughter is married well in dynastic terms (indeed, it must be said that she, though strong-willed, shares this view), and twenty messengers sent in suit of the girl, Hilde, are hanged. Once again the point is that the suitors as such do, or can do, nothing about it. The inference is that they are therefore not strong enough to make an appropriate match.

The successful wooing of Hilde is the subject of the second focus of the work. King Hetel, a king at the centre of what seems to be a network of alliances in northern Germany and Denmark, sends his envoys, notably the singer Horant and the warrior Wate to Ireland. The *Brautwerbung* motif, travel in pursuit of a bride, is familiar in the so-called minstrel epics and to an extent in the romance, but it is in origin a political motif, here very clearly so. Of special interest is the interplay of force and cunning on the part of the warriors, and also the involvement of Hilde herself in the plot to abduct her.

Horant (who appears in the far earlier Anglo-Saxon poem of *Deor* as a *leoðcræftig monn*, a notable singer) and Wate (in some Germanic legends a giant, or the father of Wayland) are within this work vassals of Hetel, and Wate in particular is representative of a fairly crude political pragmatism.[168] These two are sent as supposed exiles to Hagen's court. Horant charms the ladies of that court with his singing, while Wate is embarrassed even to be with the ladies, preferring the activities of a warrior. Indeed, he pretends to take lessons in swordsmanship from Hagen and in doing so comes close to defeating him. Meanwhile, Hilde has assured herself that Hetel is a powerful and worthy king. When she has been lured to their ship and abducted, she clearly throws in her lot with Hetel, even though her angry father now gives chase across the seas. A pitched battle is fought between Hagen and his pursuing army and Hetel and his men, and Hilde and her retinue watch this genuine battle just as they watched the jousting and swordplay earlier. When it comes to a—this time again genuine—fight between Hagen and Wate, Hilde intervenes, asking King Hetel to stop the fight. He does so, and the situation recalls that at the end of *Waltharius*, even though in that case Hildigunda was helpless and it is effectively the poet who stops a fight which could only end in pointless death, leaving Hildigunda to care for the wounds.

---

168 On the backgrounds of these and other characters see George T. Gillespie, *A Catalogue of Persons Named in German Heroic Literature* (Oxford: Clarendon, 1973); and for Wate the study by Winder McConnell, *The Wate Figure in German Medieval Tradition* (Berne: Lang, 1978).

Hilde in this case has a more positive role. The warriors are all exhausted, and the death of her father—who is by now seriously wounded—would jeopardise her position as Hetel's queen. Hilde is a diplomat, however, rather than a healer, and she calls upon Wate to tend the wounds of Hagen, something which he refuses to do until a formal treaty has been made. This happens only when Hilde goes to Hagen himself (using Horant as an intermediary in the first instance) to seek his forgiveness.

The delicate political negotiations in all this are quite clear, but a reconciliation *is* brought about and a somewhat reluctant Hagen is then treated to an exhibition of Hetel's power. The objective audience becomes aware that Wate the doer and Hilde the adviser are equally indispensible to the process. The pattern of battle or other show of strength, followed by acquiescence when politically expedient has been worked through, and Hagen, we are told quite explicitly, has achieved his aim.[169] Indeed, he takes his leave of his daughter (and the epic) with an admonitory speech on the nature of ruling not unlike that of Hroðgar to Beowulf, although this is directed at a queen, and addresses itself both to government and to reputation:

> Er sprach zuo sîner tohter 'ir sult krône tragen,
> daz ich und iuwer muoter iemen hœren sagen
> daz iuch iemen hazze, ir sît sô guotes rîche,
> liezet ir iuch schelten, daz stüende iuwern hôhen
> namen unlobelîche'. (strophe 568)

[He told his daughter: 'bear the crown in such as way that your mother and I shall not hear that you have incurred anyone's hatred. You are now so rich and powerful that it would be a disgrace to your good name if anyone had cause to make accusations against you'.]

---

169 Strophe 548 begins 'Hagnen was gelungen als er hête gegert', [Hagen had succeeded in getting what he wanted.] Most editors and some of the translations (including my own) amend the name to 'Hetelen', which makes equally good sense (since he has also achieved his aim in a more immediate manner). I am now inclined, however, to retain the manuscript reading, in line with Winder McConnell, *Kudrun*, p. 56.

Hagen returns to Ireland and continues his rule; we are not told whether he has sons to succeed him.

The whole work consists of thirty-two chapters, and the first eight have been covered so far. The rest of the work is concerned with Hilde and her daughter, Kudrun, and although there are certain similarities with the early portion of the work, the political implications of this major part (in which Hilde and Kudrun play equally important roles to the end) are rather different and more ramified. Hetel and Hilde have a son and a daughter, and it is assumed that the son (who is brought up by Wate) will succeed Hetel. The focus, however, is on the daughter once more, where the question is not one of succession but of a suitable marriage, suitable, that is, in political terms since marriage to Kudrun implies alliance with a larger unit than that controlled by Hagen, for example. Three suitors present themselves, and all three are favourably viewed by Kudrun herself, though all three are turned down by Hetel. The first of them, a Saracen king with the somewhat unlikely name of Sivrit is rejected and swears vengeance, as does, a little later, Herwic of Zeeland, when he too is rejected. Thirdly, Hartmuot of the Normans is dismissed because of his status—his father had been a vassal of Hagen. It is interesting that any of these would be acceptable to the still very young Kudrun. Herwic returns with an army, takes Hetel by surprise, and once again wins by a demonstration of superior power, using also the element of surprise, the right to the marriage. The pair are betrothed, but Hilde asks for a period of time—a year—to prepare Kudrun for queenship. In the event, the delay in the actual marriage proves unfortunate, but it is difficult to condemn Hilde for this. Her reasoning is sound. The delay is utilised by the first rejected suitor, Sivrit, however, to attack the successful one. Hetel, Kudrun's father, goes to Herwic's assistance, and while his own country is undefended, the other rejected suitor, Hartmuot the Norman, returns, together with his father, Ludewic, and abducts Kudrun.

In this abduction, which differs from that of Hilde because it is not a direct demonstration of strength, but rather a subterfuge, a new factor has to be mentioned. Hartmuot has been supported in his plans by his father—reluctantly—and more especially by his mother, Gerlint, with enthusiasm. There is a parallel here with the very first part of the *Nibelungenlied*, where Siegfried's parents—in this case together—warn him against an attempted liaison with the Burgundians, and are eventually proved right. Yet it is equally difficult to criticise Gerlint for anything except misjudgement at this stage. She is, admittedly, characterised by the narrator (not by other characters in the work, as is Kriemhild at the end of the *Nibelungenlied*) as a she-devil, but her concern is to have the best match for her son, and she is still smarting under the rejection on grounds of social inequality.

Kudrun is abducted, then, and word of this is sent to Hetel and Herwic, who at once conclude a treaty with Sivrit. The whole new alliance sets out to pursue Hartmuot and Ludewic, catching up with them on a sandy islet in the mouth of the Scheldt. In an extended battle, on difficult ground and in mists and darkness, Hetel is killed and the Normans escape with Kudrun. This particular battle appears in a number of earlier analogues as a battle for Hilde, in which Hagen dies,[170] but such reflections of the saga—in languages ranging from Latin to Orkney Norse—need not affect our reading of this version, for which the battle is a turning point, and not a tragic conclusion.

The incidence of Christianity in *Kudrun* is of interest at this point. While the work is mostly secular, there are some indications by the narrator that the loss of Hetel at the battle on the sands is a judgement by God, since Wate—who is not noticeably Christian at any point—had commandeered ships from a group of pilgrims. Hilde in fact offers a kind of penance for this, by founding and endowing a cathedral, but she has to give her mind now to the question of damage limitation. She has lost her husband, although Wate and the others are bound in loyalty to her as much as to the dead king. Her son is too young, however, and she has no army. Her situation is a little like that of Kriemhild, but there is one difference: Kudrun is still alive. Hilde thus elects to wait for a number of years until enough boys have grown up to be warriors.

---

170 There is a detailed summary of the many analogues (Latin, Old Norse, German, Anglo-Saxon and others) in the introduction to the Bartsch/Stackmann edition.

Kudrun is alive, but she is Hartmuot's prisoner. Hartmuot himself behaves honourably towards her and refuses to take her as a concubine, affected, in spite of his overt declaration of indifference, by her taunt of what others will think of him. She is, however, virtually enslaved by Gerlint, Hartmuot's mother, in the name of tutelage. This in a sense is the education of Kudrun, but it does not lead, as Gerlint hopes it will, towards acquiescence and the realisation that she should agree to marry Hartmuot, but rather to fortitude. Kudrun maintains her chastity and her self-esteem in the steadfast refusal to dishonour her betrothal. Although the geography of the whole is a little odd, the two countries *are* some distance apart (by Normans it is more likely that the poet means the Norman kingdom of Sicily than mainland Normandy), and the Normans cannot attack Hetel's lands any further. At this stage in the work, incidentally, Kudrun is referred to frequently (and more or less equally) as 'Hilde's daughter' or 'Hagen's granddaughter', underscoring the dynastic point, and reminding us of the earlier vassal status of the Normans. Indeed, at one point she even declares herself to be kin to Hagen: 'ich bin daz Hagenen künne' (1486,3).[171]

Eventually, after Kudrun has been forced to wash clothes on the sea shore, she gets word (first by miraculous means, in fact) that rescue is imminent. Herwic and her brother arrive, reassure themselves that Kudrun has not become Hartmuot's wife or mistress, and return with an army, including Wate and the other allies, besiege Hartmuot and Ludewic, and defeat them. Within the broader working-out of the political situation, the final part of work contains several individual scenes of immense literary effect—first when Kudrun, aware of the impending rescue, openly defies Gerlint and hurls her washing into the sea; secondly when Hartmuot, realising he is trapped, but has to fight, turns on his still-scheming mother and asserts his own dignity once and for all; and thirdly when the vengeful Wate strikes off the head of the old queen in the centre of the great hall.

171 Most critics draw attention to the point. See, on the political implications, Ian Campbell, *Kudrun* (Cambridge: CUP, 1978), p. 279.

In the evaluation of the work as a whole, probably too much has been made of the supposedly gradual moderation of the political attitudes of the successive generations in *Kudrun*. At this last battle there are indeed representatives of what is seen as an earlier, pragmatic and crude forcefulness in the figure of Wate in particular. It has been perceived too in the Norman King Ludewic, who, when defied by Kudrun, had grabbed her by the hair and hurled her into the sea, from which Hartmuot had to rescue her. But in some respects Wate's pragmatism is allowed to take its course throughout the work. Ludewic is already dead, but the killing of Gerlint is left to him, nor indeed is he stopped (although there is a mild protest from one of the other warriors) from killing the young children in the Norman fortress. Wate explains (with an initial irony in his mode of address):

> 'du hâst kindes muot.
> die in der wiegen weinent   diuhte dich daz guot
> daz ich sie leben lieze?   solten die erwahsen,
> so wolte ich in niht mêre   getrouwen danne einen
> wilden Sahsen'. (strophe 1503)

['Don't be so childish! Do you really think it is a good idea if I allow those babies to live? If they grew up I would not trust them any further than I would trust a wild Saxon!']

Given the fact that Hilde's people have had to wait precisely for a new generation of warriors to grow up, the point is taken, although blood now flows through the castle. Although he is allowed to kill Gerlint and also one of Kudrun's own women who has turned traitor, however, a stop is put on Wate's (preemptive or revenge) killings eventually, when Kudrun herself prevents him from killing Hartmuot, the would-be husband. Wate very much wants to kill him, but Hartmuot had always behaved honourably towards her. Interestingly, she calls upon her betrothed, Herwic, to stop Wate from killing Hartmuot in battle (just as Hilde had persuaded her betrothed to stop a battle), but even afterwards, when it is decided that Hartmuot should be taken as a prisoner back to Kudrun's own country, Wate continues grumbling, and suggests that if Hartmuot wants to stay in his own country, then he, Wate, will be happy to arrange this on an absolutely permanent basis. It is Kudrun's brother, in fact, who makes a final and clearly political statement on the situation:

> 'Waz hulfe, ob ir si alle'.   sprach her Ortwîn
> 'hie zu tôde slüeget   in dem lande sîn?
> Hartmuot und sîn gesinde,   die suln baz gedingen
> ich wil sie lobelîche   ze lande mîner muoter Hilden
>   bringen.' (strophe 1559)

['What would be the point of killing everybody in the whole country?' said Ortwin. 'It is better to let Hartmuot and his men hope for better things, and I propose to take them back in honourable fashion to the lands of Hilde, my mother'.]

Ortwin is the senior male in rank, and takes the initiative, but Kudrun has been the spirit of reconciliation precisely as her mother was between Hagen and Hetel, and this can now be worked out again for this new generation, or rather: for this new situation. The distinctions between the acts done or sanctioned by the different generations *as such* are not that great, and should not be stressed too much.[172] Hagen, for example, accepted the situation when it became clear that expediency demanded it. There is every point in removing Ludewic, Gerlint, and possibly even the children (as a possibility of a new force). There is, however, little point in removing the ruling house, and every point in keeping them alive to employ another policy, that of marriage.

Bellum gerant alii, tu felix Austria nube was not a Habsburg exclusive, but the diplomatic use of marriage to prevent war did not always work. The *Nibelungenlied* makes the point clearly enough, and Beowulf himself, too, is dubious about marriage as a policy if it is not thought through. À propos of the marriage between the Danish princess Freawaru and Ingeld he comments that this might not be enough to reconcile on a lasting basis two peoples who are old enemies, and old quarrels might flare up again later. Beowulf's

---

172 Campbell, *Kudrun*, pp. 149–79, rightly plays down the point, which is stressed by Hoffmann, *Kudrun*, and more recently by Ellen Bender, *Nibelungenlied und Kudrun* (Frankfurt/M.: Lang, 1987), p. 191.

conjectures *in the context of the poem* (although they are based presumably on the Ingeld saga) are voiced as a suspicion only. Wate's actions in killing the children is designed to obviate such a possibility, whatever marriage alliances are entered into.[173] Marriages have, too, to be desired on all sides. Rather later, and in the North, Barbara Crawford, in her illuminating study of marriage in Norse society comments that 'there are five famous marriages in saga literature which take place against the stated will of the girl concerned. All five were unmitigated disasters, ending with the death, maiming or divorce of the husband'.[174] This might, indeed, have been the case had Hartmuot forced a marriage to Kudrun. That he does not do so, nor indeed take her as a concubine, is what saves him. His own marriage now to Kudrun's old friend and fellow captive Hildeburc, who has seen the courteous side of Hartmuot, cements the alliance between the two, especially as Kudrun's brother marries Hartmuot's sister.[175] This can only come about after Kudrun herself has arranged for her mother to embrace the Norman princess Ortrun. The actual arrangement of the marriages, however, is

---

173 See *Beowulf,* lines 2026–69. On marriage in *Kudrun,* see Otto Zallinger, *Die Eheschließung im Nibelungenlied und in der Gudrun* (Vienna and Leipzig: Hölder-Pichler-Tempsky); Eckhart Loerzer, *Eheschließung und Werbung in der Kudrun* (Munich: Beck, 1971); and Winder McConnell, 'Marriage in the *Nibelungenlied* and *Kudrun*'. in *Spectrum Medii Aevi: Essays . . . in Honor of George Fenwick Jones* (Göppingen: Kümmerle, 1983), pp. 299–320.

174 Crawford, 'Marriage and Status'. p. 78. She cites too (p. 87) the case of Cecilia, sister of the Norwegian King Sverre, married to a Swedish noble against her will for political reasons. The marriage was declared illegal, but only when she acquired powerful supporters. Far earlier, Tacitus refers in the *Annals* to the famous enmity between Arminius—Hermann—and Segestes, leaders of the Germanic tribes of Chatti and Cherusci, who were linked by the marriage of Segestes' daughter to Arminius, who had, however, reputedly stolen her from another man: see his *Annals,* i, 54. On the question of abduction (which happens in the romance on a fairly regular basis, of course), see Nolte, *Kudrunepos,* p. 17.

175 Hildeburc, unfortunately, shares in the text we have not only the exile of Kudrun, but the abduction of her mother and indeed the island sojourn of her grandmother; in the development of the story, the poet has clearly neglected to provide different names to differentiate three characters. The age of Kudrun's brother is also somewhat variable.

presented in a great deal of detail, and in the clearest of political terms. The arrangements are placed before the two Normans by Kudrun herself, who prefaces her proposals with the words:

> 'welt ir folgen, Hartmuot,   also ich iuch lêre,
> tuot ir daz willichlîche,   sô scheidet ir iuch von aller
>   hande sêre.' (strophe 1635, 3–4)

['If you agree to what I am going to suggest, my Lord Hartmuot, and do so willingly, then this will be a way out of all your difficulties'.]

The word *willichlîche*, 'willingly', is vital, but Hartmuot has at this point very little choice. Still he agrees that Hildeburc is an honourable match for him, and he can rule with her at his side without shame. Kudrun, incidentally, has already obtained the agreement of her brother to the marriage with Hartmuot's sister. The last stage comes, however, when Wate—without whose strong arm none of this could have happened—points out that the agreement of Hilde needs to be sought, and that this will involve the complete submission of the two Normans. They do, however, agree to this, aware that the solution provided by Kudrun is both politically sound and honourable—that is, acceptable. The work ends then (after a somewhat *ad hoc* marriage of the third suitor, sometime enemy and later ally Sivrit, to an otherwise unmentioned and unnamed sister of Kudrun's betrothed) with a well-established network of alliances, brought about by force when necessary. But the clearly strong dynasty of Hagen the Wild, his daughter and his grand-daughter, who are still able to command and when necessary to subdue the force of arms represented by the still absolutely essential Wate, has prevailed. Wate, the loyal warrior vassal, is vital to the whole: he has brought up Hetel and also Hetel's son Ortwin, and he was instrumental in winning Hilde for Hetel. He may have been at fault in his attack on the pilgrims (when there was no one to restrain him), but it was in human—if not in theological—terms still a calculated gamble, without which any pursuit of Kudrun would have been impossible. Wate also manages the rescue of Kudrun, and (stopped only when he seems to want to go further than is politically necessary) he ensures the maintenance of later stability, again by a pragmatic exercise of force. Before killing the treacherous Heregart, Wate had announced that he was the Lord Chamberlain of Hilde's court—'ich bin kamerære' (strophe 1528, 3),—and indeed he continues to act as a very powerful politician to the end, still controlling at least the public expression of Kudrun's organisation behind the scenes. The final reconciliation (supposedly associated with Kudrun and not Wate's generation) is actually spelt out by Wate:[176]

> Dô sprach Wate der alte 'wer möhte ez süenen ê,
> unz Ortrûn und Hartmuot für froun Hilden gê
> und biete sich ze füezen der edelen küniginne?
> Und lobet siz al eine, sô müge wirs alle wol ze
>   hulden bringen.' (strophe 1646)

[Wate the Old said: 'How can this reconciliation be completed until Hartmuot and Ortrun go to Queen Hilde and prostrate themselves before the queen? Only if she gives her approval can everything be sorted out'.]

Tragedy, or even the tragic ending, is a misleading notion when associated with the Germanic hero, and here the supposed contrast between the *Nibelungenlied* and *Kudrun* needs at least to be kept in proportion. Both are political works, and the first ends in disaster. Siegfried is a disruptive force within an established society. Against his entry, and the limited powers of a weak king, Hagen tries to keep the balance of the state. Even *Diu Klage* is a kind of acknowledgement of his power, and in the political context it is Hagen who stands beside Byrhtnoð, Beowulf, Ernst, Charlemagne and the rest. Siegfried is the anomaly, Grendel invited to Hroðgar's table. *Kudrun* does not actually *end* in disaster, but there are enough political problems on the way: Hetel is killed and his fighting force all but wiped out, and Kudrun is kept virtually imprisoned for many years. Politically, Gerlint, Ludewic and Hartmuot all fail in their attempt to force an alliance with Hetel through marriage with

---

176 See Brian Murdoch, 'Interpreting *Kudrun*'. *New German Studies* 7 (1979), 113–27, esp. p. 123; and McConnell, *Epic of Kudrun*, p. 84.

Kudrun. It must be said that the situation is somewhat different—more civilised, that is—than it was in the *Völundarkviða*, where Völundr established his place in the succession by rape. But that would in any case have called forth revenge rather than alliance in *Kudrun* had Hartmuot tried to force Kudrun. The work is an affirmation of the dynastic hierarchy of power, power associated with a specific class, and the politics are in the strictest sense conservative and pragmatic, relating to a warrior society or to a social system predicated also upon the power of arms, from which man has not yet moved completely. But the underlying notion in all the works we have examined is the warrior hero's primary aim (an aim shared by women in a position of power) to maintain and develop a stable society as a bastion against chaos and against any forces from outside or from within that might work against this stability. In pursuing that aim, the warrior will maintain a reputation that is not just his, but which belongs to his family and his society. That he is called upon to do so indicates already his high status in that society, and this makes him a hero. In *Kudrun*, women seem to be foregrounded far more than elsewhere, it is true, and there is a concluding emphasis on political successes, so that the future in *Kudrun* will be, it is hoped, a time of peace, just as there was peace outside the literary work as such under the rule of Beowulf or Waltharius. But what is *really* foregrounded in *Kudrun* is the political context as such, that forms the basis of definition for the Germanic hero. It offers a paradigm of coping, and that will necessarily involve damage limitation. The hero operates in a real, and therefore in an imperfect, world.

Bibliography of Primary Texts

I have listed a convenient original version of texts used (there are often many more), plus one or more translations into English (and where appropriate also into modern German). Access to secondary studies consulted may be had through the name index.

Old and Middle High German

Hildebrandslied

Elias v. Steinmeyer, *Die kleineren althochdeutschen Denkmäler* (Berlin and Zurich: Weidmann, reprint 1963), no. 1; and in Wilhelm Braune, *Althochdeutsches Lesebuch*, 16th edn by Ernst Ebbinghaus (Tübingen: Niemeyer, 1965), no. 28. With modern German translation in Horst Dieter Schlosser, *Althochdeutsche Literatur* (Frankfurt/M.: Fischer, 2nd edn, 1989), pp. 264–7. English translations by Francis A. Wood, *The Hildebrandslied* (Chicago: U. Chicago P., 1914); in Charles W. Jones, *Medieval Literature in Translation* (New York: McKay, 1950), p. 499f; Bruce Dickens, *Runic and Heroic Poems of the Old Teutonic Peoples* (Cambridge: CUP, 1915), pp. 78–85; Brian Murdoch, *Lines Review*, 109 (1989), 20–22.

Ludwigslied

Steinmeyer, *Denkmäler*, no. 16 and Braune, *Lesebuch*, no. 36. With modern German translation in Schlosser, *Literatur*, pp. 274–7. English translation in J. Knight Bostock, *A Handbook on Old High German*, 2nd edn by K.C. King and D.L. McLintock (Oxford: Clarendon, 1976), pp. 239–41.

Herzog Ernst

Herzog Ernst, ed. Karl Bartsch (Vienna: Braumüller, 1869); *Herzog Ernst, in der mittelhochdeutschen Fassung B*, ed., trs. Bernhard Sowinski (Stuttgart: Reclam, 1970). English translation by J.W. Thomas, *The Legend of Duke Ernst* (Lincoln, Neb. and London: University of Nebraska Press, 1979).

Pfaffe Konrad, *Rolandslied*

Das Rolandslied des Pfaffen Konrad, ed. Carl Wesle, 2nd edn by Peter Wapnewski (Tübingen: Niemeyer, 1967). With modern German translation by Dieter Kartschoke (Frankfurt/M.: Fischer, 1970; now Stuttgart: Reclam, 1994). English translation: J.W. Thomas, *Priest Konrad's Song of Roland* (Columbia, SC: Camden House, 1994).

Nibelungenlied

Das Nibelungenlied, ed. Karl Bartsch, 15th edn by Helmut de Boor (Wiesbaden: Brockhaus, 1959; 21st edn by R. Wisniewski, 1979). With modern German translation, ed. Helmut Brackert (Frankfurt/M.: Fischer, 1970); edition and modern German prose version by Werner Hoffmann, *Das Nibelungenlied/ Kudrun* (Darmstadt: WBG, 1972). English translations by D.G. Mowatt, *The Nibelungenlied* (London: Dent, 1962) and A.T. Hatto, *The Nibelungenlied* (Harmondsworth: Penguin, 1965).

Diu Klage

Der Nibelunge Noth und Die Klage, ed. Karl Lachmann, 6th edn by Ulrich Pretzel (Berlin; de Gruyter, 1960). English translation by Winder McConnell, *The Lament of the Nibelungen* (Columbia, SC: Camden House, 1994).

Kudrun

Kudrun, ed. Karl Bartsch, rev. edn by Karl Stackmann (Wiesbaden: Brockhaus, 1980). German translation by Karl Simrock, rev. Friedrich Neumann, *Kudrun (Gudrun)* (Stuttgart: Reclam, 1958); see also editions of the *Nibelungenlied*, above. Recent English translations by Brian Murdoch, *Kudrun* (London: Dent, 1987); by Marion E. Gibbs and Sidney M. Johnson, *Kudrun* (New York: Garland, 1992); by Winder McConnell, *Kudrun* (Columbia SC: Camden House, 1992).

Konrad von Würzburg, *Heinrich von Kempten*

Kleinere Dichtungen Konrads von Würzburg I, ed. Eduard Schröder (Berlin: Weidmann, 2nd edn 1930). With German translation in *Konrad von Würzburg*, trs. Heinz Rölleke (Stuttgart: Reclam, 1968). English translation in J.W. Thomas, *The Best Novellas of Medieval Germany* (Columbia SC: Camden House, 1984).

Old Saxon

Heliand

Heliand und Genesis, ed. Otto Behaghel, 8th edn by Walther Mitzka; 9th edn by Burkhard Taeger (Tübingen: Niemeyer, 1984). English translation by Marianne Scott, *Heliand* (Chapel Hill: U. North Carolina Press, 1966); and G. Ronald Murphy, *The Heliand* (London and New York: OUP, 1992). German translation by Felix Genzmer, *Heliand* (Stuttgart: Reclam, 1966).

Anglo-Saxon

Beowulf

F. Klaeber, *Beowulf and the Fight at Finnsburg* (Boston: Heath, 3rd edn, 1950); A.J. Wyatt, *Beowulf*, rev. edn by R.W. Chambers (Cambridge: CUP, 1952); C.L. Wrenn, *Beowulf*, rev. edn by W.F. Bolton (London: Harrap, 1973); Michael Alexander, *Beowulf* (Harmondsworth: Penguin, 1995). With English translation by Michael Swanton, *Beowulf* (Manchester: MUP, 1978). Facsimile of the manuscript with a transcription, ed. Norman Davis, *Beowulf* (London: EETS, 1966). English translations by Michael Alexander, *Beowulf* (Harmondsworth: Penguin, 1973); Stanley B. Greenfield, *A Readable*

Beowulf (Carbondale: S.I.U. Press, 1982); John Porter, *Beowulf* (Pinner: Anglo-Saxon Books, 1990).

The Battle of Maldon

The Battle of Maldon, ed. E.V. Gordon (London: Methuen, 2. corr. edn, 1954), with supplement by D.G. Scragg (Manchester: MUP, 1976); ed. D.G. Scragg (Manchester: MUP, 1981) and in *The Battle of Maldon AD 991*, ed. Donald Scragg (Oxford: Blackwell, 1991). English translations by Michael Alexander, *The Earliest English Poems* (Harmondsworth: Penguin, 1966), pp. 111–23; Kevin Crossley-Holland, *The Battle of Maldon and Other Old English Poems*, ed. Bruce Mitchell (London: Macmillan, 1966); Bill Griffiths, *The Battle of Maldon* (Pinner: Anglo-Saxon Books, 1991).

Deor

Deor, ed. Kemp Malone (London: Methuen, 1933). English translation by Alexander, *Earliest English Poems*, pp. 43f.

Guthlac

The Guthlac Poems of the Exeter Book, ed. Jane Roberts (Oxford: Clarendon, 1979). English translation by R.K. Gordon, *Anglo-Saxon Poetry* (London: Dent, 1926; rev. edn, 1954), pp. 256–79.

Old Norse

Edda Poems (Grípispá, Völundarkviða, Atlakviða, Hávamál, Hamðismál)

Sæmundar-Edda, ed. Finnur Jónsson (Reykjavik: Kristjánsson, 2nd edn, 1926), pp. 268–84, 141–53, 385–97; *Edda: Die Lieder des Codex Regius*, ed. Gustav Neckel, 4th edn rev. by Hans Kuhn (Heidelberg: Winter, 1962); some ed. and trans. Ursula Dronke, *The Elder Edda* i (Oxford: Clarendon, 1969). English translations by Henry Adams Bellows, *The Poetic Edda* [1923] (repr. New York: Biblo, 1969); Paul B. Taylor and W. H. Auden, *The Elder Edda* (London: Faber,

1969) [selection]; Patricia Terry, *Poems of the Vikings* (New York: Bobbs-Merrill, 1969). German translations by Felix Genzmer, *Heldenlieder der Edda* (Stuttgart: Reclam, 1952).

Latin

Tacitus, *Germania*

Cornelii Taciti opera minora, ed. Henry Furneaux and J.G.C. Anderson (Oxford: Clarendon, 1900; repr. 1939). English translation by H. Mattingly, *Tacitus on Britain and Germany* (Harmondsworth: Penguin, 1948).

Einhard, *Vita Caroli Magni*

Einhard's Life of Charlemagne, ed. H.W. Garrod and R.B. Mowat (Oxford: Clarendon, 1915). English translation by Lewis Thorpe, *Two Lives of Charlemagne* (Harmondsworth: Penguin, 1969), pp. 47–90.

Waltharius

Poetae Latini Medii Aevi vi, ed. Karl Strecker and Norbert Fickermann (Hanover: Monumenta Germaniae Historica, 1951; repr. Munich: MHG, 1978); Gæraldus, *Waltharius,* ed. A.K. Bate (Reading: University Medieval and Renaissance Latin Texts, 1978). With English translation by Dennis M. Kratz, *Waltharius and Ruodlieb* (New York: Garland, 1984); with German translation by Karl Langosch, Ekkehard, *Waltharius* (Frankfurt.M.: Insel, 1987); and by Gregor Vogt-Spira, *Waltharius* (Stuttgart: Reclam, 1995). English translation by Brian Murdoch, *Walthari* (Glasgow: Scottish Papers in Germanic Studies, 1989). German translation by Felix Genzmer, *Das Waltharilied* (Stuttgart: Reclam, 1953).

Modus Ottinc

Karl Strecker, *Die Cambridger Lieder* (Hanover: Monumenta Germaniae Historica, 1926, 2nd edn, 1955), poem 11. Text and facsimile in Karl Breul, *The Cambridge Songs* (Cambridge: CUP, 1915). With German translation in Horst Kusch, *Einführung in das lateinische Mittelalter* (Berlin: VEB Verlag der Wissenschaften, 1957), i, 210–17. English translation by Jan M. Ziolkowski, *The Cambridge Songs* (New York: Garland, 1992).

Gesta Francorum et Aliorum Hierosolimitanorum

Ed. with French translation by Louis Bréhier, *Histoire anonyme de la première croisade* (Paris: Champion, 1924).

Carmen de prodicione Guenonis

Gaston Paris, "Le *Carmen de prodicione Guenonis*", *Romania* 11 (1882), 45–518. English translation by Arthur Livingston, "The *Carmen de prodicione Guenonis*", *Romanic Review* 2 (1911), 61–79.

Old French

Chanson de Roland

Das altfranzösische Rolandslied nach der Oxforder Handschrift, ed. Alfons Hilka, 4th edn by Gerhard Rohlfs (Tübingen: Niemeyer, 1953); *Chanson de Roland*, ed. F. Whitehead (Oxford: Blackwell; 2nd edn, 1946). English translations by Dorothy Sayers, *The Song of Roland* (Harmondsworth: Penguin, 1957); D.D.R. Owen (London: Unwin, 1972); Glyn Burgess (Harmondsworth: Penguin, 1990, with part of the original text).

Gormont et Isembart

Gormont et Isembart, ed. Alphonse Bayot, 3rd edn (Paris: Champion, 1931).

Index to Secondary Literature

Alexander, Michael 15, 21, 54
Andersen, Hans Erik 25
Anderson, J. G. C. 161
Andersson, Theodore M. 17, 150
Arndt, W. 11
Ashcroft, Jeffrey 128
Ashdown, Margaret 22
Auerbach, Erich 130, 134

Backes, Herbert 132
Baesecke, Georg 125
Bartless, Robert 142
Bartsch, Karl 73, 147, 168
Bate, A. K. 91f
Bately, Janet M. 22
Batts, Michael 151
Bayot, Alphonse 114
Beck, Heinrich 38, 109
Bédier, Joseph 125
Beer, Frances F. 122
Behaghel, Otto 28
Bekker, Hugo 152, 157
Bellows, Henry Adams 17, 53
Bender, Ellen 171
Berg, Elisabeth 108
Bernhardt, John W. 80
Berry, Francis 25
Bessinger, J. B. 31, 116
Bittner, Franz 13
Blake, N. F. 25, 31
Blamires, David 74f
Bloomfield, Morton W. 6
Boer, R. C. 20
Bolton, W. F. 15, 67
Boor, Helmut de 147, 158
Borghart, Kees H. R. 151
Bostock, J. Knight 13, 103, 159
Bowra, C. M. 7, 10, 26
Brant, Rüdiger 86
Braune, Wilhelm 13, 36, 103

Bréhier, Louis 138
Breul, Karl 13
Bril, Jacques 36
Brill, George 12
Brodeur, Arthur G. 63
Bruce-Mitford, Rupert 65
Brunhölzl, Franz 92
Bull, George 11
Bulst, Walter 93
Burns, Norman T. 6, 9
Burgess, Glynn 12
Busse, W. G. 30

Cam, Helen 8
Campbell, Ian 169, 171
Canisius-Loppnow, Petra 128
Chadwick, H. M. 7, 10
Chase, Colin 63
Cherniss, Michael D. 33, 70
Cluzel, I.-M 125
Cooper, Janet 21, 24, 28, 30, 107–10, 116
Craik, Elizabeth 162
Crawford, Barbara E. 162, 172
Crossley-Holland, Kevin 21

Deegan, Marilyn 21
Delbouille, Maurice 125
Derolez, René 67
Dickens, Bruce 36
Diebold, Markus 5
Dobozy, Maria 62
Dodwell, C. R. 27, 116
Dronke, Ursula 20, 46–48
Duggan, Joseph J. 126
Dümmler, Ernst 89

Earle, John 22
Ehrismann, Otfried 150, 158
Eicke, Theodor 125

Elliott, Ralph W. V. 41, 137
Ernst, Ursula 93

Fajardo-Acosta, Fidel 63, 70
Fellmann, Ulrich 38
Fenik, Bernard 3
Fickermann, Norbert 91
Finch, Ronald G. 28
Fleet, Mary 154
Flood, John L. 60, 107
Foerster, Wendelin 120
Folz, Robert 128
Fornara, Charles William 8
Fouracre, Paul 107
Frank, Roberta 7, 10, 23, 32, 71
Fulk, R. D. 63
Furneaux, Henry 161

Galster, Georg 24
Ganshof, F. L. 11
Gardner, John 15
Garrod, H. W. 124
Geith, Karl-Ernst 128
Genzmer, Felix 28, 53, 92
Georgi, Annette 13
Gibbs, Marion E. 147
Gillespie, George T. 53, 165
Gillingham, J. B. 98
Girvan, Ritchie 65
Glatz, Gabriele 128
Gneuss, Helmut 25
Goffart, Walter 51
Gooden, Malcolm 7
Gordon, C. D. 52
Gordon, E. V. 21, 33
Gordon, R. K. 105
Göttert, Karl-Heinz 85
Gotzmann, Carola 47, 152
Gouchet, Olivier 157
Gregoire, Henri 90
Grierson, Philip 11
Griffiths, Bill 21
Grose, M. W. 26
Groseclose, J. Sidney 36, 111, 115
Gutenbrunner, Siegfried 35

Haberling, W. 102
Haidu, Peter 128
Händl, Claudia 108
Hare, R. M. 152

Harms, Wolfgang 38, 43, 102
Harris, Joseph 3, 60
Harvey, Ruth 108
Hasenfratz, Robert J. 63
Hatto, A. T. 35f, 52, 147
Hauck, Karl 60
Heselhaus, Clemens 74
Heusler, Andreas 46, 111, 150
Hilka, Alfons 12, 112, 126
Hoffmann, Werner 147f, 171
Holtei, R. 30
Homann, Holger 107
Honemann, Volker 52, 60, 128
Howarth, Patrick 52
Huppé, Bernard 9

Ihlenburg, K. H. 20

Jackson, W. H. T. 7, 62, 87f, 129,
    134, 137, 144, 152
Johnson, Sidney M. 147
Jones, Charles M. 36
Jones, George Fenwick 128, 135, 138
Jones, Gwyn 7, 68, 118
Jónsson, Finnur 17, 20, 46

Kartschoke, Dieter 126
Keller, Hans-Erich 130
Kellermann-Haaf, Petra 160
Kemper, Raimund 107
Kennedy, Alan 27
Ker, W. P. 7, 10, 25, 53, 122, 127
Kindermann, Udo 92
King, K. C. 13, 155, 157
Klaeber, F. 15, 65
Koch, H. W. 11
Koch, Karl-Heinz 47
Kocher, Paul 32
Köhler, Erich 128
Kohlschmidt, Werner 109
Kokott, Hartmut 80
Kolb, Herbert 38
Kolk, H. van der 36
Köster, Rudolf 128
Kratz, Dennis M. 92f
Krogmann, Willy 35, 149
Kuhn, Hans 17, 53
Kurth, Lieselotte E. 107
Kurze, Friedrich 123
Kusch, Bruno 11

Kusch, Horst 13

Lachmann, Karl 147
Langosch, Karl 92
Lapidge, Michael 7, 27
Laski, Marghanita 23
Lawrence, William W. 63
Leake, J. A. 65
Lean, W. 24
Learned, Marion Dexter 90, 92
Lefrancq, Paul 116
Le Gentil, Pierre 122, 127–30, 137
Lejeune, Rita 122
Levison, W. 11
Leyen, Friedrich von der 115
Leyser, Karl 108
Livingston, Arthur 126, 132
Loerzer, Eckhart 172
Lord, Albert B. 3
Löschnigg, Martin 7
Louis, René 125
Luft, Wilhelm 38
Lühr, Rosemarie 36
Lührs, Maria 93

Mackensen, Lutz 150
McConnell, Winder 7, 147, 149,
    158, 165f, 172, 174
McDonald, W. 42
McEvedy, Colin 51
McKenna, D. 2
McKitterick, Rosamund 103
McLintock, D. L. 13
Maes-Jelinek, H. 67
Malone, Kemp 54
Mattingly, H. 161
Maurer, Friedrich 109
Meinecke, Birgit 38
Menéndez Pidal, Ramón 124
Metcalfe, D. M. 24
Mettke, Heinz 43, 115
Mewes, Uwe 74
Meyer, Marc A. 51
Mickel, Emmanuel J. 130
Mills, A. D. 26
Mitchell, Bruce 21, 63
Mitzka, Walther 28
Mohr, Wolfgang 60
Monecke, Wolfgang 86
Mowat, R. B. 124
Mowatt, D. G. 7, 50, 147, 152, 154f

Münkler, Herfried 41, 59, 70, 90
Murdoch, Brian 13, 36, 91, 111, 115,
    132, 134, 139, 147, 174
Murphy, J. Ronald 28, 104

Neckel, Gustav 17, 53
Nedoma, Robert 53
Nellmann, Eberhard 128
Nelson, Janet 107
Neumann, Friedrich 147
Newton, Sam 65
Nicholson, Lewis E. 11, 62
Niles, John D. 63
Nolte, Theodor 161, 172
Northcott, Kenneth J. 42
Nöther, Ingo 128

O'Donoghue, Heather 28
Ott-Meimberg, Marianne 128, 132
Owen, D. D. R. 12

Paris, Gaston 126
Parker, Mary A. 63
Pàroli, Teresa 10, 67, 120, 157
Plummer, Charles 22
Porter, John 65
Pretzel, Ulrich 147, 149

Rau, Reinhold 123, 125
Reagan, Christopher 6, 9
Reichert, Hermann 150
Renoir, Alain 3, 42
Roberts, Jane 105
Rohlfs, Gerhard 12, 112, 126
Rolfe, John C. 52
Rölleke, Heinz 80
Rosenfeld, Hans-Friedrich 77
Ross, David 45
Routh, H. V. 138
Rubin, Stanley 21
Rupp, Heinz 152, 155
Rutherford, Andrew 30

Sacker, Hugh 7, 50, 152, 154f
Samouce, W. A. 26
Sandrock, Lucie 11
Sayers, Dorothy L. 12
Schieffer, Rudolf 92
Schilter, Johannes 115
Schlosser, Horst Dieter 13, 36, 103,
    115

Scholler, Harald 93, 130
Schramm, Percy Ernst 7
Schröbler, Ingeborg 160
Schröder, Eduard 80
Schröder, Werner 9
Schubel, Friedrich 63
Schücking, Lev 41
Schütte, Bernd 92
Schützeichel, Rudolf 38, 107
Schwab, Ute 28, 40, 107, 116
Scott, Marianne 28
Scragg, Donald G. 21f, 27, 30, 32
See, Klaus von 4, 6f, 51
Selwyn, Victor 1
Shippey, T. A. 9
Short, Douglas D 63
Siebert, Barbara 148
Simon-Pelanda, Hans 73
Simrock, Karl 147
Sisam, Kenneth 63, 67, 71, 79
Smalley, Beryl 112
Smith, Julia M. H. 123
Sowinski, Bernard 73
Spear, Hilda D. 7
Stach, Walter 93
Stackmann, Karl 147, 168
Stanley, Eric Gerald 63
Stanzel, Franz Karl 7
Steinmeyer, Elias von 13, 36, 163
Stiennon, Jacques 122
Stout, J. 157
Strecker, Karl 13, 91f
Stuart, Heather 44
Süßmann, Gustav 36
Swanton, Michael 15, 65
Szarmach, Paul 109

Taeger, Burkhard 28
Taylor, Paul Beekman 53
Terry, Patricia 17, 20, 53
Thomas, J. W. 80, 126
Thomas, Neil 154
Timmer, B. J. 7, 90
Tolkien, J. R. R. 7, 26, 32, 62f, 91,
  155

Trask, Willard 130
Trevelyan, George M. 8
Tripp, Rymond B. 70
Turville-Petre, G. 53
Tuso, Joseph F. 63

Uecker, Heiko 19
Ullmann, Walter 11

Vance, Eugene 128, 137
Vogelsang, Thilo 161
Vogt-Spira, Gregor 92
Vries, Jan de 7, 90, 114, 148

Wallace-Hadrill, J. M. 110–12
Wapnewski, Peter 126
Warnock, Mary 45
Weber, Gerd Wolfgang 71
Weber, R. L. 36
Wedgewood, C. V. 8
Weege, Magdalena 149
Wehrli, Max 109
Wesle, Carl 126
Whister, Charles W. 27
Whitehead, Frederick 25
Whitelock, Dorothy 63
Wickham, Chris 84
Williams, David J. 25
Williams, Jennifer 47
Williams, R. Deryck 4
Wipf, Karl 115
Wisniewski, Roswitha 147
Woelcker, Eva-Maria 5
Wolf, Alois 20, 46, 53
Wolfskehl, Karl 115
Wood, Francis A. 36
Woolf, Rosemary 28
Wrenn, C. L. 15, 31, 65
Wyatt, A. J. 15, 65

Yeandle, David N. 107

Zallinger, Otto 172
Zinsli, Paul 109

Index

Abbo of St Germain 109
Achilles 4, 163
Æneas 4
Ætius 46
Æthelred II, the Unready 22, 24, 30,
    32, 48, 50, 136
Alcuin 89f, 110, 146
Ammianus Marcellinus 52
Anglo-Saxon Chronicle 22, 27
Aristotle 45
Arnold, Matthew 35
Asimov, Isaac 74
Asmundarssaga Kappabana 43
Astronomer, The 125
Atlakviða 33–35, 46–52, 58f, 94–97,
    103, 151
Atlamál in Groenlenzko 51
Attila: see Atlakviða, Nibelungenlied,
    Waltharius

Battle of Maldon 9. 20–32, 40f, 49f, 1,
    68f, 71, 84, 95, 99, 101, 106, 109,
    112, 118f, 122, 127, 134–40, 174
Beowulf 7, 12, 15f, 61–73, 77–79, 82,
    86–89, 91, 94, 105f, 118f, 127,
    143, 162, 171, 174f
Beroul 15
Berthold von Thiersberg 80
Boso of Provence 106, 108
Brookes, John 1–3, 23
Byrhtnoð: see Battle of Maldon

Captain Marvel 6
Carlyle 6
Carmen de prodicione Guenonis 132, 136
Charlemagne 80, 89, 120–46, 174
Cnut 30
consors regni 161
Crusade, Anonymous History of the
    First 138

Dædalos 53f, 57
Deor 54, 57f, 165
Dietrich-epics 4, 20

Edda, Elder 17, 21, 46, 52
Einhard 123f
Ekkehart I of St Gall 91
Eliensis, Liber 22
Erkambald 91, 93
Ernst: see Herzog Ernst
Ernst of Swabia 75
Ethelred: see Æthelred

feudalism 11
Franks Casket 53
Frauenroman 161
Fredegonda 17
Fulda, Annals of 108

Gæraldus 91–93
Ganger-Hrolf 120
Geats 72
Gelimer 60
Gibbon 74
Gibicho 95
Goethe 43
Golß, Joachim von der 1
Gormont et Isembart 113f
Gregory of Tours 11
Grípisspá 16–20, 25, 31, 64, 69, 120,
    150, 152
Gundahari 46, 52, 95, 150
Guthlac, Life of 104f
Guthrum 113

Habsburgs 86, 171
Hacks, Peter 75
Hamðismál 20
Hardt, Ernst 148
Hartmann von Aue 73

Index

Hávamál 16
Heinrich der Glichezâre 85
Heinrich von Kempten: see Konrad von Würzburg
Heliand 27f, 104
Hephaistos 53
hero, concept of 5–7, 9, 12, 33
Herzog Ernst 10, 61f, 72–78, 83, 87f, 127, 143, 174
Higbald 89
Hildebrandslied 8f, 11, 33–46, 53, 59, 66, 71, 73, 90, 99–103, 116
Hildebrandslied, Jüngeres 43f
Hincmar of Rheims 106, 114
Hollywood 6f
Hucbald of St Amiens 106

Icelandic prose sagas 4
Ingeld 89, 171

Jonas of Orleans 112

Kant 45
Karlamagnussaga 125
Karloman 106, 108
Kipling, Rudyard 23
Klage 159f, 174
Kleist 143
Konrad, Pfaffe 113, 121–46
Konrad II 75
Konrad von Würzburg 61f, 72, 78–88, 119, 143
Kudrun 10, 147–75

Leonidas 1–3
Lewis, C. S. 78
Liudolf of Swabia 75, 78f
Louis the Pious 125
Louis III: see *Ludwigslied*
Ludwigslied 9, 12f, 31, 70, 91, 104–117, 122, 127, 136–39, 141
Luther 89

Machiavelli 12
Maldon: see *Battle of Maldon*
Medea 50
Miller, Thomas 22–24
minstrel epics 10
Modus Ottinc 13–16, 31, 65, 79, 86

Nibelungenlied 16f, 46, 48, 51, 59, 70, 118, 120f, 147–75
Nietzsche 45
Northumbria, sack of 89

Odoaker 35, 39
Olaf Tryggvason 30
oral-formulaic style 3
Oswald, Life of St 22, 27
Otto I, the Great 13f, 75, 79
Otto II: see *Modus Ottinc*
Otto III 13
Otto mit dem Bart: see Konrad von Würzburg
Owen, Wilfred 6

Paul, St 10f
Philip of Swabia 82
Plato 4
Pliny 77f
Procopius 60

Rambo 7
Regino of Prüm 108, 115
ring-composition 3
Roland: see next entry
Roland, Chanson de 10, 12, 26, 31, 118–46, 150
Rolandslied: see Konrad, Pfaffe
Roncesvalles: see *Roland, Chanson de*
Royal Annals 122f

St Bertin, Annals of 107f, 111, 113
St Vaast, Annals of 107f, 110
Saxo Grammaticus 43, 154
science fiction 74
Siegfried: see *Nibelungenlied*
Siegfried, King of the Franks 16f
Sigurðr: see *Grípisspá*
Smaragdus of St Michael 112
Staatsroman 9
Star Wars 74
Stricker 125
Superman 6, 11, 163
Sverre, King of Norway 172

Tacitus 160–62, 172
Taillefer 120
Theoderic the Great 35, 37, 39, 42, 44f

Thermopylæ 1–3
Thidrekssaga 53
Tristan 68
Turpin, Pseudo- 125

Vesper, Will 148
Vikings 89, 160 and see: Battle of Maldon, Ludwigslied
Virgil 89
Völundr: see next entry
Völundarkviða 7, 33f, 52–60, 73, 165, 175

Wace 120

Waise, der 77, 83
Waldere 91
Walja, King of Toulouse 90, 94f, 117
Waltharius 9, 15, 47, 52, 59, 89, 91–104, 110, 116f, 129, 134, 154, 160, 162, 175
Wanilo of Sens 145
Wayland: see Völundarkviða
Westerns 7
Wieland: see Völundarkviða
Wilde, Oscar 128
William of Malmesbury 120
William the Conqueror 120
Wolfram von Eschenbach 73